Reconstruction Bonds & Twentieth-Century Politics

DUKE HISTORICAL PUBLICATIONS

GOVERNOR DANIEL L. RUSSELL
1897-1901

North Carolina State Department of
Archives and History.

RECONSTRUCTION BONDS & TWENTIETH-CENTURY POLITICS

South Dakota v. North Carolina

(1904)

ROBERT F. DURDEN

ranklin

DUKE UNIVERSITY PRESS

Durham, North Carolina _1962_

Printed in the United States of America
by the Seeman Printery, Inc., Durham, N. C.

FOR

Anne Olber Durden

PREFACE

Preparing a projected book about Senator Marion Butler and North Carolina Populism, I had returned to the splendid Southern Historical Collection in the University of North Carolina Library in order to examine relevant papers of Governor Daniel L. Russell. Russell, who holds the distinction of being North Carolina's only Republican governor since the Reconstruction era, collaborated in the late 1890's with Marion Butler in the Populist-Republican program of co-operation which Democrats labeled for posterity as "Fusion."

Disappointed in the rather skimpy material for my purposes in the Russell papers, I was preparing to move on to another collection when Dr. James W. Patton, director of the Southern Historical Collection, informed me that he had just brought up from Wilmington an old trunk full of Russell material, mostly letters, which I could examine as soon as his staff completed processing them.

The new material, saved over the long years since Russell's death by his last young law partner, proved to be a complete and intimate history of the famous interstate lawsuit which figured prominently in North Carolina politics in the first decade of this century and echoed importantly long after Russell himself had died. Proud of his legal skill and ingenuity in masterminding South Dakota's lawsuit against North Carolina—or as he put it, against Tarheel Democrats who had captured control of the state in 1898 and 1900—Russell apparently saved every incoming scrap of correspondence about the case and carefully made, or had made, handwritten copies of his outgoing letters when typed carbons were not available. As the intricate story unfolded through the hundreds of old letters, quite a few of them being of the type which the writers wanted burned, I realized that the "South Dakota bond" story deserved telling.

The unprecedented lawsuit and the United States Supreme Court's decision in the case are significant in constitutional history. The story illumines North Carolina, and indirectly Southern and also Western, politics in the years after Populism and Bryanism had spent most of their powers. In North Carolina certainly, and in South Dakota to a lesser extent, the bond case became a major political issue and made headlines over a number of years. Finally, the subject attracted me because, along with all the legal and economic and constitutional intricacies which were involved, a vast display of fascinating human nature emerged from the candid letters which revealed the ideas, hopes, fears, hates, and quarrels of the men who were involved in the affair.

Strangely enough, at the time of the bond suit contemporaries believed Marion Butler more responsible than Russell for the troublesome problems which the suit dumped into the laps of the dominant Democrats in North Carolina. Butler, who became an energetic Republican in the Theodore Roosevelt era, suffered many a Democratic attack for three decades about his connection with the lawsuit. The new Russell material now shows clearly that not Butler but Russell originated the bold plan and called the signals for its execution from 1901 through the settlement of 1905.

Newspapers, both in North Carolina and South Dakota, cast considerable light on the story; legislators and other politicians figured largely in the bond suit, and consequently, public opinion played a significant role. North Carolina newspapers dealt first and always extensively with the bond affair; but the South Dakota journals furnished, among other things, a clear reflection of how Northerners in the early years of this century came to accept the Southern Democratic version of Reconstruction and the race problem. The official and personal papers of key North Carolina Democrats yielded an inside view of what Russell called "the enemy's" thinking and planning. But the central figure and the one whose papers form the backbone of the study is the complex Daniel L. Russell, who emerges as a sort of unique Tarheel blend of Machiavelli and Falstaff.

Governor Russell concocted his bond plan partly to cause trouble for the North Carolina Democrats, who, under the leadership of Furnifold M. Simmons and Charles B. Aycock and others, had defeated the Fusionists in the "White Supremacy" crusades of 1898 and 1900. Russell also needed money. Although other Southern repudiated bonds were originally involved in the scheme, Russell's plan succeeded only with a certain issue of North Carolina railway-construction bonds which had been authorized by a legislature composed of native Tarheels during the interval between the end of the Civil War and the beginning of the "Radical" phase of Reconstruction in 1868. These bonds, which the state legislature backed by a second mortgage on state-owned railway stock, were not repudiated but drastically scaled down by the Democrats in their debt readjustment act of 1879.

Since the Eleventh Amendment to the Federal Constitution prevented the private holders of the North Carolina "second mortgage" bonds from suing the sovereign state of North Carolina, Russell hit on the idea of having the New Yorkers who owned most of the outstanding bonds donate ten of them to another state. This sovereign donee could then, under the Constitution, sue North Carolina in the United States Supreme Court. Marion Butler, in the last days of his term in the Senate, helped secure South Dakota as the donee. Russell brought other lawyers from New York, South Dakota, and elsewhere into the complex, novel case.

From the minute the affair began in 1901, it was front-page news—and political dynamite—in North Carolina. Josephus Daniels, then at the height of his power as the editor of the fiercely Democratic Raleigh *News and Observer,* exploited the "South Dakota bond" affair for all it was worth, and a bit more too. For five years, from 1901 through 1905, Daniels' newspaper charged, without ever offering proof, that the Southern Railway corporation and its "higher ups" were connected with the "bond conspiracy." Then in later years the *News and Observer* and other Democratic newspapers continued to exploit the episode, through news columns and headlines as much as editorials, for partisan purposes.

By the time the Supreme Court rendered its decision in February, 1904, the case had attracted national attention. The five-to-four decision against North Carolina revived widespread interest in the whole vast field of repudiated bonds. But Russell, after escaping a close brush with death, still had the tedious chore of securing a compromise settlement from the North Carolina Democrats on the privately held second-mortgage bonds, since the Supreme Court had ruled only on the ten held by South Dakota.

Governor Aycock passed the bond headache on to his successor, Robert B. Glenn. The affair lasted longer than Russell had dreamed it would, and his final plans for again using South Dakota against the Tarheel Democrats did not succeed. Political circumstances in the Western state in 1905 were, to Russell's misfortune, considerably changed from what they had been in

1901. In the spring of 1905, Glenn, after overcoming vehement opposition from the *News and Observer* and its allies, agreed to a compromise settlement with the private bondholders and full payment to South Dakota of the Supreme Court's judgment against North Carolina.

Russell and his fellow lawyers received much less from the final settlement than they had anticipated, and the ensuing quarrels among the fee-hungry lawyers were both ferocious and funny. Russell died in 1908, proud to the end of his part in bringing discomfort on those whom he regarded as Democratic repudiationists. But Marion Butler, in his vigorous prime during the bond suit, lived on until 1938 and bore the brunt of repeated Democratic attacks, many of them distorted and inaccurate, about the bond affair. Even in South Dakota the affair became controversial after 1905, but in North Carolina "Butler and bonds" became the irresistible slogan and symbol for Democrats who wished to keep alive as long as they could their own mythical versions of the Reconstruction and Fusion eras.

*   *   *

The key role of Dr. Patton of the Southern Historical Collection in the inception of this book has already been suggested, and Dr. Carolyn Wallace especially and others on Dr. Patton's staff were helpful. Dr. Mattie Russell, director of the Duke University Manuscript Department, furnished kind assistance, and Miss Florence Blakely, Miss Mary Canada, Mr. Emerson Ford, and Mr. Elvin Strowd of the Duke University Library staff were generous with their aid. Mr. H. G. Jones, State Archivist, facilitated the use of important papers in the North Carolina Department of Archives and History, and Mr. Will G. Robinson, secretary of the South Dakota State Historical Society, helped arrange the use of South Dakota newspapers. Professor Herbert S. Schell, Dean of the Graduate School in the State University of South Dakota, not only supplied copies of his notes on South Dakota matters but read the manuscript and made valuable suggestions. Professor Joseph F. Steelman of Eastern Carolina College utilized his intimate knowledge of North Carolina history in a close reading of the manuscript; Dr. Benjamin U. Ratchford, formerly professor of economics in Duke University and now Vice President of the Federal Reserve Bank in Richmond, who wrote earlier studies which were indispensable to the writing of this one, read this manuscript and offered encouragement and advice.

In Duke University, Professors Richard H. Leach, William T. Laprade, Richard L. Watson, and I. B. Holley have been kind enough to read the manuscript and make suggestions. Professor W. B. Hamilton served efficiently in his capacity as editor of the Duke Historical Series and kindly as a friend who listened patiently to much about bonds long before a word was written. Mrs. Elizabeth McConnell typed the various drafts, and Anne Oller Durden listened, read drafts, and helped with the index.

The Duke University Research Council has subsidized both research and publication. A summer fellowship from the Council allowed an uninterrupted season for writing. The Research Council's policies, together with the kindnesses of its individual members, were, in short, important incentives to and aids in the writing of this book.

ROBERT F. DURDEN

Duke University
June, 1961

CONTENTS

Reconstruction Bonds & Twentieth-Century Politics

chapter one

DEFEATED LEADERS PLAN FOR VENGEANCE—AND PROFIT

DANIEL LINDSAY RUSSELL of Wilmington had always dreamed of being governor of North Carolina. And Republican though he was, a series of strange circumstances allowed the dream to come true in 1896 when, for the first and only time since the Reconstruction era, the Democrats failed to elect their candidate for North Carolina's top executive position. "You know you always told me that you would be satisfied if you were elected Governor to quit politics when your term was out," an old friend wrote Russell. "You are victorious and can afford to, and must be, charitable," the friend continued, for the truth was that "thousands of Democrats in the State would prefer any other man to you, especially in Wilmington. You know what a bitter pill it will be for the gang there."[1]

Republican victory was indeed a bitter pill for Democrats long accustomed to power, but the paradoxical fact was that the governorship brought no joy to Russell. The old dream became, as a reality, something of a nightmare; and before it was over, escape from his political misery and economic peril (North Carolina then paid her governor the sadly inadequate sum of $3,000 a year) became Russell's overwhelming desire.

Russell's Republicanism was, in one sense, only skin-deep. In long-memoried Southern fashion, he was still a Whig—a half century after that once-powerful party had disintegrated —and he came of proud Whig stock. He was born in 1845 on

[1] Sol C. Weill to Russell, Nov. 6, 1896, in Russell MSS, Southern Historical Collection, University of North Carolina Library.

a tidewater plantation in Brunswick County near Wilmington. His slave-owning father served several terms as a Whig representative in the North Carolina legislature, and his maternal grandfather, David W. Sanders of Onslow County, North Carolina, enjoyed political prominence as an active Whig in the ante bellum years. Russell's father strongly opposed secession, as did many other Southern Whigs, but when the Civil War came sixteen-year-old Daniel abandoned his studies at the University of North Carolina and rushed home to help organize and equip a militia company which he headed as captain.

Zealous Confederate though he was, young Russell's impulsiveness and hot temper got him into military trouble. His company sat quietly at Fort Fisher near Wilmington while the great armies battled savagely in Virginia; after trying every means he could devise to be transferred, and failing, Russell took the lead in hiring a ship to take the company to Virginia, only to be arrested and court-martialed for flagrant insubordination. His extreme youth and family connections enabled him to escape punishment this time. Yet it was not long before Russell's military career floundered again, and permanently.

His father, still dissenting freely and no doubt blaming Southern Democrats as much as Yankees for assorted crimes, vocally opposed Confederate conscription. The provost marshal in Wilmington therefore denounced the elder Russell as a traitor. Angrily calling upon the provost for satisfaction, in a miscarried version of the code duello, young Dan Russell lost his head and fired upon and wounded his superior officer. This time he was court-martialed and sentenced to be stripped of his rank. But Confederate military justice could hardly hope to overcome the bold obstructionism of stubborn Tarheels. Russell, at the age of nineteen, got himself elected to the state legislature. Under the sheltering wing of the popular war-governor, Zebulon Vance, who held that civil authority was superior to that of the military, the youth once more escaped the punishment he apparently so richly deserved.[2]

After his convenient term as legislator, Russell, now a Republican according to the postwar political labels that many North Carolinians switched around with surprising facility, gained admission to the bar. In 1868 he was elected a superior-court judge. Though still only in his twenties, the precocious judge held his post for six years, from 1868 to 1874, returned to the North Carolina legislature in 1876, and in 1878 successfully campaigned for election to the United States House of Representatives. He was not a candidate for renomination in 1880, possibly because the Democrats appeared unbeatable as they sedulously set about perfecting their hold on the "solid" South. Russell's political career appeared to be at a dead end when he was still only in his late thirties. He kept his interest in politics but turned increasingly to law and his plantation until totally unforeseen chaos descended on North Carolina politics in the troubled decade after 1890.

The chaos derived from the agrarian revolt which shook North Carolina as it did few other Southern or Western states. Ignored by the probusiness conservatives who dominated both major parties, the farmers were victimized by commodity prices, among other things, which steadily declined as money became scarcer and credit dearer. The long-suffering farming majority in North Carolina and the nation finally exploded in the early 1890's. The explosion first took the form of the militant Farmers' Alliance and then metamorphosed into the short-lived but highly influential Populist party. In both phases of the farmers' struggle for reform, North Carolina figured prominently; it furnished first Leonidas L. Polk as the acknowledged national leader of the Alliance and Marion

[2] Most of the above is based on the short biographical sketch in typescript by Louis Goodman, Russell's last law partner, in the Russell MSS and on a biographical account in the *News and Observer*, Oct. 30, 1896. Many of the standard North Carolina biographical compilations ignore Russell, but there are sketches in the *Biographical Directory of the American Congress, 1774-1927* (Washington, 1928) and John E. Brown, ed., *Lamb's Biographical Dictionary of the United States* (Boston, 1903).

Butler as the later National Alliance president, national chairman of the People's party, and Populist senator from North Carolina.[3]

Strangely enough, Populism made it possible for Daniel Russell, ex-Whig turned Republican, to realize his old dream of becoming governor of North Carolina. The Populists drew strength away from the somnolent Democrats, who too long had ignored pressing realities while they embroidered the myth of a virtuous and noble Democratic party which had "redeemed" the South from a horror-filled Reconstruction. The irate agrarians co-operated with the Republican party in the state in order to achieve certain reforms, such as an honest election law, and simply to beat the Democrats. This policy of limited co-operation, known by the partisan Democratic label of "fusion," led to Populist-Republican capture of the legislature in 1894 and to Marion Butler's election to the United States Senate. Two years later, when the Democrats became further demoralized by the deep split between "goldbug" admirers of Grover Cleveland and "silverite" followers of William Jennings Bryan, Daniel L. Russell was elected governor in a three-way race among Republicans, Populists, and Democrats.

"There is retribution in history," Governor Russell declared in beginning his inaugural address. Thus too had Governor Zeb Vance spoken after the North Carolina Democrats had defeated the Republicans in the heated contest of 1876. Leaving the matter of retribution, whether in history or elsewhere, to others, Russell would better have avoided reference to the bitter past. It was the memory of Reconstruction, a memory now freshened by certain aspects of the "fusion" era and kept throbbingly alive in a highly distorted and exaggerated fashion by Democratic politicians and writers, which would help to end Populist-Republican rule, bring the

[3] The author is currently preparing a study of Marion Butler and North Carolina Populism. Stuart Noblin, *Leonidas LaFayette Polk: Agrarian Crusader* (Chapel Hill, 1949), is the best treatment of the early phase in North Carolina.

"White Man's Party" back into power, and cause Governor Russell to confess, in despair and disillusionment, that "the irritations incident to being a Republican and living in the South, are getting to be too rank to be borne. . . ."[4]

Some of Russell's troubles as governor were, of course, of his own making. His hot temper was as notorious as his stubborn loyalty to his friends; the former led him into rash, ill-advised actions and the latter characteristic caused him to stand beside certain of his appointees who hardly deserved such steadfastness. But aside from his personal shortcomings, which were, after all, counterbalanced by intelligence and courageous independence, Russell's political difficulties sprang from more deep-seated and impersonal circumstances. "Fusion" by no means meant that the Republicans had swallowed the Populists, Democratic partisans to the contrary notwithstanding. It was true that together the two parties had overwhelming control of the legislature; but the togetherness implied by the term "fusion" proved impossible from the first month of Russell's term. Republicans and Populists fell into an angry quarrel about the re-election of Republican Senator Jeter C. Pritchard, whose questionable attachment to the silver cause made him anathema to the "goldbug"-hating majority of the Populists. Pritchard won, thanks to support from a bolting Populist minority, but co-operation between the two parties was now made even more difficult.[5]

Russell had pledged an all-out fight against the ninety-nine-year lease of the North Carolina Railroad to J. P. Morgan's newly created Southern Railway system. Russell's Democratic predecessor, Governor Elias Carr, had sprung

[4] Russell to Benjamin Newton Duke, Dec. 2, 1898, in the B. N. Duke MSS, Duke University Library.

[5] The fullest printed account of North Carolina political history in this period, and still valuable despite an obvious bias in favor of white Democrats and against Negro Republicans, is J. G. deRoulhac Hamilton, *North Carolina since 1860*, Vol. III in R. D. W. Connor, *et al.*, *History of North Carolina* (3 vols.; Chicago, 1919). Dr. Joseph F. Steelman's carefully documented dissertation at the University of North Carolina, "The Progressive Era in North Carolina, 1884-1917" (1955), is being prepared for publication.

the lease of the strategic railroad, in which the state of North Carolina owned a majority of the stock, on a surprised and largely indignant public. Russell's bold assaults on the "midnight lease" made this the most important issue during the first year of his administration; but in the end, after endless political and legal maneuvering, he was forced to accept the lease and to make peace with some of the powerful Republicans whom he had offended while, at the same time, he quite failed to make any real friends among the desperate Democrats.

The most fundamental source of Governor Russell's political woe lay in the Democratic party's strategy of resorting to a calculated policy of exploiting racial fears and passions to enable the "White Supremacy" party to regain power in the anti-Negro campaigns of 1898 and 1900. North Carolina Negroes, in the main, voted Republican for the same sort of historical, sentimental, and essentially irrational reasons that so many Southern whites had voted Democratic before the economic storms of the 1890's had blown a significant number of white agrarians into the crusading third party. While Negroes were by no means the only Republicans in North Carolina, they did furnish a large part of the total Republican vote, and in the eastern counties of the state Negro Republicans abounded while the white ones like Russell were scarce enough to suffer ostracism and scorn from Democratic neighbors.

It was ironic, in a way, that Russell should have to stand by and watch the Democratic Red Shirts raucously "save" North Carolina from Negro "domination." The truth was that the Republican governor was no special friend to his fellow Republicans of slave ancestry. A group of prominent Negro Republicans had openly and vigorously opposed his nomination in 1896, because of certain harsh statements which Russell had made concerning the mythical "average" Negro. Russell provided precious few political plums in the form of salary-paying offices for the estimated 120,000

Negro Republicans in North Carolina, and this was an era of painful deflation and depression when the appetite for patronage grew ravenous among the faithful of all parties, irrespective of race, color, or previous condition of servitude. Russell declared in his message to the 1899 Legislature that of all the commissions issued from the Executive Office during the first two years of his administration, it could be shown that he had appointed 818 persons to civil offices "of whom not more than eight (8) were colored."[6]

To be sure, when the call for troops came from Washington in the Spanish-American War, Governor Russell boldly appointed Negro officers to a Negro regiment from North Carolina. This action pleased Negroes and the few racial liberals who were left among the white population in the nation by 1898, and it no doubt annoyed some of the more doctrinaire white supremacists.[7] It was also true that in eastern North Carolina, where Negroes often outnumbered whites in some towns and counties, many petty offices—such as register of deeds, justice of the peace, school board, and the like—were held by Negroes. One of the ten congressmen from the state was a Negro, while a few of the Federal appointments to post offices and revenue collectorships fell to Negroes.[8] Altogether, it would be an unparalleled feat of sheer imagination to envision North Carolina in Governor Russell's time as being under "nigger domination." Yet the vivid imaginative powers of North Carolina Democrats quite rose to the challenge.

Under the vigorous and ruthlessly efficient leadership of Furnifold M. Simmons of New Bern in the east, the Democracy in 1898 launched a racist campaign such as had not

[6] Governor Russell to the Senate and House of Representatives, Jan. 4, 1899, in the Governors' Letterbooks, North Carolina Department of Archives and History.

[7] See, for example, the congratulatory telegram from the New England Baptist Missionary Convention to Russell, June 18, 1898, in the Governors' Papers, North Carolina Department of Archives and History.

[8] The best recent study of this matter is Helen G. Edmonds, *The Negro and Fusion Politics in North Carolina* (Chapel Hill, 1951).

been seen in North Carolina since the Reconstruction elections of the 1870's. The Republicans had no established daily newspaper in the state and rather few weeklies. The Democrats had Josephus Daniels' Raleigh *News and Observer,* which was without peer for exciting partisanship in both news and editorial columns. Other dailies and a host of weeklies took their cues from the powerful politician-editor in the state capital. Since 1898 was not a presidential election year, the divisive economic issues which had rent the Democrats into Cleveland and Bryan wings could be swept under the rug; and such conservative, "goldbug" Democratic papers as Joseph P. Caldwell's dignified Charlotte *Observer* and Robert M. Furman's impressive new Raleigh *Morning Post* could join in the passionate and desperate bid to "save" the Old North State from the oft-retold horrors of Negro rule and Republican-Populist misgovernment.

Democratic orators by the dozen proceeded to launch a new myth about "Fusion rule," a myth that was gradually to take its place alongside the older Democratic tales about the Reconstruction era. Chairman Simmons quietly promised certain powerful business leaders that corporation taxes would not be increased by a Democratic legislature; he assured the influential Baptist and Methodist leaders from the denominational colleges that there would be no increase in appropriations for the state-supported institutions of higher learning.[9] While Simmons maneuvered behind the scenes, Charles B. Aycock from the east and Robert B. Glenn from the west headed the roster of Democratic speakers who electrified vast audiences as they pictured, in colorful but exaggerated fashion, the unspeakable horrors which threatened white women, and indeed all lovers of "good" and "decent" government, if Fusion rule were not ended. The strategic appearance of mounted and armed Democratic Red Shirts in many parts of the state completed the program for what was

[9] J. Fred Rippy, ed., *F. M. Simmons, Statesman of the New South: Memoirs and Addresses* (Durham, 1936), p. 29.

really more of a coup d'état in the best Balkan style than it was an orderly, peaceful election in the Anglo-American tradition. Thus the "White Man's Party" in North Carolina regained control of the legislature and proceeded to prepare the way for the constitutional amendment of 1900, which virtually eliminated Negroes from the electorate and effectively curtailed the political activity of many whites through the poll tax and other devices. The break in Democratic control in North Carolina had not lasted long; it would not occur again in a twentieth century span which, by 1960, was already twice as long as the interval between Reconstruction and Fusion.

If Russell had known troubles during the early part of his administration and the bitter 1898 campaign, they must have seemed small in the grim aftermath of the election. He faced the prospect of a legislature controlled by the Democrats. An earlier Republican governor of North Carolina, William Woods Holden, had suffered impeachment, conviction, and expulsion from office at the hands of a Democratic legislative majority in 1871. The prospect of a similar fate was something which Russell, proud and fiery as always, contemplated with horror. Some of the more partisan Democrats began to discuss the possibility of impeachment after the 1898 victory.

Russell, lonely and inwardly frightened, apparently unburdened himself to very few people. One of these was his friend and fellow-Republican, Benjamin N. Duke, millionaire industrialist of Durham and New York. Inhibited from going to Durham himself by Democratic newspapers, which would have dramatically exploited such a trip as proof of the Republican governor's alleged subserviency to the malevolent, omnipresent "tobacco trust," Russell frequently invited the kindly Ben Duke to "run down" and spend the night at the Mansion. "I am lonesome," Russell once wrote Duke when Mrs. Russell had gone to visit the plantation.[10] But

[10] Russell to Duke, April 21, Oct. 19, 1898, in the Duke MSS.

a new note of near-despondency crept into the governor's hastily scrawled letters to his friend after the election of 1898. First there was the suggestion that the slanders and cruel attacks of the opposition had only affected Mrs. Russell, who was apparently a quiet person well-known for her activities in the temperance cause. "She has borne this ordeal well," Russell declared as the campaign ended, "but, I fear, is about to break down."

The truth was that the governor himself had fallen into a gloomy, half-fearful state, and this he finally confessed to Duke: "I am in deep distress. Not that I am afraid of disgrace, not that I have done anything wrong. My troubles have come because I have been honest and unpurchasable and have tried to help the common people. You are the only friend to whom I feel like uncovering and explaining all. No body else knows anything about it except my wife." Then the governor explained that he and his wife, who were childless and on the far side of middle age, had "been looking to retiring from here at the end of the term to a comfortable and happy home." But now the "devils," that is, the more fanatic Democrats, were "breaking up our business and it looks like we will be driven from our home."[11]

These words of the distraught governor's might well be dismissed as momentary exaggeration if it were not for the fact that as he wrote the dozen or more Negroes who had been killed in the Wilmington race riot and municipal coup of November 10-12, 1898, were being buried. A group of armed Democrats, led by Alfred M. Waddell, the veteran United States congressman whom Russell had defeated in 1878, had forcibly overthrown the Republican municipal government, driven the white "carpetbagger" Republicans out of the town and state, and bloodily intimidated the Negroes after preventing many of them from voting in the election on November 6, 1898.[12] Such frightful events in the

[11] Russell to Duke, Nov. 11, 19, 1898, *ibid.*

[12] Hamilton, *North Carolina since 1860*, pp. 292-297; Edmonds, *The Negro and Fusion Politics*, pp. 158-174. It was reported that a prominent

governor's home town understandably produced deep fore-
boding in his mind.

Apparently Russell contemplated resigning as governor
and moving to New York where he might practice law and
enjoy whatever business Ben Duke and his brother James
B. Duke could steer his way from the mighty American Tobacco Company. "Things are so in Wilmington," Russell
explained, "that we do not feel like living there, or trying
to do so." Furthermore, he was in bad shape financially,
"not desperate" but "not satisfactory" either. And Russell
never wrote what was the case: being a proud but poor Republican governor on the pittance which North Carolina then
paid entailed face-saving expenditures which a frugal Democrat might possibly have avoided. Worst of all, he dreaded
leaving Raleigh "in such a shape that I would be compelled
to struggle for a reasonable income down there [Wilmington]."
Russell insisted that impeachment fears did not motivate him:
"I am not afraid of any deviltry from these Democrats in the
way of impeachment. They have abandoned all that, at
least all the indications are that way. Indeed all their leaders
say so." But the whistling-in-the-dark quality of his words
is inescapable. He would not, at any rate, resign until after
the session of the legislature which would begin early in 1899.
In the meantime, Ben Duke would be in Durham for the
Christmas holidays, and the governor would be "lonesome
in this palace and anxious to see my friends."[13]

What persuasive words the loyally Republican Duke used
over those Christmas holidays to dissuade Russell from the
idea of resigning will probably never be known. Indeed, the
governor's prospects and spirits may well have brightened
sufficiently so that his friend did not have to dissuade. At
any rate, in his correspondence with Duke, Russell never
again mentioned quitting before his term expired in January,

Wilmington Democrat threatened that if Russell should dare to visit his
home in 1898 "his corpse would be floated down the Cape Fear river."
News and Observer, May 15, 1908.
[13] Russell to B. N. Duke, Dec. 2 and 22, 1898, Duke MSS.

1901. One thing Duke definitely did do was to help the governor borrow money, which was not an easy thing in the credit-scarce days of the late nineteenth century. Russell made deeds of trust for some of his lands in the Wilmington area to secure eight notes of $1,000 each. Wilmington friends lent him the $8,000, and B. N. Duke endorsed four of the notes.[14] Later in 1899 Duke favored Russell, as he had other friends in North Carolina, by investing in stock of the Continental Tobacco Company the $1,000 margin which Russell sent. The governor felt that he could find no appropriate words to thank his rich benefactor but would "try it some of these days."[15]

Clearly the Durham millionaire's friendship and financial assistance must have helped deter Russell from taking the drastic step which he had earlier contemplated. If the exuberantly partisan Democrats had known for a fact, what the *News and Observer* and others charged anyway, that "The Trust's" own B. N. Duke both extended favors to Russell and received them from him, impeachment would no doubt have quickly become a reality. Yet the many and intimate letters which the governor wrote to Duke do not show that the relationship was improper. Indeed, Russell remained his stubborn and independent self even where his powerful friend and benefactor was deeply concerned.

The best example of this independence is also an important one. Late in 1900, after the Democrats had triumphed in the election with their full slate of candidates as well as with the disfranchising amendment to the state constitution,

[14] John S. Armstrong, President of the Atlantic National Bank of Wilmington, to B. N. Duke, Feb. 27, 1899, *ibid.* It is somehow both sad and amusing that President Armstrong shortly afterward wrote the Durham capitalist in his own, that is Armstrong's, behalf: he was looking for a "first class business opening somewhere North." The bank in Wilmington was most successful, and Armstrong had about $100,000 to put into the right kind of enterprise, but "for certain reasons, I prefer moving into a section possessing more enterprise and opportunities."

[15] Russell to B. N. Duke, Aug. 10, 1899, *ibid.* Russell later claimed that his four years as governor cost him $11,000 in excess of his $3,000 annual salary. *Morning Post,* Jan. 10, 1905.

Chief Justice William T. Faircloth of the North Carolina Supreme Court died suddenly. Here, about two weeks before Russell would be succeeded by Governor-elect Charles B. Aycock, the Republican governor was faced with the necessity of appointing a chief justice who would serve until the regular election scheduled for the fall of 1902. Aside from the prestige of the office, it carried with it real power, for vital matters having to do with the economic and political life of the state would hinge on the court's decisions in the years immediately ahead. Specifically, and perhaps most crucially, the constitutional amendment, which was carefully and legalistically designed to accomplish the illegal feat of disfranchising illiterate Negroes while allowing illiterate whites to register and vote under the "grandfather clause," was expected to have to undergo the judicial tests which some elements of the state's Republican party would strongly demand. With two Republicans already seated on the five-man tribunal, the appointment of the chief justice would perhaps determine how the majority of the court would decide on a large number of fundamental issues.

Russell's indifference to the disfranchisement of the great mass of Negro voters was widely known, although he had kept silent during the 1900 struggle, which had been essentially a repetition of the "White Supremacy" and Red Shirt campaign of 1898. It was this fact of his acceptance of the disfranchisement scheme, the cornerstone of the plans for undisturbed Democratic hegemony in North Carolina, which prompted an influential and large group of North Carolinians, including perhaps as many Democrats as Republicans, to come up with the suggestion that the ideal candidate to fill the supreme court vacancy was none other than Daniel L. Russell himself! His great legal ability was widely recognized, even by some of the most partisan Democrats; furthermore he was a Republican from the eastern part of the state, and it was assumed that, in view of the circumstances and existing composition of the court, whomever he appointed would have to possess these qualifications.

The Raleigh *Morning Post,* influential spokesman for the conservative wing of the Democratic party, declared that since the chief justice would have to be a Republican from the east and since Russell was the pre-eminently able and available lawyer from that section, his clear "duty is to resign his present position and accept the appointment" as chief justice from the lieutenant-governor, Charles A. Reynolds, who would of course become acting governor. Distinguished lawyers in various towns, including both Republicans and Democrats, hurriedly signed petitions requesting Russell to adopt this plan. In Winston-Salem, for example, Robert B. Glenn, already a leading Democrat and destined to succeed Aycock as governor in 1905, joined Cyrus B. Watson, the Democratic gubernatorial candidate whom Russell had defeated in 1896, and others in endorsing the plan.[16]

While Democrats worried about the fate of their disfranchisement scheme, businessmen looked at the crucial appointment from a different angle. Colonel Alexander B. Andrews, locally influential as a vice-president of the Southern Railway Company and one of the most powerful men in North Carolina if not the South, dashed off a hurried and confidential note to B. N. Duke. It is "very important," Andrews avowed, that the trust-hating and Populistically inclined Democrat, Justice Walter Clark, should not dominate the court. But if Governor Russell appointed his friend and fellow Republican from Warren County, Charles Cooke, Andrews feared precisely the worst—Clark's control of Cooke and the court. "The thing to do," Andrews urged, "is for Gov. Russell to resign and have Lt. Gov. Reynolds, who then becomes Governor, to appoint Gov. Russell the Chief

[16] Raleigh *Morning Post,* Jan. 2, 1901; and see issues of Jan. 3 and 5, 1901. Glenn's explanation that he endorsed Russell because he (Glenn) was one of the key authors of the suffrage amendment, and his "heart was bent upon its ultimate legal adoption," is in the *Morning Post,* June 10, 1904.

Justice. I know this would be very gratifying to Gov. Russell, he only needs a little backing and encouragement from friends to make him agree to pursue this course." Duke should write the governor at once or send an agent to see him.[17] A Concord industrialist shared Andrews' concern about the appointment and urged Duke to see his friend the governor quickly: "We would at least like to have a friend on the bench. Of course this is strictly between ourselves."[18]

While these powerful forces, some acting publicly and some quite privately, converged in urging the plan of Russell's making himself chief justice, the Raleigh *News and Observer* exploded angrily in its strongest "tocsin-sounding" manner. With Aycock's inauguration so near yet so irretrievably far, Editor Daniels' frustration and suspicion were clearly beyond all limits. "Who is it that wants to foist Russell, the irascible, vacillating, corporation tool upon the people in the office honored by Taylor, Nash, Henderson, Ruffin and other great jurists?" Clearly it was all a "plot" of the Southern Railway, since Russell had long ago put on the yoke of A. B. Andrews and "rendered 'villein service' as is required of all vassals." Furthermore, the "Tobacco Trust" Dukes preferred Russell, Daniels declared, because the celebrated libel case of the Reverend T. J. Gattis versus President John C. Kilgo of Trinity College (which many regarded as a case, in reality, of Justice Walter Clark against Kilgo, Trinity College, and the Dukes) was slated to come before the Supreme Court in the near future.[19]

Gathering steam as it proceeded, the *News and Observer* threateningly trumpeted, on the very day that Russell finally settled the matter, that justice would surely overtake those who were "concocting this degradation" and "retribution when it comes will be in proportion to the outrageousness of

[17] A. B. Andrews to B. N. Duke, Dec. 30, 1900, in Duke MSS.
[18] W. R. Odell of Odell Cotton Manufacturing Company to B. N. Duke, Dec. 31, 1900, in *ibid.*
[19] *News and Observer*, Jan. 4, 1901. For the Gattis-Kilgo case, see Paul N. Garber, *John Carlisle Kilgo* (Durham, 1937).

their offense." "It would, be a fitting conclusion to the tragedy, the farce and shameful humiliation begun in Reconstruction and ended in Fusionism for the scalawag Governor, within one week of the close of his term of office, to appoint himself Chief Justice . . . as the pliant creature of the Southern Railway and the Tobacco Trust." And if Russell's other and more recent crimes were not sufficient to disqualify him from the chief justiceship, the then leading racist organ in the state capped the climax of its indictment by asserting that as superior court judge back in 1868-1869 young Russell's "pre-eminent ability" had led him to decide that a "negro buck" in Wilmington could take his sweetheart in to sit among "white gentlemen and ladies" in a local theater on the grounds that whites had no right to exclude Negroes from the place; it had been left to the United States Supreme Court "without a Southern man among them, to overthrow this outrageous and humiliating doctrine."[20]

What had Russell decided and to whom had he listened for advice? He did what he apparently wanted to do and what no one had exactly predicted: he moved Justice Daniel M. Furches, a Republican, up to the chief justiceship and named his friend Charles Cooke as the new justice. B. N. Duke had apparently shared A. B. Andrews' wariness toward Cooke. Russell received word from Senator Jeter C. Pritchard, the North Carolina Republican whose term would not expire until 1903, that Pritchard, Duke, and Andrews agreed that it would be best not to appoint Charles Cooke to the supreme court. Rather, Russell should elevate Furches and name Edward W. Timberlake, judge of the superior court in the fourth judicial district, to fill the vacancy that Furches' promotion would leave. Then Russell could reward his friend Cooke with Timberlake's post. But the stubborn governor retorted that Cooke did not live in Timberlake's district and besides he would not "betray" his constantly loyal and "disinterested" friend, Cooke, who was "safe" and reliable any-

[20] *Ibid.,* Jan. 5, 1901.

how. Cooke, the governor explained, was "as loyal and sincere and true a man as I, with all my wide knowledge of men, have ever known." Duke might be told that the governor mismanaged the whole affair. "*I know that I did* [manage it rightly]," Russell insisted. "I made no mistake in that affair."[21]

Actually the Durham capitalist had cared much less about the controversial supreme court matter than Josephus Daniels could have imagined. Duke had had preferences and had let them be known. But when Governor Russell followed his own counsel, Duke, now returned to his Manhattan base, admitted to a close associate in Durham that he did not really feel much concerned about the judicial appointment; he had heard from Russell. Besides, "Stocks are booming & I don't know when the end of the advance will come."[22]

Why Russell had resisted the urging of so many who wanted him to become chief justice cannot be dogmatically explained. He took great pride in his acknowledged legal prowess and could but have been flattered to occupy the seat for which Josephus Daniels declared him so grossly unfit. Furthermore, while Russell had recovered from the gloomy depression that followed the 1898 election, he had by no means solved his financial problems. Trying to recoup enough to pay at least some of his nagging debts, he had speculated in cotton futures only to get "badly caught." He confessed privately, about a year before his term was to expire, that he was "awful anxious to make some money to pay my debts. We can get home & quit spending money. I am *badly worried* about money."[23]

Yet he rejected the honor and security, however temporary, which would have been his as chief justice. One probable factor was that, realistic as he was, Russell feared, and correctly, that his tenure as chief justice would by no means be safe. Having, as he felt, barely escaped the humiliation of the impeachment which Democratic extremists had threat-

[21] Russell to Duke, Jan. 5 and Feb. 2, 1901, in Duke MSS.
[22] Duke to Ed Stagg, Jan. 8, 1901, in *ibid.*
[23] Russell to Duke, Jan. 9 and Sept. 7, 1900, in *ibid.*

ened in 1898, he had no appetite for further exposing himself
and his reputation to the enemy's fire. Well might he have
so calculated, for the chief event of the forthcoming 1901
legislative session was the impeachment and trial of Chief
Justice Furches and Justice Robert M. Douglas, distinguished
Republican from Greensboro and son of Illinois' "Little
Giant," Senator Stephen A. Douglas. Democratic extremists,
goaded by a combination of partisan zeal and apprehension
about the constitutional amendment, failed to carry enough
of their own party with them to convict the judges; but
Russell could hardly be blamed for wanting to escape the
ordeal which the *News and Observer* and other Democratic
spokesmen had so clearly foreshadowed.

Another possible factor in the denouement of the chief-
justiceship story is the position taken by the lieutenant-governor, Charles A. Reynolds of Forsyth County. If Russell
were to be made chief justice, Reynolds would necessarily
have had to play a co-operative and prominent part. Years
after the event, in 1929 in fact, and when he was almost
eighty-one years old, Reynolds reminisced concerning his
political past with a Tarheel newspaperman. He recalled being summoned to Washington for a conference with Senator
Pritchard, A. B. Andrews of the Southern Railway, Superior
Court Judge E. W. Timberlake, and several other prominent
North Carolinians. The proposition advanced there, according to Reynolds, was that he should sit tight while Russell
resigned to accept appointment as chief justice from Reynolds,
who would have become, in perfectly legal fashion, the governor in fact as well as name. Reynolds remembered keeping
quiet while the plan was discussed but growing more and
more irate. Finally, "with his entire being shaken with
pent-up anger," he responded to the assembled Republican
mighty with a "powerful explosion of wrath": "Gentlemen,
I won't do it. What would it mean to the reputation of each
man concerned? It would mean the ruination of every person

implicated, I'll have nothing to do with it." That ended the interview.

To the reporter, Reynolds explained that he would have liked the governorship, even so briefly, but "the idea of getting the office by a trade seemed to me to be about the most contemptible practice in which one could indulge"; and furthermore he felt that "the Supreme Court was the highest authority to which the people could appeal and that it ought not to be filled by a trade."[24]

That there was such a conference in Washington as Reynolds described is corroborated by what Russell himself wrote to Duke, although, as explained above, Russell's version deals with a plan whereby Timberlake rather than Cooke would be named to the Supreme Court after Associate Justice Furches had been elevated to the chief justiceship. Lieutenant-Governor Reynolds no doubt attended that meeting, and it is quite likely that the Washington conferees considered, as would any group of prudent string-pullers, several plans, alternative plans no doubt arranged in order of preference and according to what various contingent circumstances might allow. Reynolds may well have opposed the idea of his becoming governor in order to make Russell chief justice. But in view of several factors—Reynolds' relative political inexperience at that time, the high-powered nature of the group with whom he met in Washington, and the evidence in the Russell-Duke correspondence—it is highly unlikely that the retiring lieutenant-governor of January, 1901, played the heroic and decisive role which he colorfully described to a no doubt awed, as well as grateful, newspaperman in 1929. The tricks that age and passing years play on memory are too well known to need elaboration; that Reynolds was no exception to the general rule is best shown by the fact that in his 1929 interview he placed the whole episode concerning the chief justiceship two years early, in 1899, and

[24] Winston-Salem *Journal and Sentinel,* Aug. 25, 1929. Dr. Nannie M. Tilley kindly called the author's attention to this item.

thereby unwittingly distorted several significant aspects of the matter.

There were, clearly, several factors, but probably the most important and tangible reason why Russell had finally abandoned the plan for making himself chief justice was that he had, at last, hit upon a plan, a "scheme" he called it, whereby he hoped to make money, very much money indeed; and in early 1901 the "scheme" appeared more substantially promising than the rewards of any post which would be held at the mercy of the overwhelmingly Democratic legislature. The plan involved repudiated Southern bonds, including some scaled-down bonds of the State of North Carolina, and would lead eventually to a precedent-making case in the United States Supreme Court, the case of *South Dakota* v. *North Carolina.* Russell had already enlisted the help of his Populist friend, Senator Marion Butler, and was all set to proceed with his "scheme." It would have the double beauty, in his and Butler's eyes, of enriching them while causing no end of trouble to the jubilant Democrats who had now taken control of North Carolina's political destiny.

[*chapter two*]

ORIGINS OF THE "SOUTH DAKOTA BOND" CASE

RUSSELL'S plan for self-enrichment and sweet revenge on the Democrats involved repudiated and partially repudiated Southern bonds and particularly certain bonds which the State of North Carolina had sold in an ambitious program of state aid for railway development. Much of the state's political and economic history since the Jacksonian era had revolved around these interrelated matters of railroad construction and bonds.[1] It was the Whigs in North Carolina, appropriately enough in view of Russell's political pedigree, who launched the railroad building which ultimately played such a vital part in the state's life. The Whigs, despite strong opposition from the more economy- and laissez faire-minded Democrats, committed the state to a program of state aid for the risky, expensive business of railway development in the late 1830's. Then in 1849 the legislature chartered the North Carolina Railroad Company to traverse much of the state by linking Goldsboro in the east to Charlotte in the west; the state initially subscribed two of the three millions of capital and private citizens furnished the remainder. By a subsequent act in 1855 the state added another million to its original subscription. With Whigs still playing the dominant roles in the matter, the North Carolina Railroad opened for business in 1856. Aside from its military utility, which would shortly be dramatically revealed, the road was the first to cross the then backward, poverty-stricken Piedmont which, thanks in part to its transportation facilities, was destined to become the industrial and financial center of North Carolina.

To pay for its expensive program of aiding the railways, North Carolina sold its bonds and invested the proceeds in the stocks of the various railway companies. Or sometimes the state's bonds were simply exchanged at par for railroad securities, and the rail company itself disposed of the state's bonds. In the case of the North Carolina Railroad the state's bonds, amounting finally to three million dollars, were made especially attractive by virtue of the fact that the bonds were secured by a direct lien or mortgage on the three mil-

[1] C. K. Brown, *A State Movement in Railroad Development* (Chapel Hill, 1928) is detailed, while Hugh T. Lefler and Albert R. Newsome, *The History of a Southern State: North Carolina* (Chapel Hill, 1954), pp. 342-349, has a convenient summary of the ante bellum railroad program.

lions of North Carolina Railroad Company stock which the state owned.[2]

Immediately after the Civil War, and before the Radical Republican phase of Reconstruction began, North Carolina, like the rest of the South, faced financial ruin and omnipresent poverty. Yet Tarheel leaders, many of whom had been anti-secessionists and Whigs, were still in control of their own affairs as they fulfilled the Reconstruction plans by which President Andrew Johnson hoped, in vain, to "bind up the nation's wounds" in the same manner and spirit favored by his predecessor, Lincoln. In order to continue the program of aiding the railroads at a time when the state had little or no income, the state legislature in 1866-1867 authorized state help for the Western North Carolina Railroad, an extension of the ante bellum line, in this fashion: the state's bonds were to be secured by a second mortgage on the state's stock in the North Carolina Railroad Company which had already been pledged as security for an ante bellum bond issue. But since each of these new "Western bonds" had a par value of $1000 they were now given a second lien on ten shares of the state's $100-a-share stock in the North Carolina Railroad. This was the origin of the "second mortgage" or "ten-share bonds" which were later to acquire a certain fame from Russell's "scheme."

The bond transactions were still in process, however, when Radical Reconstruction began in North Carolina and nine other Southern states in 1867-1868. The financial shenanigans that accompanied the political and racial changes of the turbulent era are well known. Suffice it to say here that North Carolina was no exception to the familiar generalization that extravagance and corruption characterized the Radical Republican regimes which temporarily ruled in the South;

[2] B. U. Ratchford, "The North Carolina Public Debt, 1870-1878," *North Carolina Historical Review,* X (Jan., 1933), 1-3. This and the successive articles in the same journal provide a more detailed account of the North Carolina debt than does the same author's authoritative but more general *American State Debts* (Durham, 1941).

at the same time "Grantism" flourished in Washington, the Democratic Tweed Ring swindled millions in New York, and, in short, much of the nation witnessed a notorious lowering of public morality and private ethics. North Carolina Republicans in a short time authorized about ten million dollars more than the bonds totaling $17,377,000 which were actually issued, mostly for various railroad projects. Since many of these bond issues carried with them, in accordance with the new constitution of 1868, special taxes to pay interest, they became known as the "special tax" bonds. It is certain that Republicans had no monopoly on shady dealings in these dollar-worshiping years, but they were in power. It became, consequently, a paramount article of faith in the Democratic credo that the "special tax" bonds constituted the leading exhibit in the partisan case against "Republican misrule" which allegedly accompanied the original and also fanciful case of "Negro domination" in the state.[3]

North Carolina Democrats were among the first in the South to move toward repudiating the debt incurred by their hated Republican opponents, a task made easier for the Democrats by virtue of the fact that most of the bonds were held in the North. The battle, with its highly charged political as well as economic overtones, raged a full decade. Finally in 1879-1880 the Democrats, now safely ensconced in both legislative and executive branches, repudiated the huge debt incurred by the Republicans and funded and drastically scaled down the prewar debt. A constitutional amendment in 1880 prohibited, once and for all time, any consideration of the "special tax" bonds. The various segments of the "honest" debt were funded at amounts ranging from 15 to 40 cents on the dollar.[4] The "ten-share bonds" that had been issued to aid the Western North Carolina Railroad were

[3] *Ibid.* The latest and liveliest account of this era in North Carolina is Jonathan Daniels, *Prince of Carpetbaggers* (Philadelphia, 1958), which centers on the high-flying and shady operations of General Milton S. Littlefield.

[4] Ratchford, *American State Debts*, p. 184.

scheduled, together with other internal improvement bonds issued during and immediately after the war, at 25 cents on the dollar despite the fact that the "ten-share Westerns" or "second mortgage" bonds carried on their face a second mortgage on state-owned railway stock which other bonds in the 25-cents-on-the-dollar class did not possess.

Repudiation, in the ears of bondholders or even would-be bondholders, has always been the most frightening and horrifying word in the language. This was never truer than in the years at the close of the Reconstruction era, when Southern Democrats, in varying degrees, appalled the financiers of New York, Boston, London, and Paris, as well as a few of the smaller financial fry scattered around Dixieland, by resorting to the drastic measure of wiping out millions in inherited debt by legislative fiat.[5] That many of the financial operations of the Radical or Republican state officials and legislatures during Reconstruction were riddled with corruption is a fact widely accepted and beyond dispute. But the complex truth was that the shady practices and corruption did not begin suddenly in 1868, were not ended abruptly when Democratic "Redeemers" regained control, and were never limited exclusively at any time to Republicans. In other words, only truth-juggling partisanship could derive simple Democratic virtue and wicked Republican vice from the financial side of the Reconstruction era.

One close student of the subject generally defends repudiation of the Reconstruction debts on the grounds of the unconstitutionality and fraud which characterized so many of the bond issues in the war-wrecked and economically prostrated Southern states. The scaling down of the pre-Reconstruction debt, however, was another matter, much harder to justify; and North Carolina, among all the ex-Confederate states acted especially drastically in seizing the opportunity to scale down its prewar or "honest" debt while totally re-

---

[5] The best general account, comprehensive as well as calm, is Ratchford, *American State Debts*, pp. 162-229.

pudiating its Reconstruction debt without even making the effort, which Alabama and Georgia did make, to deal with each bond issue on its merit.[6]

Repudiation in the "New South," in short, aroused bitter controversy in the nation and was, despite dramatic over-simplification by most Southern Democratic politicians at the time as well as by their later spokesmen, a complex, many-sided affair. Yet all the howling of a thousand Wall Streets could not overcome one fundamental fact: the sovereign states, albeit newly limited in several key areas by the postwar constitutional amendments, were still sovereign in the matter of state finances and taxes. And the Eleventh Amendment, which had been ratified in 1798, still constituted an apparently insurmountable fortress around the states' invulnerability to suit from individual citizens of other states, no matter how outraged or defrauded the individuals might consider themselves to be. That amendment, born in the angry aftermath of the case of *Chisholm* v. *Georgia* (1793), declared: "The Judicial power of the United States shall not be construed to extend to any suit in law or equity, commenced or prosecuted against one of the United States by Citizens of another State, or by Citizens or Subjects of any Foreign State."

It was this constitutional barrier, more than anything else, which protected Southern repudiators and confounded their enemies. Various efforts were made to breach the wall by court action, but invariably the United States Supreme Court ruled, as the Eleventh Amendment required, against the frustrated bondholders. In one of the more outstanding of the legal assaults on repudiation, the State of New Hampshire, acting merely as the agent for some of its citizens who held repudiated Louisiana bonds, sued that Southern state in the Supreme Court; but the Court ruled that New Hampshire's action was a transparent effort to circumvent the Eleventh

[6] *Ibid.*, 193-196.

Amendment and dismissed the case.[7] Southern Democrats, of course, applauded such decisions and rejoiced in the wisdom of the Constitution and its unimpeachable interpreter, the Supreme Court, but in the North the Eleventh Amendment came in for a steady drumming. Newspapers and such influential journals as the *Nation* loudly protested the Court's decision and urged in vain that the Eleventh Amendment be amended right out of the Constitution. *The Independent* declared in 1883: "The repudiation of State debts under the cloak of this Amendment has become the shame and disgrace of our country, and the proper remedy to arrest this enormous evil is to give to the Federal Courts [by a new amendment] the power which the Eleventh Amendment took away, and authorize Congress by appropriate legislation to carry that power into full and complete effect."[8]

Such verbal outpouring and teeth-gnashing were about the only recourse left to the holders of the repudiated or scaled-down Southern bonds. As the years passed, the controversy subsided. Most holders of the repudiated bonds probably became sadly reconciled to the loss of their investment—or failure of their speculation—and most of those whose Southern bonds were still worth something reluctantly accepted whatever fraction of the face value that could be obtained in refunded bonds. But at least one creditor of North Carolina refused to accept that sovereign state's arrangements as enacted in 1879. This was a New York banking firm, Schafer Brothers, which controlled 234 of the North Carolina "second mortgage" or "ten-share" bonds that had been issued to help build the Western North Carolina Railroad. Each bond had a face value of $1,000, but North Carolina offered only 25 cents on the dollar or $250 per bond. Indignant but helpless, Schafer Brothers decided just to wait —and hope.

[7] *New Hampshire* v. *Louisiana*, 108 U. S. 76 (1883), is discussed in Charles Warren, *The Supreme Court in United States History* (3 vols.; Boston, 1923), III, 387-388.
[8] As quoted in *ibid.*

Meantime, the bonds issued before the war to help build the North Carolina Railroad, known as the "construction bonds" and secured by a first mortgage on the state's stock in the railroad, had fared far differently and better. When the state failed to pay interest on these ante bellum bonds, despite the fact that the railroad paid dividends to the state and the dividends had been specifically pledged for the payment of the interest, one A. H. Swasey, a holder of some of the "construction" bonds, brought suit in 1871 against the railroad in a Federal circuit court. Swasey asked for an injunction restraining further dividend payments to the state, the appointment of a receiver to receive the dividends for the benefit of the bondholders, and a sale of a portion of the state's stock if the dividends were not sufficient to pay all the interest due. The railroad, a majority of whose directors were named by the state, admitted that the construction bonds had a lien on the state's stock but argued that the stocks were more clearly and specifically pledged as security for the bonds which had been subsequently issued to help the Western North Carolina Railroad; in other words, the railroad in this instance contended that since a formal mortgage had been executed in the case of the "second mortgage" bonds and only a statutory pledge in the case of the "construction" or "first mortgage" bonds, the formal mortgage should have precedence over the pledge. The Federal court did not agree. It issued the injunction as asked by Swasey, and named a receiver to pay out the railroad's dividends to the bondholders according to the court's instructions.

When the case was brought again before the Federal court, because the dividends were not sufficient to pay certain accumulated arrears in interest, the defendants insisted that the state was a party to the suit through its direct interest in the railroad, and, therefore, the suit could not be prosecuted by an individual. The Federal court, however, denied this argument on the grounds that the Eleventh Amendment applied only when a state was a party of record and that Federal courts regularly heard cases affecting the property of a state in the hands of its agents without making the state a party to the suit. The circuit court again ruled against the defendants, who appealed in vain to the United States Supreme Court.

The legal position of these "first mortgage" bonds being what it was, plus the fact that many of North Carolina's most influential citizens owned some of the ante bellum bonds, it is no wonder that not even the debt-slashing Democrats dared include them in the adjustments and repudiation acts of 1879. Some provision concerning them had to be made, however, for they would mature in 1883-1885; and if no arrangements were made for them by that time the holders would be able to sell the stocks pledged as security. Consequently, after several years of negotiation and delay by the state, the bondholders accepted the state's offer to exchange new forty-year, 6 per cent bonds for the original "construction" bonds. Any surplus of dividends from the state's stock over interest payments on the bonds was to go into a sinking fund to retire the bond issue; and the new bonds were specifically given not in payment but only in extension of the old bonds and without prejudice of the old bonds' lien on the state's stock in the North Carolina Railroad. In other words, no chance was taken that the "second mortgage" bonds could acquire a first lien on the state's increasingly valuable railroad stock. The "second mortgage" bondholders were not consulted in any way concerning the arrangements which the state had made with the "first mortgage" holders; the unlucky Schafer Brothers, as previously stated, were merely offered 25 cents on the dollar under the 1879 adjustment, and this they would not accept and had never accepted in the two decades after North Carolina made the offer.[9] These Schafer bonds would ultimately furnish Gov-

---

[9] This summary account of the Swasey suit and the final arrangements for the "first mortgage" bonds is based on Ratchford, "The North Carolina Public Dept. 1870-1878," pp. 5-7; and "The Adjustment of the North Carolina Public Debt, 1879-1883," *North Carolina Historical Review*, X (July, 1933), 163-165.

ernor Daniel L. Russell his opportunity to strike a doubly sweet blow, both profitable and revengeful, at North Carolina Democrats.

Precisely when or how Russell hit upon his "scheme" is not clear. Indeed, although it appears improbable from the abundant documentary evidence available, one of his political advisers or friends may have first put him on to the plan. At any rate, in the early part of his gubernatorial administration, it will be recalled, Russell vigorously opposed the "midnight" lease of the North Carolina Railroad to the Southern Railway. He finally lost this fight and backed away from the whole matter, which had created a political storm in 1897; but in the course of it he apparently learned a great deal about North Carolina's finances, past as well as current, and their intimate relation to the railroads in the state. For one example of how Russell had opportunities to learn much, it appears that the state government did not actually come into physical possession of the certificates of stock in the North Carolina Railroad, for which bonds of the state had long ago supposedly been exchanged, until 1897, when the lease fight raged.[10] Russell could insist, and with much justification, as will be shown, that he indeed knew the intricate ins and outs of one of the most complicated aspects of North Carolina's history: "It is not vanity or egotism in me but the simple truth when I say that I am the only man in North Carolina to-day who understands all the points, all the facts and all the law with regard to the capitalization, the stock, private and public, the bonds, the mortgages, the history and present status of the North Carolina Railroad Company. There are other lawyers as capable of understanding it as I am but they have not studied it as I have."[11]

The heart of Russell's "scheme," which he proudly and carefully kept as secret as possible until it was matured, was simply this: since the Eleventh Amendment barred individual

[10] Phillip W. Averitt to Governor Charles Aycock, June 9, 1902, Governors' Papers.
[11] Russell to John Graham, Jan. 23, 1901, Russell MSS.

citizens of other states from suing a sovereign state, and
since the sovereign state naturally prohibited its own citizens from suing, why not arrange for another state to sue?
The Federal Constitution gave the Supreme Court original
jurisdiction in controversies between states. Russell took to
his law books, as undated memoranda in his personal papers
show, and found numerous cases where the Supreme Court
had acted under this grant of power; true, most of the cases
had involved boundary disputes between states, but there were
some other types of cases and, after all, "controversy" is a
broad word.[12] If another state should sue one of the repudiating Southern states for full payment, with interest, on one
or more of the repudiated bonds, it might just be possible that
the United States Supreme Court itself would order the Southern state to pay her sovereign creditor. If so, surely the repudiating state would rush to compromise with any individual
holders of the other bonds rather than be forced to pay
full principal and interest to a state which could collect;
and, Russell further reasoned, even a small amount in
compromise would still represent a vast sum of money.

Moreover, the North Carolina "second mortgage" bonds
were an even better bet; for not only did they have a second
mortgage on valuable railway stock owned by the state, but
they also were of "honest" or pre-Carpetbag origin. There
were many complications and one or two especially puzzling
aspects about which Russell would spend many thought-
filled hours, but this, in brief, was the crucial "invention"
of his "scheme." It was, in actuality, two schemes, one involving the millions of dollars worth of Southern repudiated
bonds and one the more limited but also more promising
"second mortgage" bonds of North Carolina. The first step,
obviously, was to convince Schafer Brothers of New York
City that a lawyer had appeared who was convinced that he
could compel North Carolina to pay more on the "second

[12] A pertinent book here, to which Russell did not, of course, have
access, is Charles Warren, *The Supreme Court and Sovereign States*
(Princeton, 1924).

mortgage" bonds than the scorned 25 cents on the dollar which had been offered since 1879. This step alone would be tricky since the New York bankers were not to know, at least initially, the secret "patent" about one states' suing another nor that the author of the whole project was none other than the incumbent governor of North Carolina.

At least a year before his term expired, Russell was privately at work on his plan. The first clear reference to the matter in his papers is a letter, dated January 31, 1900, from Schafer Brothers to the state treasurer of North Carolina, William H. Worth. This letter, which was a reply to Treasurer Worth's inquiry, stated that Schafer Brothers did indeed "own and control in our possession" 210 of the Western North Carolina Company bonds and, in addition, controlled but did not own 25 of the bonds. (This was an error, by one bond, for the total number of bonds then in Schafer Brothers' control was 234 rather than 235.)

For belling the Schafer Brothers cat, Russell had just the man. His law partner for many years, Addison G. Ricaud, had earlier abandoned Wilmington to practice law in New York City. Ricaud, a Democrat and mayor of Wilmington in the early 1890's, apparently sought a different, and better, "climate" during the white supremacy campaign of 1898. As Ricaud later expressed it, he had come to regard Wilmington as "the most proscriptive and intolerant community I know of, and, as always the case, the concomitants of selfishness and duplicity also abound." Trying to live there would mean perpetual involvement "in brawls."[13] It was during the 1898 campaign, which also caused Russell to consider removing once and for all to New York, that the governor wrote a strange recommendation for his old friend and partner. After praising Ricaud's learning, honesty, and other sterling virtues, Russell, apparently facetiously, declared: "His devotion to truth is his most serious professional defect. He hardly ever tells a lie; indeed, I am inclined to think he never

[13] Ricaud to Russell, June 26, 1900, Russell MSS.

does, and as a result [he] has made some failures where he might have been successful."[14] Ricaud returned this strange testimonial and probably got another and more suitable one from the governor of North Carolina. At any rate, Ricaud found a law partner in New York and was available to perform invaluable services for the old associate whom he apparently respected, admired, and faithfully served. It is possible that Ricaud went to New York in 1898 with the bond plan already in mind; it is improbable that he did so, for Russell seems to have saved all of the written record about his beloved "scheme," and the first written mention of it to Ricaud, although this was clearly not Ricaud's introduction to the subject, came in May, 1900. Russell learned that Treasurer Worth had received inquiries about the "second mortgage" bonds, and the governor feared that two prominent Raleigh attorneys, Fabius Busbee and Robert Gray, might themselves be trying to make a deal with Schafer Brothers. "You better hustle," Russell warned Ricaud, and, meantime, perhaps a kind word or two from Benjamin N. Duke to Schafer Brothers might help.[15]

Russell began his request to Duke carefully: "I hope that you are not so very busy that you cannot give a little attention to the matter that I now want to write to you about." Then the governor explained that he thought he had found a way to make some money. Since nothing about it would come up until after his term expired there really was no harm in "having a chance at it" and, in one sense (and a misleading one), he was just "looking a little ahead to get control for my friend [Ricaud] as attorney in the matter." Russell then explained about Schafer Brothers' block of "second mortgage" bonds and about Ricaud's desire to get a contract for collection of the bonds on a contingent basis of 50 per cent of all money collected above the 25 cents on the dollar that North Carolina offered. Russell did not want Duke himself to incur

[14] Governor Russell to the Bench and Bar of New York State, Sept. 21, 1898, *ibid.* This is the signed original.
[15] Russell to Ricaud, May 9, 1900, *ibid.*

any pecuniary liability "but simply to vouch for the standing of Mr. Ricaud and to influence Schafer Bros. to give him the business."[16]

Ricaud, in the meantime, had begun what would be a long and tortuous business. He had learned, upon tackling the bond matter as requested by Russell, that "some Raleigh attorney" had indeed made an appointment to see Schafer Brothers, but Ricaud had managed to get the New York bankers to agree to do nothing in the matter until they had seen him. When Ricaud finally got to the Schafers, he began to learn a lot, and the process was not an unmixed pleasure. For one thing, he found that it would be difficult to get the brothers to concede even one-third, much less half, of any amount collected on the bonds above the amount that North Carolina had long offered to pay. Secondly, the Schafers were quite familiar with the whole subject of the Southern bonds and especially with the history of North Carolina's bonds and the various lawsuits connected with them. "They are keen, active Wall Street operators," Ricaud reported, "who are on the alert, very suspicious, optimistic in their views, and professedly occupy high moral grounds in business transactions, and seem disposed to sacrifice their holdings in these Bonds, rather than encourage State repudiation, by accepting the beggarly pittance which North Carolina offers, but with all things [they] are courteous, clever and successful Hebrews, with whom a bargain once made will be fulfilled."[17]

After Ben Duke visited Schafer Brothers and vouched for Ricaud as the former law partner of Duke's friend, Governor Russell, the prospect for Ricaud brightened.[18] Still, there was trouble about the profit that Ricaud, and his silent partner, should receive. Furthermore, convincing the Schafers that the bonds could be collected without at the same time even mentioning the secret "patent," which Russell hoped to save for bigger game, proved to be exceedingly difficult. At

[16] Russell to Duke, May 9, 1900, Duke MSS.
[17] Ricaud to Russell, May 11, 15, 1900, Russell MSS.
[18] Ricaud to Duke, May 16, 1900, Duke MSS.

this stage of the negotiation, Russell thought that it would be best if Ricaud merely proposed this plan of action: a petition from Schafer Brothers to the North Carolina Supreme Court for a ruling on the validity of the bonds; then, after the state court had upheld these bonds of impeccable ancestry, the North Carolina legislature could hardly refuse to pay off the state's honorable and just debt. But Ricaud found that the Schafers were reluctant to divide generously that which they strongly felt to be rightfully theirs anyhow; they had grown suspicious, Ricaud believed, that he was "concerting with the Powers that be" in North Carolina and came to them like a debtor who comes with the cash in his hand to pay an obligation and asks for a compromise. "Wall St[.] robbers are the keenest alive," Ricaud moaned, "and if they think there is a 'nigger in the wood pile' they will burn the wood if necessary to run him out. I would be willing to die if I could only do them once to the Queen's taste."

For all his wishing, Ricaud hardly "did" the Schafers. The best contract which he could get, making him their lawyer for the collection of the North Carolina bonds, gave him (and, in effect, Russell) only one-third of the excess collected over and above the 25 cents on the dollar already offered by the state. But actually Ricaud and Russell would get even less because of a secret agreement, on which the Schafers insisted, whereby Ricaud promised to return to the Schafers one-tenth of his fee, as a "commission." In other words, Ricaud finally had to agree to take only 30 per cent of the excess. And since Lawyer Fabius H. Busbee in Raleigh had also written to the Schafers proposing a plan similar to the one Ricaud had presented and could himself be useful on the scene at the state capital, Busbee now became the Raleigh representative of Schafer Brothers and of their senior counsel in the bond matter, A. G. Ricaud.[19]

Neither Russell nor Busbee, both of whom were well

[19] Ricaud to Russell, May 18, 19, 25, June 2, 5, and July 23, 1900, Russell MSS.

qualified to know, had any real confidence in the idea of a petition from Schafer Brothers to the North Carolina Supreme Court. For one reason, Russell knew from what Justice Walter Clark told him that Clark would be bitterly hostile to the petition and there seemed "no way to get any of the others [on the state supreme court] to stand up against him in that matter." The case was "honest and just," Russell insisted, "but these elements amount to nothing."[20] Russell had played with the petition idea and had Ricaud use it in his negotiations with the Schafers mainly to protect his secret "patent." Why use it for the relatively small sums to be made from the "second mortgage" bonds when the "hundred millions," as Russell referred to the mass of repudiated Southern bonds, promised vastly more rewarding profits? Ironically enough, from the beginning Russell's two "schemes" got in the way of each other. And it was the widespread confusion, in North Carolina and elsewhere, as to the distinction between the "second montgage" bonds and the subsequently issued "carpetbag" bonds which was soon to help transform Russell's bond case into a political explosion, the reverberations from which were to last long after Russell himself had died.

Russell at this point saw no reason why his two plans could not be pursued at one and the same time. In fact, he pressed Ricaud to explore with the Schafers, whom Russell himself met during a trip to New York in the late summer of 1900, the possibility of that firm's undertaking the tremendous task of trying to pool significant chunks of the repudiated Southern bonds, but without Ricaud's telling "the law point" that Russell had "invented." Ricaud, however, found the Schafers uninterested in the broader, more speculative field until something definite had been accomplished with their "second mortgage" bonds. "We will have to go slow in this [repudiated bond field]," Ricaud reported them as saying, "and if we could show some definite results in our matter it

[20] Russell to Ricaud, Aug. 24, 1900, and Busbee to Ricaud, Aug. 25, 28, 1900, *ibid*. See also Russell to Ricaud, Sept. 4, 1900, *ibid*.

would inspire confidence with the holders of the other bonds. We could then say that we have succeeded in ours, and have taken up this." Ricaud responded that the two matters were independent, delay was dangerous, and if the Schafers did not boldly seize the opportunity it would have to be offered to some other firm.

During a conversation, which was long in duration but short on candor, the Schafers threw out feelers to extract information about Russell's "scheme." Ricaud merely affirmed that "we had a final scheme to submit" after petitions to the state supreme court or to the legislature had failed. Here one of the Schafers asked directly if one state could not sue another and added: "I don't know whether I am hot on the trail of your final scheme or not, but I suppose that it is in connection with this idea that you now speak." Ricaud concluded that they had obviously been talking with other counsel, muttered something about the comity between states which precluded aggressive relations, and beat a hasty, expedient retreat from the conversation and the Schafer office.[21]

Since the Schafers were close to knowing the secret "patent" and since Russell had so little faith in the petition idea anyhow, the Schafers were made privy to the whole plan shortly after Ricaud's embarrassingly hurried exit from their office. Even the full knowledge of Russell's plan failed to interest the financiers in the repudiated bonds. Ricaud peevishly concluded that the brothers had "attained an age of physical decline, and they almost go into nervous hysterics over this matter. Simon Schafer is almost crazy on this NC Bond subject and displays so much irritation in discussing the matter that I avoid seeing him as much as possible."[22] Himself quite eager for slightly different reasons, Russell, without dropping his larger project, began to push the "second mortgage" matter with greater vigor and associated several significant new figures with the enterprise.

[21] Russell to Ricaud, Sept. 7, 1900, and Ricaud to Russell, Sept. 7, 10, 1900, *ibid.*
[22] Ricaud to Russell, Oct. 30, 1900, *ibid.*

One of these new associates was a distinguished lawyer in Detroit, Michigan, Alfred Russell, an acquaintance of Governor Russell's but no relation. Alfred Russell wrote requesting the governor to endorse the new book which he had just had published on *The Police Power of the State*.[23] The sort of man who headed a variety of clubs and societies, from the Michigan Political Science Association to the Sons of the American Revolution, Alfred Russell had graduated from Dartmouth and the Harvard Law School before the Civil War. After a fling at Michigan Republican politics in the 1860's, he had developed a substantial practice in corporation law, serving in such capacities, for example, as the chief attorney in Michigan and Canada for the Wabash Central Railroad Company. Alfred Russell furnished several important suggestions about the bond suit and remained associated with Governor Russell throughout the matter; consequently the early letters exchanged between the two men are worth close examination.

Governor Russell replied, first, that sending a testimonial to Alfred Russell's publisher would be a pleasure, even with the most perfunctory examination of the book, "as I am ready at all times to endorse any thing that you will write." Then getting straight to business, as was his fashion, the governor explained that he wanted to submit a scheme for Alfred Russell's confidential judgment and with a "view to our co-operative professional action, in case you think well enough of it to desire the association." At any rate, Alfred Russell was fond enough of legal points to consider the "invention" even though he might "declare it to be 'wild-cat', and render judgment accordingly."

"As you know, I shall go out of this office of Governor early next January," Russell continued. "I have been almost financially ruined by being Governor of this State for four years and my anxiety to make some money probably warps

[23] Chicago: Callaghan & Company, 1900. To avoid confusion in the remainder of the narrative, Alfred Russell will be referred to as such and the name used alone will refer to Governor Daniel L. Russell.

my judgment as to the practicability of my invention, which not being patented, is liable to be lost, if my secret should leak out before I can get things shaped up. Indeed I strongly suspect that I am not the only lawyer who ever thought of the scheme. Indeed I am almost sure that others have thought it out just as I have but have regarded it as impracticable, and so have never attempted to put [it] into operation."

Then Russell noted that there were "hundreds of millions" of repudiated Southern bonds held in the United States and Europe, "about all of them dishonestly and many of them outrageously repudiated by the debtor States." After a detailed account concerning the "only instance of State repudiation in the antebellum period," where Mississippi Whigs had fought the Democrats over repudiation of state bonds issued during the 1830's, Russell came to the "second mortgage" bonds of North Carolina. He explained that they amounted to $234,000 principal and nearly double that amount in interest and were secured by a second mortgage or statutory lien given by the state on state-owned railroad stock with a current market value of about five million dollars. The first mortgage, which the state recognized and on which it paid interest, amounted to $2,700,000. The state "arbitrarily offered" for the second mortgage bonds 25 per cent of the principal and nothing for the coupons, but the bondholders refused; at that time, 1880, the railroad stocks had not been worth enough to pay the first mortgage, much less the second, but since then the mortgaged property had risen in value sufficiently to pay for both mortgages and still leave a million and a half to North Carolina. "But the State holds on to the property, enjoys its income, and repudiates the debt."

As Alfred Russell knew, the Constitution gave the United States Supreme Court original jurisdiction in all suits between states, between the United States and a state, or between a state and a foreign state. Now suppose the vast amount of repudiated bonds were gotten together, and since they "are now simply trash" the holders would be willing to do anything that did not involve much personal cost to them. Then the bondholders could select some state to "accept a good big donation of this stuff" for the benefit of its university or "some public charity." The donation would have to be "complete and irrevocable and without any sort of agreement or reservation in favor of the assignor [donor]." When the bond-receiving state sued, Governor Russell concluded, the defendant state would have no "legal or equitable" defense. "All that ever has been said along that line is that the money derived from their sale was dishonestly handled, and that some of the Legislatures were reckless in authorizing the issue of the Bonds. But in every one of these States, large amounts of the money derived from sales of the Bonds were received and enjoyed by the State." Surely when the repudiating states saw that they could be sued by other states, they would agree to compromise with the bondholders who would stoutly declare that "before we will be robbed, we will donate all this hundred millions to States of this Union or to foreign States who can and will bring you to the bar." Actually, "the scheme is to get the compromise out of them at a very low rate, depending in each case on the ability of the debtor to pay. Five cents on the dollar would be a big thing and all of them are able to pay very much more than that."

"My own judgment is, that there is just one and only one snag in this scheme," Governor Russell concluded, "and that is, the difficulty in finding the State, or States which will accept the donation, bring the suit and stick. The Southern States would make an outcry about 'carpet-bag' Bonds and talk loud about good-fellowship and comity which should exist between States. They would dicker with the politician[s] of the plaintiff State and buy and bribe and bully, if they could." But if a plaintiff state could be found, the first suit to bring would be on the "second mortgage" bonds because "there is upon them no taint of fraud" and they were secured by ample collateral. The suit would be on the equity side. Some lawyers would say that a judgment against a state is not enforceable because the

Supreme Court "cannot by executionable process take from the State that which is necessary to its sovereignty or governmental function." Admitting the principle, Russell pointed out that the states had "lots of assets" outside of those which were essential to state administration, so he felt no fear on that score either. What did Alfred Russell think?[24]

The Detroit lawyer promptly replied that he was "ready to take hold of it with vigor." Indeed, he had gone over the whole matter about fifteen years earlier when a friend was the United States minister to Belgium and had "arranged to have a suit brought against one of our States in the name of the King of Belgium [Leopold II, of Belgian Congo fame] but dropped the matter when it appeared that the defendant state apparently had no property subject to execution." "Thro a Dutch banker of my acquaintance," Alfred Russell suggested, "we might get the Queen of Holland to take bonds and bring suit." Also, why should not Wheeler H. Peckham of New York City join in the legal fray? He had appeared for the bondholding plaintiff in the earlier case of *New Hampshire* v. *Louisiana*; and aside from being a friend of Alfred Russell's, he had the attractive distinction of being a brother of Justice Rufus W. Peckham of the United States Supreme Court. Wheeler H. Peckham might even assist in obtaining New York State as the plaintiff, but, regardless, "the fact of his fraternal relation with the court would be a help to us."[25]

Alfred Russell thus became associated with the project. His liveliness, quick intelligence, and candid cupidity were to shine through the many letters which he scrawled to Governor Russell in the years ahead. Wheeler H. Peckham of "Peckham, Miller, and King—Cable Address 'Lawful,' " also agreed to become associated with the venture. Aside from the brother, who loomed so large in Alfred Russell's thinking, Wheeler H. Peckham brought great prestige to the "scheme." In 1894 President Grover Cleveland had nominated him for a seat on

---

[24] Russell to Alfred Russell, Oct. 9, 1900, Russell MSS.
[25] Alfred Russell to Russell, Oct. 13, 1900, *ibid.*

the Supreme Court only to encounter the immovable, and triumphant, opposition of Senator David B. Hill, Democrat of New York. Although his brother Rufus was confirmed by the Senate after Cleveland nominated him in 1895, Wheeler Peckham enjoyed both a reputation as a foremost expert in municipal and constitutional law and a lucrative practice as counsel for some of the largest corporations in New York. Despite the addition of eminent counsel to help with the projected lawsuit, there was still one small chance, in which Russell had little faith, that the "second mortgage" bonds could be compromised with North Carolina and the "patent" saved for the "hundred millions" of repudiated bonds. The chance had to be at least explored.

When Russell yielded the governorship to Charles B. Aycock in January, 1901, bonds, "second mortgage" or otherwise, were of no great interest to the North Carolina public. With the "White Supremacy" Democrats sweeping back into full control of both the executive and legislative branches of the state government, few paid any attention to Russell's last message on January 9, 1901. Aside from recommending that the legislature should hasten to raise his successor's salary, which was promptly done, Russell also dealt at some length with bond matters.[26] He mentioned that certain holders of

[26] From Governor Russell's Whig-Republican point of view his bond ventures were quite respectable and certainly more honest than the wholesale repudiation which the Democrats had perpetrated at the close of the Reconstruction era. As long as he was governor, Russell refrained from any formal, written association with Schafer Brothers, or any other bond firm, and he did not legally replace Ricaud as the Schafers' chief counsel in the bond matter until an agreement was signed in March, 1901, two months after Russell had retired from the governorship. The one clearly dishonest use of his office which Russell made in the bond matter came late in 1900: he acted on inside information and used his authority as governor to halt the cancellation of eight "second mortgage" bonds which a New York holder had sent in for redemption at 25 cents on the dollar; that is, for bonds worth on their face $8000 in principal alone the New Yorker had applied for the $2000 which North Carolina authorized for the series. Russell not only arranged to halt the redemption but hurriedly contrived to borrow money from his Wilmington banker so that the governor himself could buy the bonds, albeit in Banker Armstrong's name, from the New York holder who needed cash in a hurry. Russell

state bonds which had a second mortgage on the state's stock in the North Carolina Railroad had presented a memorial with the request that he transmit it to the General Assembly. After reciting a concise history of the "second mortgage" bonds, the retiring governor suggested that if the courts should ever rule in favor of the bondholders, the bondholders themselves might agree to surrender their bonds for, say, $300,000, a sum which could be taken from the proceeds of the sale of state railway stock. To pay off both the first and second mortgages would require about $3,000,000 but this would still leave the state holding unencumbered stock worth about $2,000,000. Or, as another possibility, the state could arrange to be the purchaser at the judicial sale of its stock and borrow the $3,000,000 needed to pay off both mortgages by issuing new bonds at a low rate of perhaps 3½ per cent. Russell reminded the legislators that the first mortgage bonds commanded high prices on the market because the collateral was worth almost twice the amount of the bonds and also because they called for 6 per cent for nineteen more years whereas money on the best securities often brought no more than 3 per cent. The legislators might consider whether in even submitting the matter to the courts there would be an element of bad faith towards the first mortgage holders who, after all, would contend that in 1880 the state of North Carolina promised to pay them 6 per cent until 1919 and that this promise should be kept regardless of the claims of the second mortgage holders. In short, the outgoing Republican chief executive more than hinted that it would be wise and prudent for North Carolina to seek a compromise with the holders of the second mortgage bonds.

---

eventually added them, together with ten bonds which Ricaud acquired, to the Schafer pool, making a total of 242 bonds after the donation of ten bonds to the plaintiff state. The Democrats subsequently devoted much attention to this negotiation, in which Russell's omnipresent fears and lust concerning money had led him into unethical conduct. See Russell to Ricaud, Nov. 1, 3, 9, and 27, 1900, *ibid.*

The Democrats faced budgetary difficulties, as Russell well knew. In the 1900 campaign they had urged the disfranchisement of the Negroes by means of a literacy test from which whites, whether illiterate or not, could escape by means of the "grandfather clause." But the loophole for whites was of temporary duration; and Governor Aycock and other Democrats had found that the only way to allay white fears of the future disfranchisement of the white boys who each year became illiterate adults was to pledge much greater, and more expensive, state support for public schools. The campaign, of course, shed no light on just how this educational program would be financed. Higher taxes were anathema to many voters, and a powerful wing of the Democratic party talked as if state bond issues, at any time and regardless of the purpose, were wicked inventions of Alexander Hamilton and the Devil. It was actually to this dilemma that Russell spoke when he concluded that portion of his last message which dealt with bond matters: if the legislature should wish to make available for educational purposes any part of the state's valuable asset in the form of its stock in the North Carolina Railroad, "there is no way to do it, except by discharging the liens upon it, because with these incumbrances out-standing, purchasers could not be found who would pay for a share of this stock the same price as that which they pay for a share of private stock."[27]

The clearest indication that many Democrats ignored the content of Russell's message, especially in its more technical portions, came when the *News and Observer* commented that it was a "clear, succinct, instructive paper, dealing with candor and judgment with the institutions and interests of the State." Furthermore, in a wild and quite rare burst of magnanimity toward the departing Fusionist, Josephus Daniels' paper concluded that his recommendations were "along right lines and calculated to advance the State and its public

[27] Governor Russell to the North Carolina Senate and House of Representatives, Jan. 9, 1901, Governors' Letterbooks.

institutions."[28] Unlike Daniels, Editor Furman of the Raleigh *Morning Post* had apparently read the message carefully. The *Post* appreciated, among other things, its relative brevity and singled out as its most important feature the statement concerning revenue and taxes in which Russell developed new issues involving the state's interest in the North Carolina Railroad. Accused by Daniels' paper of being the tool of the trusts and accordingly nicknamed the "Wheezy Old Railway Organ," the *Post* stated simply its belief that "the State will not sell its interest" in the railway, and "whatever of equity may exist in the [bondholders'] claims mentioned will have to be adjusted otherwise."[29]

Despite the genuine Democratic thirst for revenue, Russell had never really believed that any short cut to get the second mortgage bonds paid off would work. As "I have told you forty times," he declared to Busbee in Raleigh, "I have no confidence in procuring legislative action, but it is worth a trial, because, if it does nothing more, it paves the way to future action."[30] The North Carolina legislature would probably never listen "until you have 'chunked' some rocks and knocked over some of their crockery." The memorial or petition from the Schafers, which Busbee also presented to Governor Aycock, who transmitted it to the legislature without any recommendation one way or the other, was in Russell's realistic eyes "all trash anyhow" except as an effort to agitate the matter and get the idea before the public that the hard-pressed state government might save some money by compromising the second mortgage bonds. Russell had tried in vain to launch a public discussion of the matter by his mes-

---

[28] Raleigh *News and Observer*, Jan. 11, 1901, which also carries the text of the message. For a later and more typical reaction toward the idea of the state's selling its North Carolina Railroad stock, which now became the Southern Railway's evil scheme, see the *News and Observer*, Jan. 19, 1901.

[29] Raleigh *Morning Post*, Jan. 11, 1901.

[30] Russell to Busbee, Jan. 23, 1901, Russell MSS. Busbee had transmitted the petition from Schafer Brothers to Russell, for the sake of the official record, on January 9.

sage to the legislature; the petition to Aycock in February, 1901, aroused no response from him or from the legislature and was ignored during the furor surrounding the Democrats' efforts to convict two impeached Republican members of the state's supreme court.[31] There seemed no alternative to "chunking" some legal rocks at North Carolina, and for that purpose a sovereign state, preferably a pliable one, became the urgent, indispensable item.

In view of the fears which Governor Russell expressed about the "only one snag" of procuring a state, it was ironic that plaintiff states turned out to be just about as easy to obtain as distinguished associate counsel had been. Alfred Russell believed that it would be safer to have a special legislative act of the state receiving the donation, that is a general act authorizing the governor and other appropriate state authorities to accept donations of bonds or other securities for the use of the university, perhaps, and on which suits in the United States Supreme Court were authorized. Alfred Russell felt confident that he could get such an act from the Michigan legislature which would sit in January, 1901, because the "governor [Aaron T. Bliss] and attorney general of Michigan are both personal friends of mine, and I could get them to accept the donation and authorize suit; but I fear the Supreme Court would hold it beyond the scope of their official power to accept donations to the State." Furthermore, it would be well to "avoid taking in too many to divide profits among," since everyone would want as large a share as possible. "How would it do not to undertake too much at first," Alfred Russell concluded, "but simply at first take up the North Carolina proposition and the rest later?"[32]

On both points, about the special legislative act and the priority for the North Carolina bonds, Governor Russell quite

[31] Russell to Alfred Russell, Nov. 2, 1900, *ibid.*, for the "crockery" reference. Russell to Ricaud, Jan. 22, 1901, *ibid.*, and Busbee to Russell, Feb. 4, 1901, *ibid.*, for the petition to Aycock. See also the petition itself accompanying Busbee to Aycock, Feb. 7, 1901, in Governors' Papers.

[32] Alfred Russell to Russell, Oct. 20, 1900, Russell MSS.

agreed. After a meeting in New York in late November or early December, 1900, the lawyers began work in earnest. Alfred Russell prepared a draft of the legislative act which he had suggested; Governor Russell improved it by deleting any mention of the university so that the state and the state alone would "get the stuff"; and Alfred Russell set about securing the measure's passage in the Michigan legislature. Michigan Senate Bill 30, "To provide for the acceptance and collection of grants, devises, bequests, donations and assignments to the State of Michigan," was introduced on January 15, 1901, and eventually signed into law by Governor Bliss in early April. Alfred Russell, chafing to move to the next step, began to prepare the bill in equity for Michigan to file against North Carolina in the United States Supreme Court. "*I think we should have some money in hand!*" Alfred Russell spluttered. "*They* [Schafer Brothers] *ought to give us at least* $500. apiece Retainer! I want money very much & so do you. Insist upon it!" Why, even Wheeler Peckham agreed that "Retainers, & the larger the better, is about the only legal principle which I never knew disputed!"[33]

However much Governor Russell might share the general legal lust for retainers, it was he, through Ricaud, who had battled to get the contract with the Schafers even on a contingent basis. One of his greatest crosses in the legal drama now unfolding was that the expensive business of launching and continuing the suit fell constantly onto his shoulders. And Russell possessed many more ideas than he did dollars. Alfred Russell itched in vain and had the additional disappointment of not seeing Michigan used, after all, in the suit against North Carolina.

Russell, while still North Carolina's chief executive and afterwards, enjoyed moving in powerful political and business circles in Washington and New York. Lacking the "down home" inhibitions which limited many agrarian-minded Tar-

[33] Alfred Russell to Russell, Oct. 20 and Dec. 14, 1900; April 3, May 28, and June 1, 1901, *ibid.*

heels, the proud Republican operated easily in the metropolitan hotels and offices where "deals" were consummated in the none-too-scrupulous, dollar-hungry world that was America at the turn of the century. After a few forays to the nation's capital in search of a plaintiff, Russell began to string up sovereign states as the successful fisherman does trout. Senator William M. Stewart, veteran Republican from Nevada, undertook to procure his home state for bond purposes.[34] But the prime mover and shaker in the state-procuring line turned out to be none other than Senator Marion Butler, North Carolina Populist, so soon to be an ex-senator at age thirty-seven.

Precisely when Russell invited Butler into the bond venture is not known, but it was apparently late in 1900, possibly in December. The time is important, for Butler would be fighting bitter political battles about when and how he became associated with the bond matter for many years after Russell had died and become a memory. At any rate, on December 22, 1900, Russell forwarded to Butler a copy of the donation bill which the governor and Alfred Russell had designed. Russell explained that the title to the bonds had to be exclusively in the state and that a general bill, with no particular bonds specified, was better "because it will catch more flies." Butler was to "talk up this thing" among the more "approachable" senators. "I am working to get an act through the Michigan Legislature, which meets in January," Governor Russell explained. "Then you push Nevada. Try Wyoming and put out feelers as to other States."[35]

Butler was in the process of transferring the vast energy and genuine political talent which had long been expended for the agrarian cause to the cause of Marion Butler's material advancement in the world. He needed no prodding. "It is sure now," he soon reported, "that we will have as many strings to our bow as we will want." Senator Clarence D.

[34] Senator W. M. Stewart to Russell, Nov. 20, 1900, *ibid.*
[35] Russell to Butler, Dec. 22, 1900, *ibid.*

Clark, Republican of Wyoming, and Senator William E. Chandler, Republican of New Hampshire, went to work on their states. When delays developed in those particular states, Butler found that his colleague and partner in many Senate battles, Senator Richard F. Pettigrew, Silver Republican of South Dakota, held out the best hope for quick action. Russell urged that it was "of the utmost importance that we should rope in two or three of these States in the next thirty or sixty days."

In Pettigrew, Butler had acquired an important new ally in the entire bond venture. Senator Pettigrew, like Butler, had been defeated for re-election and would leave the Senate in March, 1901; but he retained some political power and influence in South Dakota. Furthermore, Congressman Charles H. Burke of South Dakota worked with Pettigrew and Butler, and Burke belonged to the more conservative or "Stalwart" wing of the Republican party which had now captured control of South Dakota. Promising his South Dakota friends that prompt action in the state legislature would be followed by prompt donation of bonds to the state, Butler urged Russell to bring the first suit from there. South Dakota was surely the most favorable state, "in as much as Pettigrew & his rep[ubli-can]. cong[ressman]. absolutely control the situation—can control the Gov. & Attorney Genl. without extra cash. . . . We have a sure thing of it in S. D. Don't waste any time, but come on at once, for we must see these parties in N. Y. before they go out to S. D."[36]

True to Butler's prediction, the South Dakota legislature proved to be quite "controllable," as were the lawmaking bodies of so many other states at that time. The coveted bill, especially designed by Governor Russell and Alfred Russell and forwarded via Butler and his friends in Washington, was

[36] Butler to Russell, Jan. 11, 18, and 30; Feb. 25, 26; and March 11, 1901, *ibid.* Russell to Butler, Jan. 30, 1901, *ibid.* In January Butler seems to have thought, or hoped, that bonds from some other state besides North Carolina, perhaps from Virginia or Georgia, would be used in the first case. See Butler to Russell, Jan. 18, 1901, *ibid.*

duly passed by the South Dakota legislature and signed by Governor Charles N. Herreid. Furthermore, and undoubtedly as part of the deal, South Dakota's attorney-general, John L. Pyle, made an agreement with Robert W. Stewart of Pierre, South Dakota, whereby Stewart would serve as South Dakota's counsel in the forthcoming litigation and receive, in return, 10 per cent of whatever amount South Dakota collected. Stewart, a prominent corporation lawyer and later a high official in Standard Oil, enjoyed great influence among the staunch McKinleyite Republicans who then controlled South Dakota along with so many other Western and Northern states. In a subsequent written, and needless to say, secret, agreement between Russell, Butler, and Pettigrew, the last-named was promised, in the event of recovery in favor of the private holders of the "second mortgage" bonds, $10,000 of the 33⅓ per cent of the amount recovered above and beyond the 25 per cent which North Carolina had long offered. Pettigrew, according to the terms of the agreement, would use this sum to "satisfy the claims" of Lawyer Stewart and Congressman Burke for their assistance in securing a settlement of the bonds.[37]

Thus South Dakota came into the "scheme." Actually, Governor Russell, as he told Wheeler Peckham, would have preferred Michigan because it would "look better to have for plaintiff a State more important than South Dakota or Nevada." But Alfred Russell had not been able to secure the new Michigan law quite as expeditiously as had Butler and his Western allies. The Schafers, now so eager after their two decades of waiting, urged as great speed as possible. They handed ten of the North Carolina bonds to Russell on March 18, 1901, for donation to South Dakota, and the former governor of North Carolina readied his far-flung legal team for the first formal, public move—a motion from South Dakota to the United States Supreme Court for permission to file a bill of complaint against North Carolina. Moving urgently

[37] A copy of the Pyle-Stewart agreement, June 17, 1901, is in the Russell MSS; Russell-Butler-Pettigrew agreement, Sept. 6, 1901, *ibid.*

to meet first an April and then a May deadline, Russell encountered the first of what would seem a lifetime of delays when Butler and Ricaud sent the distressing news that, under the referendum provision of the South Dakota constitution, the bond-donation act would not go into effect until four months after the legislature had adjourned, making the effective date June 2. The bonds, however, were already in possession of the South Dakota authorities and probably could not be withdrawn in order to make Nevada the plaintiff. "Of course the idea of a new donation is out of the question," Ricaud declared. "Simon Schafer is nervously prostrated at Atlantic City. His brother tells me this matter has caused his trouble."[38] Under the circumstances, no move about the second mortgage bonds could be made until the fall session of the Supreme Court. The "hundred millions" of repudiated bonds were, however, another matter, and Russell together with Ricaud, Butler, and Pettigrew moved ahead vigorously, and so hopefully, with this phase of the scheme.

[chapter three]

CHASING THE ELUSIVE "HUNDRED MILLIONS"

"IN A FEW WEEKS I shall probably be on the list of two or three of whom you are one,—the only living Republican ex-Governors of Confederate States. This consideration perhaps nerves me to request that you will take a little time and trouble to give some information, or to direct me how I can get the information, concerning the repudiated debt of Louisiana." Thus Governor Russell applied to ex-Governor

[38] Russell to Peckham, March 13, 1901; Russell to Butler, April 23, 1901; and Ricaud to Russell, May 9, 1901, *ibid.*

Henry C. Warmoth, who had presided over Louisiana during the most turbulent phase of Radical Reconstruction. A similar plea went to ex-Governor Rufus B. Bullock of Georgia, who promptly replied with both information and a stout defense of his own role in Georgia's bond transactions during Reconstruction.[1]

Russell did not, however, merely wait for others to enlighten him concerning the tangled matter of repudiated Reconstruction bonds. He pored over old North Carolina records, digging out obscure data about the controversial bonds. He and his private secretary corresponded with lawyers in Virginia about the bonds of that state. The inquiry to Florida went somewhat agley, for it brought back this tremulous comment: "We hope you do not intend to try and make our State liable under this bond issue, as the same bears interest at 8 per cent and by this time, would bankrupt us if we had to pay the same."[2]

Russell certainly did intend to make Florida and any other repudiating Southern state as "liable" as he could. The plan for the "hundred millions," as he outlined it to Alfred Russell, was to get all the repudiated bonds, or the bulk of them, deposited with some trustee in New York with a written agreement that "the stuff" should be controlled by a committee. After the bonds were safely deposited and under control, Russell and his associates would meet with the committee and say: "We have a plan by which we believe we can pump some value into this old trash of yours. Before we develop it, you must make an agreement with us, thus: we are to state our plans, you are to say whether you are to undertake it or not. If not, then we are to have an option at twelve months on your stuff at a very low price, say one fourth of one percent. on the principal, the coupons thrown in. If you say that you think our plan is feasible, and you will

---

[1] Russell to Warmoth, Oct. 22, 1900; Russell to Bullock, Oct. 23, 1900; and Bullock to Russell, Oct. 25, 1900, in Russell MSS.

[2] Liddon and Eagan, Lawyers of Pensacola, Florida, to Russell, Sept. 29, 1900, *ibid.*

undertake it, then you are to pay us an agreed retainer and give us the contract of collecting at an agreed percentage."[3]

Russell made it sound simple. And the coveted retainer was almost palpable. This phase of the "scheme," however, proved to be impossibly difficult, although Russell was long in realizing this and at first regarded the repudiated millions as promising much more cash return than the second mortgage bonds. In the first place, Schafer Brothers, as previously explained, had no interest in the larger project until their own matter had been settled satisfactorily. Pressure from them, among other things, compelled Russell to plan to use his "patent" concerning the detour around the Eleventh Amendment in the contemplated suit against North Carolina. But long before any knowledge of that had reached the public, gossip about Southern bonds began to fill Wall Street, where the grapevine always outpaced the tickertape. To his and Russell's consternation, Ricaud found, for example, that John B. Manning, a prominent New York banker, had a keen interest in the North Carolina "special tax" bonds; Manning believed that they could be collected and had a plan on foot to have the Wyoming School Board bring suit in the United States Supreme Court to test North Carolina's liability. Furthermore, John S. Wise, former Virginia Republican also with a Whiggish background, had an interest in the rival scheme. Ricaud could only implore Russell himself to visit New York and see what could be accomplished in the repudiated-bond field.[4]

Russell did visit New York. He apparently called on Henry Clews, whose company had figured largely in the bond ventures of several Southern states during Reconstruction and who reportedly still controlled a large number of the repudiated bonds of Georgia and North Carolina. But Clews had played the bond game for a long time, as Russell quickly perceived, and seemed in no hurry whatsoever to tip his hand one way or the other. The "retainer and a fat contingent"

[3] Russell to Alfred Russell, Oct. 16, 1900, *ibid.*
[4] Ricaud to Russell, Dec. 4, 1900, *ibid.*

glittered beckoningly to lawyers, but the task of pooling significant numbers of the old bonds was formidable and the field a busy, crowded one.[5]

Russell, after leaving the governorship, may have had the inclination to linger indefinitely in New York financial circles, where he would have been at less of a disadvantage than he was by being on his plantation near Wilmington. He simply did not possess the means. The case differed, however, with Marion Butler and Richard F. Pettigrew. Both of them left the Senate in early March, 1901, and entered various business ventures (such as gold-mining operations in the American West and Mexico) which necessitated offices in New York and Washington. Consequently, they undertook the task of organizing the chase of the "hundred millions," and by April, 1901, seemed to have made a promising start. First they sold the idea to W. N. Coler and Company, bankers and dealers in municipal bonds—cable address "Hopeful"—and then, with Coler and Company's help and connections, the "committee" persuaded the North American Trust Company, one of the strongest in New York according to Butler, to undertake to pool the repudiated bonds with a view towards negotiating and compromising with the various Southern states that had issued them. "If we win our test suit," Butler concluded hopefully, "the thing is now a big thing & will be dead sure."[6]

With both phases of Russell's bond plan now well under way, they began to get in each other's way. When Russell still hoped to begin the "second mortgage" suit in the spring of 1901, that is, before South Dakota's referendum requirement had cropped up to necessitate delay, Butler and those in the pool committee, or syndicate as it was also known, begged for

---

[5] Russell to Peckham, March 13, 1901, *ibid.*

[6] Butler to Russell, April 13, 1901, *ibid.* Pettigrew had discovered a history of repudiated bonds which Russell requested to borrow. This could have been a University of Wisconsin doctoral dissertation by William A. Scott, *The Repudiation of State Debts* (New York, 1893). See Russell to Pettigrew, April 8, 1901, *ibid.* Byrd S. Coler of the Coler Company was a prominent New York Democrat and unsuccessful candidate for governor in 1902.

time in order to round up Southern bonds before their holders saw the legal rainbow of hope on the horizon. "Our New York friends," Butler explained, "whose interests are identical with ours in this matter think that if any move is made before they have gotten matters sufficiently in hand, that it may seriously interfere with their success in assembling the matters in interest." To show that the trust company had gone to work, even abroad, Butler enclosed Associated Press dispatches from London which reported that a London firm was "promoting the old scheme" of buying up repudiated Southern bonds, and since the bonds were "largely held here" there was considerable local interest.[7] Russell quite understood Butler's point and tried to explain to his overeager associate, Alfred Russell, that an early suit in the Supreme Court "would let out the secret and word would go out all over the world that the Bonds were good and the holders would get 'stiff' and make all sorts of demands and try to get all sorts of cuts on my contingent."[8]

On the other hand, there were the Schafers. Their two-decade wait for North Carolina's fiscal "repentance" left them utterly impatient with any idea of delaying the suit. Furthermore they insisted, quite wisely as events were to show, that the second mortgage bonds were significantly different and vastly more promising than the repudiated variety. Ricaud, who always needed cash and who still had the job of dealing frequently with the Schafers, pushed for speed in launching the Supreme Court suit. He finally declared, perhaps in a moment of passing frustration, that he believed Simon and Samuel Schafer were "little short of maniacs & will round the circle completely unless some bow of promise soon gilds their hopes in this matter. I really begin to believe that they have held to their bonds so long in the expectation that the state would ultimately awaken to a full sense of righteousness, as they conceived it, & pay in full." Now the several interviews and correspondence with Russell, which

[7] Butler to Russell, April 25, 1901, *ibid.*
[8] Russell to Alfred Russell, June 4, 1901, *ibid.*

had dissipated the Schafers' long-held faith, had simply "occasioned their collapse."[9] Frustrated as they understandably were, the Schafers had to accept the postponement of South Dakota's opening move until the fall. This delay gave the bond syndicate a whole summer's grace to seek among the unknowing for Southern bonds which could be brought easily into the pool.

The North American Trust Company sent out a circular letter and published advertisements concerning the Southern bond committee and its plans. Wall Street gossip materialized into a rash of printed stories, which ranged from hopeful to scornful depending largely on the geographic origin of the writer. The New York *Times*'s financial reporter had the story garbled at first and wrote that he found Southerners on Wall Street who regarded the advertised offers to buy certain Southern bonds as "reflections upon the credit of the South" and merely "an attempt on the part of shrewd speculators to make money." These Southern spokesmen were reported as insisting that money was now available in at least some Southern treasuries "to redeem in full any bonds that may be offered." The Boston *Evening Transcript* asserted that an "interesting chapter" of the country's financial history had begun with the syndicate's efforts to pool the Southern bonds; it explained that the syndicate asked for half of whatever might be recovered on the pooled bonds. Individual holders had made numerous efforts to collect in the past, but now the New York committee believed that by securing a majority of the bonds it could persuade the Southern states to settle. For its troubles in making the arrangement, the syndicate asked an "unusual" commission of 50 per cent, "although probably many of the holders of these bonds would prefer to have half a loaf than no bread." The Boston paper also declared that there were many persons in the South who believed that the Reconstruction bonds were legally issued and should be paid. "The New York syndicate apparently believes in the general

[9] Ricaud to Russell, Dec. 28, 1901, *ibid.*

honesty of the Southern people, and thinks that although the [state] courts are prohibited from taking up the issue, the Legislatures of those States may properly review the matter. An impartial investigation at this time may be had without allowing differences as to local policies to warp the judgment."[10]

Bond gossip and publicity reached into the hinterland, too, and in the South at least, the whole matter appeared in a rather different light from that of New York or Boston. The Raleigh *News and Observer* reported the bond development, but without any inkling that certain North Carolinians were connected with the matter. The paper flatly asserted that it would take the value of all the personal property in North Carolina to pay the state's estimated $80,000,000 of repudiated debt, principal and interest.[11]

Despite all the newspaper speculation, the pooling operation progressed slowly—dishearteningly so. No one knew exactly how many millions of dollars worth of bonds had been repudiated. One careful, later estimate of the Southern states' total repudiated principal, exclusive of any interest, is $62,466,000.[12] Thus it is clear that the very magnitude of the undertaking posed tremendous problems. Many of the bonds had been destroyed or cast aside as valueless. Aside from these factors, however, it soon developed that the various interested groups, especially on Wall Street, worked at cross purposes. Henry Clews, to name one important example, proved highly elusive and unresponsive to Russell's overtures.

And, as if there were not already sufficient obstacles, differences developed within the committee which the North American Trust Company represented. No angry quarrels

[10] Clippings from New York *Times,* July 25, 1901, and Boston *Evening Transcript,* Aug. 8, 1901, *ibid.*

[11] *News and Observer,* July 31, Aug. 14, 1901.

[12] Ratchford, *American State Debts,* p. 192. Louisiana topped the list of eight repudiating Southern states with $14,442,000 in principal, and North Carolina came second with $12,655,000. Ratchford also estimates the reduction of principal by scaling down and the accrued unpaid interest on the scaled-down debt.

erupted at this early stage, or at least there is no written record of any open dispute between Russell and his various colleagues; but it seems clear that the seeds of later schism had been planted. Butler and Pettigrew, it will be remembered, had engineered the contracts with Coler and Company and with the trust company. In the agreement of April, 1901, between Butler, Pettigrew, and Coler and Company, on the one hand, and the North American Trust Company on the other, it was specified that the trust company would receive at least 50 per cent of any amount which might be collected on the pooled bonds; this amount was to be divided by giving one-seventh each to Russell, Pettigrew, Butler, Coler and Company, the trust company, Pettigrew and Butler jointly, and the remaining one-seventh was to be held by the trust company to cover all contingent and other expenses, with any residue being prorated among the several interested parties "in accordance with their respective interests in the total amount as herein indicated."

In other words, Butler and Pettigrew were to fare significantly better than Russell under the terms of this agreement, a copy of which Russell received and apparently approved. Still, it may have irritated Russell that in addition to their one-sevenths and their joint seventh, the two ex-senators would probably share largely in the withheld seventh, the residue of which was to be prorated among the parties in accordance with their respective interests. Consequently, after a meeting of Russell, Butler, and Pettigrew in September 1901, the three of them concluded and signed a formal agreement concerning the division to be made of the profits in both the second mortgage and repudiated bond ventures. Concerning the former the agreement specified that in the event of recovery in favor of the private bondholders, $10,000 of the $33\frac{1}{3}$ per cent of the amount above the 25 per cent that North Carolina already offered was to be paid to Pettigrew to be used by him to satisfy the claims of Attorney Robert W. Stewart and Congressman Charles Burke, both of South

Dakota. Then, after the payment of attorney fees and other expenses, the remainder of the 33⅓ per cent was to be divided by alloting ⅕ to Butler, ⅕ to Pettigrew, and ⅗ to Russell, with Russell paying Ricaud whatever amount that might be agreed upon between them. (Russell proposed giving Ricaud ⅓ of whatever amount Russell netted, and Ricaud vowed that he preferred to "avoid any scramble or contention for swag.") As for the repudiated bonds, the September, 1901, agreement stated that Russell was to be consulted about and have equal voice in the distribution of the "certain undivided one-seventh (⅐) interest" as set forth in the April, 1901, agreement to which Russell had not been a party. Any residue of the said ⅐ was to be divided equally among the three parties, and in case of any disagreement about the distribution the majority should decide.[13]

Clearly, the arithmetic between friends in the bond business had gotten a bit complicated, and no doubt relations among the parties had become strained, albeit temporarily. The September, 1901, agreement was later to become a source of angry discord, but for a long period after its signing Russell and his partners seem to have worked together harmoniously.

But not completely so. Russell, feeling no doubt that his interests had not been adequately consulted in the Coler Company-North American Trust Company project, entered into negotiations with other parties interested in repudiated Southern bonds. Andrew McKinney and Company, bankers and brokers in New York, corresponded with Russell first about repudiated Georgia bonds; after several letters had been exchanged, Russell encouraged the McKinney firm to tackle the task of syndicating the Southern bonds held in England and on the continent. "If I could get them together," Russell boasted, "I could show them a scheme that is even better than the South Dakota suit."[14]

[13] Agreement of Sept. 6, 1901, between R. F. Pettigrew, Marion Butler, and D. L. Russell, Russell MSS. Ricaud to Russell, Dec. 18, 1901, *ibid.*

[14] Russell to McKinney and Company, Nov. 23, 1901, *ibid.*

Another connection which Russell utilized in the repudiated-bond field was with one T. A. Darby of Darby, Glave and Company, "Southern Securities a Speciality." Darby put Russell into touch with McKinney as well as with at least one rich man, who was interested in bond speculation and who had a millionaire brother-in-law in California from whom large sums might be borrowed for just such purposes. The renewed interest in Southern bonds had driven their prices upward, as Russell and the other "insiders" had feared, but now Russell tried assiduously to capitalize on this development. He learned, for example, of a large block of the North Carolina repudiated bonds which were reportedly purchaseable at $5.00 for each $1000 bond, that is, half of 1 per cent. Russell then hoped to sell these to his rich acquaintance for not less than 4 per cent or possibly 5 per cent of their face value, with Russell of course sharing the nice profit from this operation with Darby, the McKinney company, and probably others.[15]

Little apparently came of all the complicated negotiations, deals, and propositions, or at least Russell never seemed able to secure the cash he so desperately needed. He and Darby, whose letters reflect an erratic and emotionally unstable personality, fell out. The quarrel is of no significance, but Russell's method of dealing with it furnishes a good insight into his blunt, direct business manner and toughmindedness. Darby had written repeatedly complaining of the awkward position in which he felt he had been put and of his hurt feelings. Russell, after earlier warning remarks, finally told Darby: "You must understand if you are going to deal with me that idle conceits of that sort do not prevail with me. They are not business. Suppose you dispose with them for a while and let us see if there is any money to be made out of this thing—if not I drop it quick." Furthermore, the apparently teetotaling Russell in Wilmington sternly advised his heavy-drinking business associate in New York to "please

[15] Russell to McKinney, Feb. 17, 1902; McKinney to Russell, Feb. 19, 1902; and Russell to A. Abbott, Feb. 22, 1902, *ibid*.

keep cool" and not "imbibe anything but water cold or hot—
occasionally a glass of butter-milk. . . ."[16]

If Russell felt serious disappointment concerning the lack
of progress with the repudiated bonds, he did not express it.
The truth was that South Dakota's suit on the second mortgage
bonds had finally commenced in November, 1901. Not only
did the nationwide publicity about the suit add to the difficulty
of pooling any significant block of the repudiated bonds, but
Russell increasingly found himself deeply involved with the
incredibly time-consuming, yet challenging, task of proving
that his "invention" could accomplish all that he had claimed
for it. When serious illness struck the former governor mid-
way the legal struggle, whether or not he could live to see his
"patent" proved became a question which haunted and tor-
mented him.

[*chapter four*]

SOUTH DAKOTA BEGINS SUIT AGAINST NORTH CAROLINA

THE SUMMER'S delay in the launching of the interstate
lawsuit on North Carolina's second mortgage bonds afforded
Russell and his associates time for preparation and study.
Russell himself did the hardest cogitation and most faithful
labor, and Alfred Russell's keen mind seems to have been the
most dependable whetstone on which Governor Russell could
sharpen the edge of his own thinking. Peckham, of New
York's Peckham, Miller, and King, may have been the most
famous legal name attached to the burgeoning lawsuit, but
he furnished more prestige than he did ideas or labor.

[16] Russell to Darby, Jan. 30, 1902, *ibid.*

Russell and Alfred Russell debated in their letters the many legal points involved in the precedent-making case. "But I confess," Russell declared, "that I get a little nervous when I consider that we are blazing through an untrodden forest in this, that no such suit as ours has ever been brought. Why? Because it is the only case where individuals have been co-parties with a State in a suit between two States." An individual could not, of course, be a coplaintiff in a suit against a defendant state because the Eleventh Amendment forbade it. Yet a state could be a plaintiff against an individual, and if the individual were a nonresident citizen the Constitution opened the United States Supreme Court to the plaintiff state. What Russell and his associates had done was to join together as defendants the state of North Carolina and two individual citizens who were not residents of South Dakota, the plaintiff state. The individuals were Charles Salter of New York and Simon Rothschilds of the same place, holders respectively of North Carolina's second and first mortgage bonds. They had been made parties to the suit for an important reason: in suits in equity all parties concerned in the matter to be decided must be represented in the suit, and the two individual bondholders served as class representatives for both groups of bondholders. "Am I wrong in saying that ours is the only case where a State is Plaintiff and a State is Defendant and individuals are Defendants? Do you know of any such case?" Russell asked his colleague in Detroit.[1]

By late July, 1901, Russell had printed copies of South Dakota's bill of complaint. "Keep it very close and keep the secret too," he cautioned his private secretary. "I am looking for it to leak every day but it must not leak from me or my friends." Russell's caution paid off, for there was no hint to warn North Carolina Democrats of the medicine being brewed for them by the former Fusionist governor.

Peckham provided the next delay. He was to appear as counsel for South Dakota and, taking advantage of other

[1] Russell to Alfred Russell, June 24, 1901, Russell MSS.

business before the Supreme Court which would require his presence in Washington, would make the motion to the court for leave to file South Dakota's bill. When his other business was postponed from September to October and finally to November, Peckham postponed his chore for South Dakota. As galling as this may have been to Russell, it had to be borne or else Peckham's expenses for a special trip would have to be paid; and Russell simply had no money. Peckham did take the precaution of having South Dakota's attorney-general write him an official letter authorizing him to act for South Dakota. Failure to conform to some technical regulation of the Court might give it an opportunity to deny South Dakota's motion. The Court, Peckham noted, was "always quite strict about the authority of people not holding official position to represent a State, and I remember in the Louisiana cases that I had the most formal authority from the Attorney General of the State of New Hampshire. . . ."[2]

Meantime, Alfred Russell's curiosity and cupidity were getting out of hand. He did not understand all the delays; nor was he comforted by the fact that, so far, he had no official connection with the case. His name nowhere appeared on the printed bill nor did he have a contract with Schafer Brothers as Russell did. Russell soothed his colleague by explaining that Senators Pettigrew and Butler had suggested it would be better to have the bill signed only by Attorney-General Pyle of South Dakota, Lawyer Stewart, and Peckham. One out-of-state lawyer was enough. "You may be assured that you shall not be prejudiced by your name['s] not being on the Bill," Russell purred. He and Alfred Russell would be needed when it came to arguing the case before the Supreme Court; it really was "not of much importance as to who signs the Bill in the first instance"; and, besides, he had a memorandum signed by Pettigrew and Butler which recognized Alfred Russell as counsel in the suit—just in case. "I care nothing for *form* only for *substance*," Alfred Russell finally

[2] Peckham to Alfred Russell, Sept. 30, 1901, *ibid.*

ventured, "& that is to *make some money!*"[3]

Others whom Russell had to console and attend were the nervous Schafer brothers on Wall Street. He had frequently warned them that when the case began the newspapers would be full of it, and people over the nation, especially lawyers and speculators, would talk much about it. "I want to impress upon you the necessity of keeping silence," Russell warned his employers; "be careful not to talk, and if newspaper men try to interview you, tell them that you have nothing to say. If they ask you as to who are your counsel, or the names of your lawyers, just tell them that that is your business and you have nothing to say for publication. Do not talk to anybody until I see you."[4]

Peckham finally sent a man from his firm to Washington and had the South Dakota motion submitted on November 11, 1901. The Supreme Court soon granted the motion for leave to file the bill and cited the defendant state to appear and answer the bill of complaint on March 3, 1902. Subpoenas were issued accordingly. Russell wrote an amusing account of the North Carolina reaction to these shocking developments when he brought Alfred Russell up to date. The former governor felt, first of all, that "the thing has got a good send off" in North Carolina. Of course, the "sensational and piratical part of the press" (meaning the *News and Observer* and its followers) started out by attempting to explain South Dakota's move as a scheme of the Southern Railroad to force a sale of North Carolina's stock in the North Carolina Railway, so that the Southern could buy it. The same sensational papers first attempted to have the public believe that the bonds involved were of "carpetbag" origin, that is of the special tax variety. Those newspapers, however, which "represent the business element" were pointing out, correctly, that the bonds were honest in origin and that their proceeds were accounted for.

[3] Russell to Alfred Russell, Oct. 7, 1901, and Alfred Russell to Russell, Oct. 10, 1901, *ibid.*

[4] Russell to Schafer Brothers, Oct. 22, 1901, *ibid.*

As for the Democratic rulers of the state, they were, in Governor Russell's judgment, quite paralyzed and demoralized. "They are less familiar with the original jurisdiction of the Supreme Court as to controversies between sovereigns," Russell quipped, "than I am with the debates of the Council of Nice. About the best they could do after the first week was to walk around the streets and swear that the Court would never grant the motion, that such a thing was never heard of before, since Jno. Hancock signed the Declaration. . . . I think that about all of them thought the case would have to be brought before a county squire and carried up by appeal before a jury in the county court house. But they will learn as they get older."[5]

Neither Governor Charles B. Aycock nor his advisers were the legal innocents which Russell made them out to be. But receiving the following formal notice from the President of the United States, Theodore Roosevelt, was truly not a cheering experience: "For certain causes offered before the Supreme Court of the United States, having jurisdiction in equity, You are hereby commanded, that laying all other matters aside and notwithstanding any excuse, you be and appear before the Supreme Court" on March 3, 1902, to answer South Dakota's bill of complaint. "Hereof you are not to fail at your peril."[6] Aycock may not have fully comprehended what was going on; he at least had the discretion to keep quiet until he did understand the mystifying move against North Carolina.

Not so with Editor Josephus Daniels, who in these early years of the century was perhaps at the height of his power in the state. Daniels' *News and Observer,* on the day after South Dakota's first move, exploded with a headlined question—"Is It Another Southern Railway Scheme?" Many news stories and editorials would still be answering the question

[5] Russell to Alfred Russell, Nov. 21, 1901, *ibid.*

[6] President of the United States, via the Clerk of the Supreme Court, to the State of North Carolina, Charles Salter, and Simon Rothschilds, Nov. 25, 1901, Governors' Papers.

affirmatively long after it had become clear to most people that the villainous corporation really had no connection with the matter. At this early stage, however, the *News and Observer* confidently explained that if South Dakota won its suit the North Carolina Railroad would be sold at public auction; all proceeds beyond what was required to pay the first mortgage would go to the holders of the second mortgage bonds; and the "manipulators" on the "inside" of the Southern Railway management, who had already bought up the bonds on which they were suing for a song, would get the state's stock for much less than it was worth, issue bonds on it for two or three times its capital stock, and pocket several millions. Only the *News and Observer*'s vigilance had thwarted the scheme when it cropped up before the legislature earlier in the year, but now the "schemers" had somehow obtained the assistance of "the rotten borough of South Dakota" to bring suit. Having warmed to its suspicion about the Southern Railway, Daniels' paper soon traced no less than nine chapters in the railway's alleged scheme to get possession of the state-owned North Carolina Railroad; the conspiracy was now said to have begun in 1895 when the Southern got its ninety-nine-year lease of the state-owned road and to have included such later developments as the plot to have Russell made chief justice and the opposition by the Southern's lawyer-lobbyists to the impeachment of the two Republican judges on the state supreme court.[7] The *News and Observer*'s elaborate conspiracy charge, in other words, contained a strange mixture of fact and wild guessing, of truth and untruth, designed to show among other things, that the paper's strongly partisan stand on many important issues since 1895 had consistently been right while those who had opposed the *News and Observer* had, rather more wittingly than not, been pliant tools of the "trusts."

One error which the *News and Observer* did not long make, although the paper blurred the matter and the error

[7] *News and Observer,* Nov. 12, 13, 1901.

was a common one that died hard, was to confuse the second mortgage bonds with the totally repudiated ones of "Carpet-bag-Negro" or Radical Republican origin. No less careful an editor than Joseph P. Caldwell of the then widely respected *Charlotte Observer* declared initially that South Dakota's suit would not amount to much because the fraudulent bonds involved had been issued by the Radicals and long ago repudiated by North Carolina. Lesser papers, mostly weeklies, also made Caldwell's mistake but were not as quick and unflinching in admitting it as he was; and in later years, as will be shown, the confusion between the second mortgage and special tax bonds became even more widespread than it was in 1901, a matter which some Democrats did not overly regret.[8]

Of the three most important papers in the state at the time —the Raleigh *News and Observer, Charlotte Observer,* and Raleigh *Morning Post*—Robert Furman of the Raleigh *Morning Post* best understood the complex matters involved in South Dakota's suit and clearly informed his readers from the outset. Furman, the state's senior newspaperman in point of service, stubbornly remained a Democrat of the Grover Cleveland variety. Close friend of such Tarheel Democrats as Senators Zeb Vance and Matt Ransom, he served as chief clerk of the state senate for several sessions and as state auditor from 1893 until 1897.[9] This background of political experience plus his journalistic talents enabled Editor Furman to enlighten, rather than inflame, concerning the affair which quickly became known in North Carolina as the "South Dakota bond suit."

Furman's *Post* asserted at the outset that the bonds involved were "never tainted with fraud, or so treated at any time by the State." If the worst came and South Dakota's suit were sustained, Furman prophesied that the state would only

[8] *Charlotte Observer,* Nov. 12, 13, 14, 1901. After his initial blunder about the bonds, Editor Caldwell generally followed the line taken by the Raleigh *Morning Post.*

[9] Obituary notice by R. H. Battle, *Morning Post,* May 13, 1904.

have to dispose of enough of its stock to pay the outstanding bonds, and the state would still be the majority stockholder in the North Carolina Railroad. "So all the slush as to the Southern road scheming to buy the State's stock in order to crush out private stockholders is worse than nonsense," the *Post* tartly avowed, "and is resorted to by the only paper in the State that will not tell the truth when it thinks its interest may be served by falsehood and slander." The officials and public of North Carolina would best understand that a "lawsuit is on which cannot be whistled down the winds nor avoided by vulgar abuse and misrepresentation." The *Post* felt sure that Governor Aycock would treat the matter as its gravity required and secure for North Carolina "the best settlement that law and equity, as adjudged by the Supreme Court of the United States, if the matter cannot be settled otherwise, may decree."[10]

In addition to its own careful news stories and editorials, the *Morning Post* published a significant letter from Fabius Busbee, Raleigh attorney for Schafer Brothers and sometime counsel for the Southern Railway. Going into the origin of the bonds, Busbee explained that in the 1866 act providing for bonds to aid the Western North Carolina Railroad, said bonds being secured by deed of mortgage for equal amount of stock in the North Carolina Railroad, no mention had been made of the fact that the stock had already been pledged before the war for the "construction bonds." Not long after the "ten share" or second mortgage bonds were put on the market, a young New York banker invested much of his capital in them, paying a large price because North Carolina's credit had not yet been ruined by the flood of special tax bonds. Young Schafer, according to Busbee, relied on the credit of North Carolina and the pledge of ten shares of stock for each bond as security and did not even know of any prior mortgage on the stock held by the owners of the construction bonds. No interest was paid on the bonds after

[10] *Morning Post,* Nov. 13, 1901.

1869, and when the state passed the 1879 act offering 25 per cent of the principal of the ten-share bonds there was already due about $600 interest upon each bond. In other words, in 1879-1880 the state offered Schafer $250 in a bond paying 4 per cent interest for a $1600 debt on a bond which supposedly paid 6 per cent interest. Since the stock-secured bonds had originally cost the holders "probably about an average" of $1200 or more, Schafer could hardly be blamed for refusing to accept about 15 per cent of the amount due.

Busbee added that for many years he had, when in New York, consulted Schafer Brothers about the bonds; and when North Carolina in 1879 compromised with the first mortgage bondholders he had advised the Schafers that the state had no right to renew a first mortgage after its maturity without the consent of the second mortgagees. He had further advised them that the equity of the second mortgagees could be easily enforced as against a person or corporation but that against a sovereign state there was no remedy.

Busbee disclaimed any knowledge of the steps taken since he had presented the memorial from Schafer Brothers to the legislature earlier in 1901; he had learned of the plan to file South Dakota's bill while in New York "last week" and his mention of the matter to Colonel A. B. Andrews on November 11, 1901, was the first that the Vice-President of the Southern Railway had heard about it. Busbee pointed out that if the railway officials had been interested in these bonds and had desired to keep their interest concealed, they would hardly have permitted one of their regular counsel (Busbee) to represent the bondholders. "So far as I have ever learned," the Raleigh attorney declared, "there is absolutely no desire upon the part of the Southern Railway to own the stock of the North Carolina Railroad Company."[11]

In addition to refuting the charge about the Southern

[11] Fabius Busbee to the Editor, *Morning Post,* Nov. 13, 1901. The *News and Observer* had refused to publish Busbee's letter, according to a *Post* editorial note.

Railway's being behind the bond suit, Editor Furman explored various aspects of the case for the "information of those who are intelligent enough to understand and honest enough to appreciate." He believed that the second mortgage bonds had been sold on the market for a valuable consideration, perhaps 90¢ on the dollar and the money, rather than being stolen by any plundering Radicals, had been applied to the construction of the western railroad, perhaps beyond Icard Station. The two important points in the new lawsuit, as he then saw them, were: (1) whether South Dakota could sustain the suit in behalf of a corporation like the state university, for whose benefit the bonds were said to be donated; and (2) what effect the extension of the first mortgage debt without the knowledge or the consent of the second mortgagees would have. Further, there was consolation in the fact that the second mortgage bonds were apparently the only ones on which any suit against North Carolina might be maintained. And the Supreme Court had theretofore invariably rendered decisions favorable to the South on "all questions specially affecting Southern interests." "Coarse, vulgar abuse and misrepresentation may serve some dishonorable purposes of one sort or another in this locality, but it will not affect the facts or the Supreme Court of the United States in determining the case."[12]

The *Post*'s various revelations concerning the origin of the bonds and the denials of the alleged conspiracy headed by the Southern Railway made no dent at all on the excited arguments of the *News and Observer*. In fact, the latter paper chortled that the stand taken by the Southern Railway's organ, "now known as the Morning Post," merely furnished the "tenth chapter in the chain of incontrovertible evidence" as to the railway's scheme.[13] It was all a bit like the when-did-you-stop-beating-your-wife gambit.

Amidst all the confusion, the charges and countercharges,

[12] *Morning Post,* Nov. 14, 15, 1901.
[13] *News and Observer,* Nov. 14, 1901.

one thing was clear: the South Dakota bond suit had quickly become an important public question in North Carolina. This was so even before it became known that Russell and Butler, the two chief Fusionists, were intimately involved in the move against North Carolina, or, as they usually regarded it, in the move against the North Carolina Democrats. The public became aroused not only because of the interesting constitutional questions but also because the case struck the railway and bond chords which had been central to the state's political life since the 1840's. The relationship of the second mortgage bonds to the Reconstruction era was not what some careless Democrats asserted, but it was still close enough to furnish an especially powerful reason for North Carolina's interest in the suit which South Dakota had begun.

Furnifold M. Simmons, Democratic state chairman who had just taken the Senate seat which he was to occupy for the next three decades, regarded the matter optimistically. In the first place, he suggested, it was apparent from the bill that South Dakota was not the absolute owner of the ten bonds but merely the agent for the state university; since New Hampshire had not been allowed to act as agent to circumvent the Eleventh Amendment, surely South Dakota would not be either. Secondly, since the complainant asked that enough of North Carolina's rail stock be sold to pay all of the outstanding bonds, and not just the ten which had been allegedly donated to South Dakota, Senator Simmons regarded it as crudely obvious that the suit had been unconstitutionally brought for the benefit of Schafer Brothers. In contrast to Simmons, Governor Aycock refused any statement on the matter beyond assuring the private citizens who held a minority of the North Carolina Railroad's stock that the state's stock would not be sold as a result of South Dakota's action. Even the *News and Observer* became temporarily calmer after Aycock affirmed what the *Morning Post* had said from the first.[14]

[14] *Morning Post,* Nov. 15, 16, 17, 1901; *News and Observer,* Nov. 19, 1901.

Governor Aycock's selection of counsel to represent North Carolina in the bond suit received praise from all the newspapers. James E. Shepherd of Raleigh, James H. Merrimon of Asheville, and George Rountree of Wilmington were the three eminent lawyers named; Shepherd was a former chief justice of the state supreme court, Merrimon the brother of a former chief justice and himself a former superior court judge, and Rountree an energetic lawyer-legislator and ardent Democrat. The *Morning Post* praised the choice of the three lawyers as clear corroboration of the *Post*'s initial conclusion that the case was one of true gravity. "There is one thing to a dead moral certainty," Furman soberly concluded, "if the Supreme Court says those bonds must be paid, they will be paid; in what way will be a matter for the State Legislature to decide." In a similar vein, the *Charlotte Observer*, having learned from Furman that the bonds in question had been issued by a legislature "composed of our own people," calmly pointed out that North Carolina had offered 25¢ on the dollar for the bonds in 1879 not because they were in any way invalid or fraudulent but because "the State was 'broke' and that was all that it felt able to pay." The *News and Observer*, with its conspiracy charge against the Southern Railway made a bit untenable but never renounced by the paper, stubbornly staked out the ground on which it would stand: the state had made a fair, just settlement of its indebtedness in 1879 and the attempt to reopen that settlement "for an ulterior purpose through the connivance of a Western rotten borough, called a state, is one which the State will resist to the very end."[15]

Despite the early attacks on South Dakota by Josephus Daniels' paper, neither the newspapers nor the politicians of that Western state seem to have paid much attention to the bond suit in its early stages. One explanation for this is that the prominent South Dakotans involved—ex-Senator Pettigrew, Congressman Burke, Lawyer Stewart, and, to a lesser

[15] *Morning Post,* Nov. 20, 1901; *Charlotte Observer,* Nov. 23, 1901; and *News and Observer,* Nov. 20, 1901.

extent, Governor Herreid and Attorney-General Pyle—had nothing particularly to gain by any special publicity concerning the matter. When the suit began, the Sioux Falls *Daily Argus-Leader,* the state's leading paper and conservative or "Stalwart" Republican in its politics, carried a brief dispatch from Washington on an inside page. "South Dakota Wants Her Cash," the small heading declared, but the matter was not deemed important enough to warrant any editorial comment.[16] Reconstruction bonds rang no bells of memory and hit no sensitive nerves of history in the distant prairie state; in fact, if they had, South Dakota reaction would have been totally different from that which predominated in North Carolina. When the *Argus-Leader* looked South or back to the Civil War period, it saw matters from a perspective that would have horrified hot Southern Democrats into speechlessness—or at least stunned them momentarily. When Alabama's disfranchisement of the Negroes was carried by a small majority, thanks to vast majorities which the Democrats had achieved in the very counties where the Negro population was heaviest (the same type of thing had happened earlier in North Carolina), the *Argus-Leader* coolly explained: "There is a puzzle here, but its all in the counting. An up-to-date southern politician doesn't care who does the voting if he is allowed to do the counting." Or again, when there was a reported increase in public opposition to lynching in the South, the South Dakota Republican newspaper explained that when so many Northerners had moved South during the 1890's they had undoubtedly taken with them "a higher plane of civilization." It seemed clear that "northern emigration strengthened the southern sense of honor and has brought about the change of view toward lynching."[17]

With views like these, polar opposites to the righteous and militant "White Supremacy" Democracy of the South, perhaps it is not strange that there was, at least until the crucial closing

[16] *Daily Argus-Leader,* Nov. 12, 1901.
[17] *Ibid.,* Nov. 13, 1901, and Jan. 24, 1902.

stages of the bond suit, little or no exchange of opinion or communication between South Dakota and North Carolina. But the truth was that North Carolina's Democratic rulers, down to 1905, simply ignored or forgot about the possibilities of appealing to public opinion in South Dakota; when the Tarheel officials did belatedly enter the arena in South Dakota they found the field quite ready for cultivation.

Daniel L. Russell never ignored any possibility of getting information and attitudes into newspapers. He realized from the first that, far from being merely a legal contest, cloistered and remote, his bond suit involved legislatures and politicians in at least two states, and newspapers were the best means of getting at the politicians as well as the voters. During the early years of the bond suit Russell necessarily concentrated his attention on North Carolina newspapers and opinion.

The weekly that had become famous in the 1890's as Marion Butler's newspaper and spokesman, the *Caucasian,* could explain about the second mortgage bonds without going into any detail about the origins of the South Dakota suit. Butler, whose name had not yet been publicly connected with the matter, had announced, quite prematurely as it later turned out, "I'm out of politics, for good and all. I am now in business, and I make money and do not get jumped on."[18] But when the *Caucasian* printed a long account of South Dakota's action, emphasizing the points made by the *Morning Post* and *Charlotte Observer,* Josephus Daniels' paper quickly declared that it began to "look like Attorney Marion Butler had something to do with getting South Dakota to sue the State, and Editor Marion Butler seems to be backing up Attorney Marion Butler and the South Dakota suit."[19]

More important and influential than anything which the

[18] *Washington Post,* Nov. 16, 1901, as quoted in Raleigh *Morning Post,* Nov. 17, 1901.

[19] *News and Observer,* Nov. 22, 1901. In the same issue of the *Caucasian* which aroused Daniels' suspicion, the announcement appeared that new owners had acquired the Caucasian Publishing Company but Marion Butler would continue to contribute to the editorial columns of the paper. *Caucasian,* Nov. 21, 1901.

Caucasian might say, under the circumstances, was the long, learned letter which Charles Price of Salisbury, North Carolina, wrote to the *Charlotte Observer*. A youthful captain in the Confederate Army and influential Democratic state legislator and speaker of the house in the 1870's, Price had become an important lawyer for the Southern Railway and would shortly be elected president of the North Carolina Bar Association. He was what a later generation would call a McKinley Democrat; in fact, he became an avowed Republican early in the twentieth century. Before the publication of his letter to the Charlotte paper, which was requested by the editor, Price wrote confidentially to Governor Aycock, explaining that he wanted to say a personal word about the South Dakota suit and had also asked Colonel Andrews to see Aycock about it. "As sure as I live," Price solemnly insisted, "there will be serious trouble to the state growing out of this suit." The case should be settled at once, for nothing would contribute more to the success of Aycock's administration.

The South Dakota suit, Price felt, aimed at establishing the jurisdiction of the Supreme Court; under well-settled rules in equity every person, whether a private citizen or not, who held one of the second mortgage bonds, would file it and participate in the distribution of the fund arising from the sale of the state's stock in the North Carolina Railroad. This, in turn, would lead to suits designed to test the validity of the 1875 amendment to the North Carolina constitution which repudiated the special tax bonds. Price insisted that if it were necessary Aycock should call the legislature into special session; but that really was not necessary if, after consultation with the leading men in the state, the "business men," Aycock himself would take the responsibility for action. "It is so plain that the result of this case will be a trouble to the state, I cannot see how you can hesitate."[20]

[20] Charles Price, Law Department of the Southern Railway, to Governor Aycock, Dec. 27, 1901, Governors' Papers.

Aycock, despite the urgency expressed by Price, apparently saw nothing to do but hesitate, once he had named the counsel for North Carolina. The Democratic governor was extremely wary of the whole matter, which carried a dangerous overtone of politics about it. When the marshal of the United States Supreme Court wrote requesting that Aycock voluntarily accept service of the subpoena, the governor replied that for "reasons appearing to us sufficient we have concluded that it is better for the subpoenas to be served on us rather than for us to accept service."[21]

Charles Price, obviously, had little or no effect on the governor. To the *Charlotte Observer* and the public, Price explained that he had given much thought to the matter involved in the South Dakota suit. Two years earlier he had been consulted by Northern citizens concerning the advisability of bringing suit on the second mortgage bonds but had declined because of the Eleventh Amendment. Nor had his prospective clients been in any way connected with the railroads. "Indeed, the railroad people with whom I am connected," Price explained, "have discouraged the bringing of this or any other suit of a similar character."

The matters involved, Price candidly asserted, were ones about which the public was surely not informed nor could it be "without such investigation as the people generally are unable to make." After making his point about the jurisdictional purpose of the South Dakota suit, as in the letter to Aycock, Price admitted that he had been a member of the 1875 constitutional convention, and like nearly all the Democrats he had voted for the amendment repudiating the special tax bonds. "At that time I was very young, being a hot-headed, intolerant Democrat and in politics had never thought of anything seriously." But looking back now at the matter, Price thought the bonds valid in law and a part of the debt of North Carolina, whose "salvation has been the want of jurisdiction in any court to enforce their payment."

[21] Governor Aycock to Marshal of the United States Supreme Court, Dec. 3, 1901, *ibid.*

Price next explained about Wheeler Peckham's distinguished record. After carefully reviewing several relevant Supreme Court decisions, Price expressed the opinion that the only real question in the South Dakota case lay in the ownership of the bonds. "If the State of South Dakota owns the bonds absolutely, and the court shall so find, there will be a recovery—there will be a decree against our State." The donor's request that any proceeds from the bonds go to the university was not obligatory on the state, and the bill of complaint seemed to show that the bonds were the absolute and unqualified property of South Dakota.

Price politely expressed his confidence in the lawyers whom Aycock had named as North Carolina's counsel. "But, looking at the case, as I do, and feeling as I do about it," he wrote to Joseph Caldwell, "I think your duty as the leading journalist in the State, is, to advise the Governor to adjust this matter at once." If South Dakota's ten bonds were paid, there would be an end to the matter. Otherwise, trouble for North Carolina would ensue. Governor Aycock should promptly take the responsibility. "Public sentiment demands it. Public good demands it."[22]

Sentiment in North Carolina was hardly what Price said it was. In fact, Tarheel opinion about the bond suit was confused and chaotic. But Price's prophecy proved to be remarkably sound, and, ironically enough, bold action along the lines he had suggested, together with strong appeals to public opinion in South Dakota, might well have saved North Carolina a considerable amount of money as well as much agitation.

The reaction to Price's letters, which were significant both because of what he said and who he was, was curious. Governor Aycock, as explained above, thanked Price for his trouble and ignored the advice. The *News and Observer*, aroused as much by Price's salute to Joseph Caldwell as the "leading journalist" in the state as by the contents of the

[22] Charles Price to Editor, *Charlotte Observer*, Dec. 29, 1901.

letter, flew into a somewhat confused dither. "This is the most remarkable letter," Josephus Daniels' journal solemnly declared, "that has appeared in North Carolina in the new century, certainly, if not in the last hundred years." After a fling at the McKinleyism of Price and the "leading journalist" and a flat rejection of the course recommended by "railway attorney" Price, the *News and Observer* concluded that the "truth is that there are deep laid schemes underneath the whole business." It might all be a scheme to demoralize Governor Aycock so that he would sell the North Carolina Railroad to the Southern, or Price could be right about his jurisdiction scheme. There was this final, and slightly misleading, consolation: "The repudiated bonds, those owned by South Dakota or owned by any other State, can have no standing in court except by a fraud on the jurisdiction."[23]

For quite different reasons, Russell was about as unhappy with a part of Charles Price's letter as was the *News and Observer*. Immediately upon seeing the document in the Charlotte paper, Russell wrote a personal letter to Furman of the Raleigh *Morning Post*. Russell approved Price's point that the South Dakota suit was soundly based and, if allowed by North Carolina to go uncompromised, would lead to recovery on the bonds. But the argument in Price's analysis which upset the architect of the bond suit was the suggestion that the best and only way for North Carolina to escape her dilemma was to walk up to South Dakota and pay for the ten bonds. Just about the last thing which Russell wanted to see was an end to the Supreme Court case which would leave the Schafer Brothers, and Russell, holding the bond-bag, so to speak. To counter Price's point, Russell suggested another possibility to Furman, with the idea, of course, of getting the counter-argument in the *Post*: "Is it not in order to ask him [Price] how this would be a 'git out' for this State, when everybody, except him, knows that just as soon as North Carolina should pay these ten bonds and coupons, there would be another

[23] *News and Observer*, Dec. 31, 1901.

donation of ten bonds, or twenty bonds, or a hundred bonds to South Dakota or some other state, and other suits would be brought on them? Then, what would he do? The net result according to his plan would be to pay the whole $700,000. for claims that could be settled for half that amount."[24]

"Everybody" hardly knew just what Russell said they did. Samuel and Simon Schafer, to name two important bodies, would hardly divest themselves of bonds which not only had some value even as matters stood but which they had tenaciously clung to for thirty years or so. Furthermore, any donation they might make to a sovereign state, as had been the case with the one already made to South Dakota, would have to be absolute and unconditional in order to meet the exacting requirements of the Supreme Court and the Eleventh Amendment. Russell himself had well understood and carefully acted on this principle. And if the Schafers were not enough of an obstacle to the course which Russell outlined to Furman, there was always the question of just how long and how far a sovereign state would be available to play the role which Russell absolutely required for the execution of his threat.

Perhaps Furman thought of these weaknesses in Russell's answer to Price. The *Morning Post,* at any rate, published neither the Price letter nor any editorial "correcting" Price along the lines which Russell had suggested. The *Post* merely abstained from the bond debate for a while. The first phase of North Carolina's public debate on the South Dakota bond suit had ended by early 1902. Though the matter was destined to become even more dramatically threatening and controversial in the near future and would last much longer than anybody dreamed, a lull had set in.

Wheeler Peckham in New York, surveying the state of opinion in North Carolina as Russell had reported it to him, took vast encouragement from that segment of Tarheel sentiment which favored paying lawful debts. "The difficulty in

[24] Russell to R. M. Furman, Dec. 30, 1901, Russell MSS.

cases of this character which have heretofore been presented
to the Court," the veteran lawyer explained, "has been in the
almost universal sentiment that it was in some way derogatory
to what they called the dignity of the State. For my part I can
never perceive much dignity in being a damned rascal. Perhaps that is rather a harsh term to apply to repudiating states,
but it is appropriate to the question of dignity."[25]

If Peckham had been content with reports about North
Carolina opinion, Russell's days would have been easier.
But Peckham, like Alfred Russell and all the others associated
with the scheme, wanted money. Alfred Russell, nervous
about Governor Russell's poor health and the painful absence
of any cash return from the project, admitted that "I pray
God to have you in his holy keeping until & after this
bus[iness] is over!!" No doubt Russell perferred being prayed
for to being dunned, especially when it was almost more than
he could do to meet the routine expenses involved in getting
his case before the Supreme Court.[26]

Marion Butler felt annoyed that Peckham refused to remember that there was no money for the lawyers unless and
until North Carolina settled for all of the Schafer bonds. But,
of course, if the distinguished New Yorker insisted on a fee
anyway, "we can do no more than share with him our part of
the S. D. fee." Butler at least lent Russell money to help him
through a temporary crisis, but ex-Senator Pettigrew extended
cold comfort when asked to share some expenses with Russell.
The South Dakotan expressed his pleasure in the idea of sharing expenses; he would make out a statement of his own expenses, and if the balance turned out in Russell's favor
Pettigrew would promptly remit, if in Pettigrew's he would
expect to hear from Wilmington. It was only "equitable and
proper that expenses should be paid in proportion to our
interests."[27]

[25] Peckham to Russell, Dec. 6, 1901, *ibid.*
[26] Alfred Russell to Russell, Jan. 17, 1902, *ibid.*
[27] Butler to Russell, Feb. 6, 1902; Pettigrew to Russell, Feb. 7, 1902,
ibid.

Pettigrew's letter apparently went unanswered. But Russell mollified Peckham as best he could, explaining again that the Schafers had given him nothing more than a contract for a contingent fee. Furthermore, by some misunderstanding, Lawyer Stewart out in South Dakota had contracted with his governor for a trifling 10 per cent contingent of whatever amount South Dakota might receive, when, according to Russell, it should have been 50 per cent so that Stewart could properly "take care" of his associates. Russell would make every effort to alter the South Dakota arrangement.[28]

This proved easier said than done. Russell, reproached by Ricaud for sending even a printing bill to Schafer Brothers, appealed to Stewart in Pierre for help in paying various costs. The Dakotan promptly replied that no provision had been made nor was any appropriation available for South Dakota to pay any costs or become obligated in any way to pay them. "This is the second time the suggestion has been made that this end of the line, or South Dakota, should pay these costs," Stewart scolded. "We hope there will be no further mistake about the proposition that all of these costs must be put up by the parties that are associated with you in the deal." Russell promptly fired back that it was unfortunate if Pettigrew had gone so far as to say that the private bondholders would pay costs for the plaintiff; the amount actually was small and could be handled easily. More seriously, there was a substantive point which Russell considered important: "This suit is well brought. The jurisdiction will stick. The defendant State has got no defense that is worth looking at except one point which it will rely on and which its lawyers will *hammer* with all their power. It is this: They will say in their answer that the donation of the bonds by Schafer to South Dakota is only colorable. They will deny that the assignment is bona fide. They will aver that it is a mere sham; that the State is not the real owner of the bonds, and that Schafer has got some resulting interest in them." Russell then predicted, correctly,

28 Russell to Peckham, Feb. 4, 1902, *ibid.*

that "they may drive us to taking depositions." Surely the South Dakotans could see that when the North Carolina counsel got "to fishing about on these depositions, it will leak out that the State has not even paid the little advance cost. . . . Now, this will not look well for us. It is one of those things that men do not like to have to explain. Indeed, there is no explanation, except to say flatly that we have paid the costs." Surely Stewart could see his governor or attorney-general and "steer us clear on this."

Russell's heaviest verbal artillery failed to crack the South Dakota position. Stewart agreed that it was indeed unfortunate that no understanding had been made earlier concerning expenses, but the South Dakota legislature had appropriated no money for the suit and the state had no incidental fund which could be tapped for the purpose. Both Governor Herreid and Attorney-General Pyle had been "great sticklers for the proposition that the State should in no way be held or become accountable for the payment of any fees or expenses, except in event of a recovery, and then only out of the amount recovered." As for depositions establishing South Dakota's ownership of the bonds, they could be supplied easily from the governor on down. But there was no cash in Dakota's hills.[29]

Just as Russell failed to secure help with expenses from South Dakota, he also found it impossible to get Stewart's 10 per cent contract changed. Russell argued soothingly that surely Governor Herreid would be justified and even commended for changing the original contract with Stewart if by so doing he could secure a much larger donation of bonds for South Dakota. But if the contract could not be changed, then ⅗ of Stewart's 10 per cent really should go to Russell so that he could pay Peckham something out of it in case recovery was made only on the ten bonds donated to South Dakota. Furthermore, the proviso in Stewart's contract giving him 5 per cent from the recoveries should not apply to the

---

[29] Russell to Stewart, Dec. 29, 1901; Stewart to Russell, Jan. 7, 1902, *ibid.*

second mortgage bonds but only to net recoveries on all bonds pooled with the North American Trust Company. The amount of the second mortgage bonds was small as compared with the others, and "we have had to make many promises on the event of recovery, so that what we recover out of the present bonds will have to bear the greater part of the expense of the litigation necessary to collect the others. . . ."[30] Russell apparently wasted his time in arguing with his distant associates; he could only moan to Butler that it was "outrageous for them to gouge us" as they were doing. Russell indeed spoke truthfully when he observed, in trying to calm Alfred Russell concerning fees, "The truth is the division is long and there is no way to help it."[31]

Aside from the constant queries and negotiations about the "division," Russell and his colleagues utilized the winter of 1901-1902 to map their legal strategy, just as counsel for North Carolina were doing in preparing the answer to South Dakota's bill. Russell decided that he and Alfred Russell should appear in the case as counsel for Charles Salter, the codefendant who represented the class of second mortgage bondholders. Anticipating the arguments of the North Carolina counsel, Russell prophesied that there would be a great to-do about the whole suit's being a fraudulent device whereby a state could be sued in defiance of the Eleventh Amendment. "All this and more will be hammered after the fashion of the 'high toned Southern Gentleman,' who is never so lofty as when he is playing the pirate." Governor Aycock's counsel might think of demurring. But that would be frivolous, and any party that would trifle with the highest court in the land by a demurrer in a case such as the one involved ought not even be allowed to answer the bill. And if they had enough sense not to demur, they would surely say that the suit was not bona fide, that the donation was only colorable and a transparent device whereby individuals could hide behind a sover-

---

[30] Butler [or Russell?] to Stewart, Feb. 10, 1902, *ibid.*
[31] Russell to Butler, April 16, 1902; Russell to Alfred Russell, April 7, 1902, *ibid.*

eign. "Then they may put in the stump speeches of Calhoun, Jeff Davis and Bob Toombs," the reconstructed Confederate surmised.[32]

The substantive point which from the very first bothered Russell more than any other aspect of the case was a subtle one which, depending on how the Supreme Court decided it, would partly determine the success or failure of the bond suit. The point was this: the second mortgage was not a blanket one on all of North Carolina's stock in the North Carolina Railroad, but each $1,000 bond had been given a mortgage on ten shares of stock, since the par value of the stock was $100 a share. Peckham and Alfred Russell argued, as Russell hoped but had his doubts, that the Supreme Court would find that the plaintiff (South Dakota) had no lien on any particular shares of stock but that all of the stock, or a sufficient amount of it to equal the par of the bond, was pledged for the payment of all the bonds; furthermore, this argument continued, the Court could not select any particular shares for the payment of the plaintiff because all of the other bondholders had the same lien as the plaintiff had on any shares that might be selected. This was a vital matter to Russell. If the Supreme Court should order the sale of only 100 shares of the stock, the case might end in the private bondholders' getting a compromise. "But, if the Court directs a sale of enough stock to pay all the bonds, we would have a 'picnic.' We would simply recover the whole $700,000. in this suit, and we would get every dollar of it."[33]

Another and related angle to this same matter bothered Russell. South Dakota's ten bonds were worth on their face, principal and interest, about $27,000. The Supreme Court, however, might order North Carolina to sell the 100 mortgaged shares of railway stock for the benefit of the plaintiff state. But since a share of the stock was worth about $170, making a total from the stock sale of $17,000, the Supreme

[32] Russell to Alfred Russell, Dec. 10, 1901, *ibid.*
[33] Russell to Alfred Russell, Nov. 21, 1901, *ibid.*

Court would have to give judgment against the defendant state for the balance of the $27,000 due South Dakota. The result of all this, Russell figured optimistically, would be that North Carolina would surely compromise the debt because it could hardly afford to go around paying $2700 on a bond that could be compromised for, say, $1500. Nor could North Carolina afford to pay off South Dakota and ignore the other bondholders; that, he predicted, would only mean that the next day North Carolina would be confronted by another suit from South Dakota or from one of the several other states which were "fixed" and waiting.[34] Governor Russell displayed a shrewd insight in his speculations about and puzzlement over this complicated matter of how the Supreme Court would decide about the curious bonds which had the second mortgage on ten shares of state-owned railway stock; this was to be one of the more striking aspects of the Court's ultimate decision in the bond suit.

A small part of the guessing and speculation ended, however, in April, 1902, when North Carolina filed her answer with the Supreme Court. A long, formal document, it began with a demand for strict proof that South Dakota truly owned "ten certain writings obligatory" and insisted that even if the complainant did possess the bonds, the transfer of ownership was "purely colorable and collusive" and made for the purpose of evading the Eleventh Amendment. North Carolina admitted the issuance of the second mortgage bonds but argued that they had not been issued and sold according to the requirements of the law which authorized them. Specifically, North Carolina now insisted that the statutory requirements that the bonds should be advertised for sale in the newspapers, sealed proposals received, and the bonds sold for not less than par—that these terms had not been fulfilled. Consequently, the Tarheel answer continued, the mortgages allegedly made by the state treasurer on the state's railway stock were not only made improperly but void anyhow because of the illegal issue and sale of the bonds. North Carolina

[34] Russell to A. A. Abbott, Feb. 10, 1902, *ibid.*

admitted the terms of the 1879 adjustment, as set forth in the complainant's bill, but the answer emphasized the "impoverished condition" of the state as a result of the Civil War, a condition which necessitated the drastic scaling down of that part of the state's debt which was not absolutely repudiated.

Admitting many other matters in South Dakota's bill, North Carolina argued that if one Charles Salter did truly hold any of the second mortgage bonds he was substantially a complainant; his interest and the interests of the class whom he represented were identical with the interests alleged by the complainant. Salter therefore should be "arrayed and treated for all purposes, and especially on the question of jurisdiction" as a complainant in the suit. (And this, under the Constitution, would have meant that the Supreme Court could not have taken jurisdiction of the case, for an individual could not constitutionally be a complainant against a sovereign state.) North Carolina denied any controversy, within the meaning of the Federal Constitution, between herself and South Dakota and closed her answer with the traditional phrase that the defendant "humbly prays this Honorable Court to enter its judgment that this defendant be hence dismissed, with her reasonable costs and charges in this behalf most wrongfully sustained."[35]

The *Morning Post* praised North Carolina's answer as a "very strong paper" and pointed out that the matter about the illegal issue of the bonds themselves had never before been raised. Furman forthrightly suggested, in a manner that probably won him no love from the state's political rulers and distinguished counsel, that if the second mortgage bonds had been illegally issued, then not only had North Carolina already needlessly given away some third of a million dollars in exchange for bonds of that issue under the compromise act of 1879, but also certain persons who were the "very best citizens" were involved in the original issuance and disposal of the bonds. In other words, Furman quietly warned that

[35] This document may be conveniently found in the Raleigh *Morning Post* or *News and Observer*, April 5, 1902.

there were no "Carpetbaggers" who could possibly be made the scapegoats if there had been any wrongdoing!

In contrast to the *Morning Post*'s careful mixture of praise and critical analysis of the answer, the *News and Observer*, still chugging down the rails of its suspicions, remarked that "certain interests" had long been trying to get control of the North Carolina Railway; they had resorted to the South Dakota suit to force North Carolina to sell her rail stock, and the state's answer made it abundantly plain, first, that there was no "cause of contest" between the two states; and second, that South Dakota's suit represented nothing more than a "fraud on the jurisdiction."[36]

Russell claimed that North Carolina's answer gave him great encouragement. "They made fools of themselves in a way that is beautiful to look at," he declared to Butler. Russell had expected to have to prove by depositions the figures on the second mortgage bonds and to try to do it in such way as to conceal his true purpose in introducing it, which would have been delicate and difficult. But now Shepherd, Merrimon, and Rountree, the North Carolina counsel, had generously given the point away. It was an important one to Russell, for it bore directly, he believed, on the "very serious point in the case and that is as to the divisability of the mortgaged stock, that is as to the danger of the Court['s] setting aside for the plaintiff ten shares for each of its bonds and refusing to pay off the individual bond holders." Grateful for the break as well as for the fact that he had not yet been publicly connected with the South Dakota suit, Russell warned Butler, "It is very important that they shall remain in their present state of mind, and that they shall never know what struck them until the argument. I will explain it all when I see you. In the mean time 'The word of our guidance is "mum." ' "[37]

The new matter in North Carolina's answer concerning

[36] *Morning Post,* April 6, 1902; *News and Observer,* April 5, 1902.
[37] Russell to Butler, April 16, 1902; see also Russell to Alfred Russell, April 7, 1902, Russell MSS.

the allegedly illegal issue of the second mortgage bonds bothered the former governor of North Carolina not at all. He had the information which he needed to counter the point almost at his fingertips; what he did not himself have he knew how to get. Russell explained to his Michigan colleague that in 1866 the state was bankrupt and bonds could not be sold on the general market at par. But the railway company said, "Give us one thousand dollars for one thousand dollars par of stock and we will give you one thousand dollars for every one thousand dollar bond, or instead of this circumlocution give us the bonds and we will give you the stock." In other words, North Carolina paid its debt by exchanging its bonds for railway stock, and "this was precisely equivalent to selling the bonds at par." The purpose of the law had been met when the bonds were sold at par, "which was about one hundred times as much as they were worth" at the time.[38]

Russell's explanation of the 1866-1867 transactions received corroboration from no less a source than the man who had been the youthful state treasurer at the time. This was Professor Kemp P. Battle, prominent historian and former president of the University of North Carolina and a member of a distinguished Tarheel family. Battle recalled that the legislature had been in session when the second mortgage bonds were issued; his memory was uncertain except "that I tried hard to comply with all the laws, and had good advisers, Gov. [Jonathan] Worth & Att'y Gen. Rogers." Battle could not recall whether or not he had advertised, but the "practice had been for years for the R. R. Co[mpanie]s to bid par for the bonds and receipts passed accordingly." If he had not advertised, "it was because I was advised that it was unnecessary." In sum, Battle insisted that he had been "advised that the plan pursued was sufficient."[39]

A deposition from Professor Battle, when the proper time came, would take care of several matters which the

[38] Russell to Alfred Russell, April 7, 1902, *ibid.*
[39] Kemp P. Battle to Edm. S. Battle, April 9, 1902, *ibid.*

North Carolina answer had raised. Furthermore, Battle might not remember whether or not he had advertised but Russell believed, or guessed, that he had. The former governor requested the confidential help of "the right man, the man of all men in the State, to dig up" the desired information, Marshall DeLancey Haywood, a prominent antiquarian and historian in Raleigh. Haywood, shuffling the post bellum newspapers in the State Library, found just the advertisements which Russell needed.[40]

Still confident of his legal ground, except for the bothersome question as to whether or not the nature of the second mortgage would force the Court to satisfy the private bondholders while satisfying South Dakota, Russell prepared for the next step. Peckham, representing the plaintiff, would take the perfunctory step of filing a general replication to North Carolina's answer. After that had been done, the Court would have to appoint commissioners to take testimony, in the form of sworn depositions, in North Carolina, South Dakota, and New York. South Dakota's replication, filed late in April, 1902, was blessed by a brevity which was lacking in most of the official documents in the case: "This replicant . . . saith, that he will aver and prove his said bill to be true, certain and sufficient in the law to be answered unto, and that the said answer of the said defendant is uncertain, untrue and insufficient to be replied unto by this replicant; . . . all of which matters and things this replicant is and will be ready to aver and prove as this honorable court shall direct, and humbly prays, as in and by his said bill he hath already prayed."[41]

Entangled with the time-consuming, tedious formalities of the United States Supreme Court, even Peckham, who had once aspired to be one of the nine august justices, growled: "If that Court would drop a little of its confounded dignity, and consult the convenience of those who practice there, it

[40] Russell to Haywood, Aug. 5, 1902, Russell to Alfred Russell, Aug. 23, 1902, *ibid.*

[41] Peckham to Russell, April 10, 1902; Russell to Peckham, April 12, 1902, *ibid.* The replication is printed in the *Morning Post,* April 29, 1902.

would be a great advance." Peckham's wishful thinking, however, did not alter the fact that, after consultation with Russell, he had to request the Court to issue an order appointing the commissioners to take testimony at the request of either party to the suit and upon ample notice to the adversary party. Russell suggested, Peckham agreeing, that the order should specify that if the commissioners were not agreed upon by the counsel for the respective parties, then the chief justice or one of the associate justices could name them.[42] The Supreme Court issued the order for the commissioners in May, 1902. The next step would be the taking of testimony. And this would publicly reveal, for the first time, that the former Republican governor of North Carolina and the former Populist senator had taken prominent roles in arranging to have the Old North State dragged, kicking and screaming, before the nation's highest tribunal. It was this testimony, which immediately made the headlines, that threw the political fat into a fire that already burned fiercely.

[chapter five]

THE TESTIMONY AND THE ARGUMENT BEFORE THE SUPREME COURT

BALANCING the scales of justice in the bond suit had turned out to be a process requiring time, money, and much patience. The advancing years and poor health of several of the key persons involved made time increasingly important. In a macabre but quite real way the slow-moving bond suit became something of a race with Death, and Death won the

[42] Russell to Peckham, April 24, 1902; Peckham to Russell, April 29, 1902, *ibid.*

first victory when Simon Schafer died in the summer of 1902. Ricaud believed that worry about the North Carolina bonds had contributed substantially to the old gentleman's demise. Praising Simon Schafer's many excellent characteristics, Ricaud could not resist the temptation to moralize: "The grasping propensity of the rich in this region is such, that they cannot bear disappointment philosophically."[1]

Whether from their own "grasping propensity" or some other motive, Russell, Ricaud, and the others were themselves behaving most unphilosophically in preparation for the taking of depositions. In fact, the author and co-authors of the bond suit were feverishly sending letters back and forth between Wilmington, New York, Washington, and Pierre trying to decide just what and how much should be explained and admitted in the testimony. Prudently anticipating this stage of the affair, Russell had written Samuel Schafer early in 1902 telling him exactly what to say in a letter which Schafer should write in his own hand to Congressman Burke. Although Russell himself had transmitted the ten bonds to the South Dakotans almost a year before he suggested this letter, he wanted Schafer to appear in the record as having done it. Schafer should declare that the bondholders preferred to donate the ten bonds to South Dakota, who could perhaps apply the money to the university or some other charitable purpose, rather than accept "the pittance" which North Carolina offered the individual holders. Furthermore, Schafer was to say that if South Dakota succeeded in collecting the bonds, the owners of the total issue then outstanding would be most pleased to make additional donations to such "governments as may be able to collect from the repudiating state."[2]

As the time neared for the depositions, Russell issued elaborate instructions and warnings to his associates. "The enemy," as he called the Tarheel Democrats who now controlled the state, would surely "fish for something to connect

[1] Ricaud to Russell, Aug. 4, 1902, Russell MSS.
[2] Russell to Schafer, Feb. 13, 1902, *ibid.*

Pettigrew and Butler with the transaction." That, he cautioned Stewart in South Dakota, "we must avoid if possible." Moreover, it would be indeed unfortunate if "the enemy" wangled an admission from any South Dakota official or witness that the state brought the suit while someone else paid the costs. "For the Lord's sake keep this out. It will not look well to the Court." Governor Herreid should say that Burke handed him the bonds together with Schafer's letter to Burke, and then the governor could put the letter in as evidence. Russell feared that the governor "may talk too much" before Shepherd and Rountree, who were going out to Pierre to represent North Carolina in the deposition-taking. Surely Stewart could "just fix it" so that his governor remained discreet and said little more than that he had gotten the bonds and Schafer letter from Congressman Burke. As for Burke himself, Russell thought it would be just as well if he could "not be within convenient reach just at this time."[3]

Peckham quite agreed with Russell's cautionary advice to South Dakota concerning the fact that the state was not paying the expenses of litigation. But the New Yorker thought it also important that "we should not in any way seem to do anything to hide it." Meantime, would Russell please advise again as to the witnesses who were to be examined in New York? "Maybe you have told me this before," Peckham airily admitted, "but the fact is, if you have [told me], I do not remember it and the weather has been so demoralizing lately that I have not looked it up."[4] Peckham, it was clear, felt little of the sense of urgency which drove Russell, Schafer, and several of the fee-hungry lawyers.

The South Dakota depositions pleased Russell immensely, but Ricaud became distressed, a bit unnecessarily as it developed, over the New York witnesses. From Pierre, Stewart reported that the North Carolina lawyers had gone away from their encounter with Governor Herreid none too happily

---

[3] Russell to Stewart, Aug. 4 and 8, 1902, *ibid.*
[4] Peckham to Russell, Aug. 11, 1902, *ibid.*

and "with a different apprehension of the salient features of this case than they came here with." Russell himself regarded Herreid's deposition as "a beauty" and, claiming that he knew "a good job" when he saw one, he congratulated Stewart upon his "excellent management of this matter."[5] Poor Ricaud, on the other hand, encountered difficulties in coaching Samuel Schafer and reported disgustedly that the New York depositions were successful only in one respect—they established "the *know-nothing-ism* of our crowd."

What Russell and Ricaud wanted to conceal in New York was the fact that Russell, while still the governor of North Carolina, had informally entered into negotiations about Schafer's bonds. This was the political dynamite which the North Carolina Democrats eagerly sought. Russell just as eagerly exerted himself to hide a part of the truth, although it was true, in a purely technical sense, that Ricaud rather than Russell had held the contract with Schafer Brothers until March, 1901. Ricaud reported that he had gone all the way out to Long Branch to drill Samuel Schafer before the examination of witnesses. "I told him there was nothing he knew which would hurt us at all but that I wanted him to forget when he first met you and our visit but otherwise he could tell anything he knew. I specially cautioned him to remember that all our dealings were with Simon and that he only incidentally knew of what arrangements were made and interviews had as a member of the firm and that it might be convenient and easy to use a defective memory &c as an excuse for inability to answer questions." Despite Ricaud's careful efforts, the excitement of the occasion must have unnerved Samuel Schafer. He "got so far away," Ricaud declared, that he was ordered to return the next day with all the letters between Russell and Schafer Brothers. Ricaud immediately took "him in charge for 2 hours and put him straight so as to claim the privilege of attny and client." After giving the firm's letterbooks to Ricaud, Schafer "tried hard to

[5] Stewart to Russell, Aug. 19, 1902, and Russell to Stewart, Aug. 23, 1902, *ibid.*

look up the private papers of Simon to see if he could not find some letters from you but after a hard struggle I got him to stop his hunt."

Sure enough, the following day the nervous Mr. Schafer testified as Ricaud had instructed. There had been no correspondence with Governor Russell before March, 1901, he declared, and after that time the letters were between client and attorney and therefore privileged. Simon Schafer's death also proved to be ironically useful, for, as Samuel Schafer told his remodeled, or Ricaud-modeled, story, the fact emerged, alas, that most of Russell's early dealings had been with the departed brother. Although Samuel Schafer had been, finally, an obliging and obedient client, rather than a candid witness, even Peckham uncharitably snapped that he was "a D——n fool."[6]

It was true, as Peckham judged, that much of the questioning done in New York by the counsel for North Carolina "was wholly irrelevant to any question at issue." But the line of questioning bore great relevance to North Carolina politics and was about to provide a sensational story for the *News and Observer*. Russell himself would soon be examined, and Peckham urged that Russell claim the same client-attorney privilege about his relationship with Schafer Brothers which Schafer had used on Ricaud's advice. In fact, Peckham argued that a "privilege of that kind is the privilege of the client and not of the attorney." Schafer could have waived it if he had so desired but Russell, being counsel, really had no power to waive it. Ricaud, too, felt apprehensive about the Raleigh questioning. He had felt in New York that "they were more earnestly endeavoring to *scalp*" Russell than to save money or honor for North Carolina; now he trembled lest Russell had imprudently left an incriminating letter or memorandum lying around in some file to which Democrats now had access. Ricaud urged the ex-governor to shy away from any mention

---

[6] Ricaud to Russell, Sept. 9 and 10, 1902, *ibid*. Also in the Russell papers is the unsigned, undated memorandum of Samuel Schafer's testimony, just as Ricaud had written it out for him.

of the relationship between Ricaud and Russell and to fix firmly on the fact that he had not been employed by Schafer Brothers until 1901.[7]

Russell felt nervous mainly about the eight second mortgage bonds on which he had arranged late in 1900 to stop the redemption so that he could buy them through a friend. He insisted in a confidential letter that he had not been in any secret deal whereby he was "going 'snooks' " with Banker John Armstrong of Wilmington, who had bought the eight bonds; that he, Russell, "never had any interest in the bonds whatever." Drawing on his formidable knowledge of legal lore, Russell cited precedent after precedent to verify, in the most casuistical manner, his argument that any agreement between the New York bondholder who sent the eight second mortgage bonds and the treasurer of North Carolina became "nudum pactum and void" when the New Yorker changed his mind, etc., etc. Then, because the man to whom he wrote was an old and close friend, Governor Russell strangely reversed his field. "I suppose I had a right to buy State Bonds if I wanted to. You see that by the transaction the State lost nothing, indeed it has gained by saving the interest on the new bonds." And anyhow, the real question was "for a great State to be trying to play a grab game on a creditor." If they asked him anything about the matter, he would just be tickled to "say some things that I would like to get into the depositions."[8]

After all his apprehensive efforts to reassure himself, Russell felt that the Raleigh depositions in November, 1902, went all right. "The enemy" questioned him closely, and for the first time publicly connected his name with the bond suit. But he wiggled as best he could, and that was none too well, around the matter of the eight bonds; he stoutly denied that he

[7] Peckham to Russell, Sept. 10 and 17, 1902; Ricaud to Russell, Sept. 23, 1902, *ibid.* In his second of two letters on the twenty-third, Ricaud urged Russell to destroy all letters from himself or the Schafers dated before January, 1901. Fortunately for history, and the present author, Russell hid the letters away instead.

[8] Russell to J. C. L. Harris, Sept. 24, 1902, *ibid.*

had officially had anything to do with the suit before March, 1901; and he slipped in one or two or his stump speeches against sovereigns who defrauded creditors and Democrats who repudiated honest debts. The 1867 officers of the North Carolina Railroad appeared in Raleigh to testify that, after exchanging railway stock for the state's bonds, they had sold the latter on the market at prices ranging from 23¢ to almost 68¢ on the dollar. Governor Aycock deposed that he had known nothing of the case until he read about it in the papers and that South Dakota had made no demand on him or any other North Carolina official before filing the bill of complaint against North Carolina.[9]

But the Raleigh questioning did not end the matter of witnesses. Counsel for both plaintiff and defendant agreed to extend the time for testimony until December 15, 1902, and Marion Butler's turn in Washington, D. C., was coming. Russell warned him that the "enemy" had been on Butler's track in the Raleigh questioning and wanted to know if Russell had not talked about the matter with Butler while both men still held state office. Russell must have felt that Butler's testimony could not be escaped, but Congressman Burke's was another matter. Russell still preferred that Burke not be examined, "because their main purpose will be to ask him if he did not confer with you and Pettigrew and some other things which, while they wont hurt the case, we would prefer to keep them out." They would try to catch Burke in the District before December 15, so it "may be that his engagements will be such he would not be in the District just at that time." Burke must have become a remarkably well-traveled, one could almost say peripatetic, congressman by this time. Butler notified the South Dakotan and fixed "things all right."[10] But while Burke traveled, Butler testified. Strangely enough, he immediately became, for North Carolina Democrats, the real villain of the piece.

[9] *Charlotte Observer,* Nov. 8, 1902; *News and Observer,* Nov. 8, 1902.
[10] Russell to Butler, Nov. 21, 1902; Butler to Russell, Nov. 24, 1902, Russell MSS.

That North Carolina was indebted primarily to Marion Butler "for the annoyance of this suit" was the conclusion drawn from Butler's testimony by the *News and Observer* and most of the ardent Democrats. Butler deposed that he himself had suggested the idea of a Dakota legislative act authorizing the acceptance of bonds and that he had done so to Senator Pettigrew while he, Butler, campaigned for Bryan in South Dakota during the 1900 presidential contest. Furthermore, the Tarheel Populist leader admitted that he had been employed as attorney for Schafer Brothers in January, 1901, a few weeks before his senatorial term expired, and that he had talked over the whole bond matter with Russell shortly before the governor's own term expired in mid-January, 1901.[11] In short, except for his claiming the authorship of South Dakota's donation act and dating it in 1900, when he actually had campaigned in South Dakota and other Western states, Butler told substantially the truth in his testimony. Russell had, by clinging to technicalities, skirted the truth more gingerly. That fact, plus the fact that Butler had been the chief architect of North Carolina's Populist-Republican rule in the 1890's, underlay the notion which now took hold in North Carolina that Marion Butler had fathered the South Dakota bond suit. Just at the height of his physical and intellectual powers and richly experienced in politics for a person of thirty-nine, Butler had long been the target of the North Carolina Democrats' most passionate hatred. Now there was fresh fuel for old fires.

The *News and Observer* waited only a few days after Butler's testimony in Washington to launch a full-scale attack. Then with glaring headlines—"BUTLER & RUSSELL. Their Own Evidence Convict[s] Them of Conduct that Will Forever Damn Them in North Carolina"—Josephus Daniels proceeded to sound the Democratic tocsin. Radical rule in 1868-1869 had sought to fasten a dishonest debt upon North Carolina, but now the "Russell Radical rule, of which Butler, Russell,

[11] *News and Observer,* Dec. 14, 1902.

and certain Southern Railway lights were the leaders, sought
—for sinister, selfish or dishonourable ends—to compel" the
state to pay par for the bonds which the state had "honorably
adjusted" more than a quarter-century ago. Why, Schafer
Brothers may have held these bonds all these years "as agents
of certain railroad manipulators who wished to hold them to
force their own terms upon the State." The "Southern Railway
speculating big men" no doubt held most of the bonds and
were behind the present suit partly for that reason but mainly
to see North Carolina, with its empty treasury and budgetary
deficit, compelled to pay about $750,000 to settle the bonds.
Then the railway "manipulators" would exert every power to
influence and bribe the legislature to sell the state's stock in
the North Carolina Railroad so that the Southern Railway
could gobble it up.

The *News and Observer*'s editorial columns, which then
differed from the news stories only in where they were located
within the paper, solemnly declared that North Carolinians
would "never know from how much of wrong they escaped
by the defeat of the Republican party in North Carolina in
1900." They knew that "they put peace in the place of law-
lessness" and that the "blight of evil and ignorant rule ended."
They knew that "race antagonisms and all forms of violence
ceased." (Actually, Governor Aycock was so appalled by the
brutality of the state's eight lynchings during the first half of
his term that he would soon make a strong appeal for a stop
to the practice in his 1903 message to the legislature.) But
Tarheels would never know fully of the "further wrongs and
corruption in contemplation" from which they had escaped
by restoring the Democrats to power in 1898 and 1900.
"The 1868-'9 gang stole more money, but if the 1895-'9 gang
had been given another lease of power, it may be well doubted
if the carpet-bagger of 1868-'9 would have far surpassed the
disgraceful gang at the helm from '95 to '99." All in all, the
conduct of Butler and Russell in the bond affair was "the
blackest page in the black book of their career."[12]

[12] *News and Observer,* Dec. 19, 1902.

Having now launched the highly emotional and history-charged attack which it would continue intermittently for many years, the *News and Observer* took the offensive with all of its angry accusations and suspicions. Lesser Democratic papers over the state took their cue from the Raleigh extremist. The *Wilkesboro Chronicle* declared that Marion Butler, "the real instigator" of the bond suit, would "do anything for the cash, provided it is against his own people." The *Tarboro Southerner* agreed that Butler's acceptance of a retainer while he was still in the Senate to force his state to pay "an unjust claim" could only lower the Populist chieftain in the eyes of "all decent men." And former Governor Russell was "but little better." The *Chatham Observer,* blithely inaccurate about the origin and nature of the bonds involved, as were many other papers, concluded: "It is not surprising that Butler and Dan Russell, who have always been against the best interest of their State, should now be trying to collect these old bonds that their crowd saddled upon the State when her people lay helpless and bleeding at the mercy of the gang who robbed our State and brought shame on her good name and suffering upon her people with all the evils of misgovernment and ruin."[13]

Confronted with the full-dress rehearsal of Democratic slogans about Reconstruction and Fusion, Russell retorted as best he could. As for Butler's employment by Schafer Brothers before his Senate term ended, Russell replied in an interview: "What of it? He was a practicing lawyer and not refusing business. . . . Is there any reason why a senator should not take a case against his own state if he believes that case to be just and fair and honest? Suppose he thinks he is doing a service to the state in trying to get it to pay or to compromise its honest debts?" Then the former governor, no doubt wistfully, reminded the reporter that everybody knew that the state had "always recognized the honesty of these bonds."

Now that he had a reporter's ear and since he had been publicly involved in the matter, Russell strove to present his

[13] The above three weeklies, together with others, quoted in *News and Observer,* Dec. 21 and 28, 1902.

views in the matter. For one thing, he insisted that if the Supreme Court upheld the contention of South Dakota and of the private holders of the second mortgage bonds that the first mortgage was due and had to be paid off, then the state of North Carolina would save rather than lose money. This was a subtle point which Russell had indirectly tried to get before the public earlier, but now he openly identified himself with it. Russell put it as a seeming paradox that if South Dakota won a judgment, North Carolina would lose only nominally and would in reality save much money. He explained it thus: if the Supreme Court decreed that North Carolina should sell enough of its railway stock to pay off both first and second mortgages, the state could, rather than sell its stock, simply borrow money on it sufficient to pay off the two mortgages. The first mortgage amounted to $2,720,000 and Russell supposed that the second mortgage could be compromised at, say, $480,000. That made a total of $3,200,000. The state's stock in the North Carolina Railroad, on the other hand, was worth $5,500,000 on the market; no banker in North Carolina would deny that the state could use the stock as collateral and borrow at 3 per cent the $3,200,000 to pay off both mortgages. But under existing arrangements, the first mortgage drew 6 per cent and would do so, unless the Supreme Court decided differently, for the next seventeen years. Therefore, Russell concluded, if the state had to pay off both mortgages as a result of the bond suit and borrowed on its stock, the state would lose the difference between $2,720,000 and $3,200,000 or, put more simply, would lose the $480,000 needed to pay the second mortgage. The state would gain the difference between 6 per cent and 3 per cent on $2,720,000 for seventeen years, which came to about $1,300,000. The net gain to North Carolina would be about $820,000; this could be the saving to the state under a Supreme Court decree in favor of South Dakota and the second mortgage bond-holders. "Let financiers figure," the former governor urged.[14]

[14] *Morning Post,* Dec. 18, 1902. The *Post*'s able Washington corre-

Russell's statement received a cautious commendation from the *Morning Post,* which conceded that Russell had presented the matter in a manner which merited the attention of North Carolina's statesmen. Purely from the standpoint of a financial transaction, the *Post* felt that Russell was right in saying that to supplant the 6 per cent first mortgage bonds with 3 per cent bonds, coupled with a fair compromise of the second mortgage bonds, would financially benefit North Carolina. Furthermore, Editor Furman pointed out that the state then received about $210,000 annually from its railway stock; the cost of settling the first and second mortgage bonds at 3 per cent would be about $90,000 each year, and this amount, when subtracted from the $210,000 income from stock, would still leave about $120,000 in the state treasury for a sinking fund to be used for the debt or for other purposes. Furman, however, did not mean for North Carolina to give anything away unnecessarily, as his closing statement proved: "But, we must wait for the decision of the court. Nothing toward this scheme, however attractive, can be done until then, and then only in case of a decision adverse to the State." The *News and Observer,* furious with Russell anyhow and apparently rather baffled by the intricate arithmetic, snapped that when "North Carolina gets rich by paying over a million dollars it does not owe, then men will lift themselves up to the top of a church steeple by taking hold of the strap of their boots."[15]

By late 1902, after Russell's and Butler's roles had been publicized, albeit in a somewhat distorted fashion, the journalistic battle lines in North Carolina had been clearly drawn.

spondent, Thomas J. Pence, interviewed Russell in the national capital and would continue to provide the best reports on the bond suit and the key personalities involved in it throughout the period. Pence later went to work for the *News and Observer,* after the *Post* had ceased publication in 1905, and was described by Secretary of the Navy Josephus Daniels, upon the occasion of Pence's death in 1916, as a newspaperman who possessed almost unerring judgment and who had "a genius for getting scoops, for men high and low gave him their confidence freely knowing he would never abuse it." *Charlotte Observer,* March 28, 1916.

[15] *Morning Post,* Dec. 19, 1902; *News and Observer,* Dec. 20, 1902.

The *News and Observer* relished the opportunity to link Butler and Russell, but especially the former, with the original Radicals of the Reconstruction era; it staunchly insisted that the whole bond affair was "a slimy creeping, round-about, Pecksniffian piece of business from start to finish" and that there was "no excuse, no palliation" for the conduct of the former senator and former governor who now sought to "mulct North Carolina" out of a vast sum of money. While the *News and Observer* blew the bond revelations into the proportions of a major political scandal, the two other leading Democratic dailies in North Carolina reacted quite differently. The then staid *Charlotte Observer*, with its old-fashioned one-column headings rather than bold headlines and its small print, carried the straight news stories of the testimony as it appeared and ignored the affair in its editorial columns. The *Morning Post*, finally, fought for a calm, middle position as best it could. The *Post* reiterated again, in the face of the *News and Observer*'s insistence on a Southern Railway conspiracy, that there was no proposition made or pending which would call for the sale of the state's interest in the North Carolina Railroad, regardless of how the bond suit might result. Nor did the *Post* believe that Aycock's administration was such that it would be influenced by threats, slanders, or cajolery. As for the rectitude of the strongly Democratic legislature, about which Josephus Daniels' paper seemed to be so apprehensive, the *Post* insisted that Democratic legislators would be "impervious to all such approaches from such corrupt and vicious sources." Whatever the Supreme Court might decide, Governor Aycock and the legislature would meet it as "honest men without the counsel or advice of the dishonest populist element whose sole ambition is to thrive by an appeal to ignorance and dishonesty." North Carolina's cause being honest, all honest people would readily yield to the decision of the United States Supreme Court.[16]

While the North Carolina newspapers debated the ins

[16] *News and Observer,* Dec. 24, 1902; *Charlotte Observer,* Dec., 1902;

and outs of the bond suit, giving off more political heat than financial light, Russell and his associates entered the last stages of preparation for the dramatic, and possibly decisive, argument before the Supreme Court. Those allegations in South Dakota's bill of complaint which had not been clearly admitted in North Carolina's answer had to be carefully proven by Peckham, Alfred Russell, and Russell. Peckham sagely pointed out, "We must be more careful than usual to clearly make out our prima facie case because the Court we may assume would rather avoid decision of the merits of the case and will be not unwilling to dispose of it on some side point."[17]

Russell felt no doubts concerning his ability to prove the lawful issue, advertisement, and sale of the bonds. His own historical research together with that done for him, as described earlier, fortified him in this area. Nor was he concerned with the whole question of how and why South Dakota received the bonds. An article about the bond suit in the *Columbia Law Review* charged that South Dakota's acquisition of the bonds was not in 'due course'; that is, that "speculative acquisition of obligations not enforceable by the persons who transferred them, is not 'due course.'" Russell tellingly retorted that the Federal government itself in an 1890 case, *U. S. v. North Carolina*, 136 U. S. 211, had sued on the defendant state's bonds, bonds which the Federal government had acquired by assignments from persons (Indian tribes) who could not sue upon them. Whatever sort of action the United States government could bring originally in the Supreme Court, Russell concluded, could most certainly be brought by a state. Nor could there be any question about North Carolina's appearing and submitting to the Court's

_____

and *Morning Post*, Dec. 20, 1902. The *Post*, again having to defend its endorsement of Russell for the chief justiceship early in 1901, delighted in reminding Daniels of the 1898 flirtation between himself and Butler, "the author of the movement to collect the bonds," which had almost led to co-operation between Butler's Populists and the Daniels-Clark, Bryanite wing of the state Democrats.

[17] Peckham to Russell, June 27, 1902, Russell MSS.

decision. "Some years ago, we did try to do otherwise down in this 'neck of the Woods,' " the unhappy Confederate remembered. "We raised an army and went to war, and got licked."[18]

Unworried about many aspects of his case, Russell still felt the greatest anxiety about the nature of the second mortgage on North Carolina's railway stock—could the Court order only enough stock sold to pay for South Dakota's ten bonds or would it have to order all the stock sold in order for any of the bonds to be paid? For the former view of the nature of the mortgage Russell used the term "in severalty," and for the latter "in solido." He admitted that his terms were probably not accurate or technical, but he felt they constituted "the best short cut that I have invented to carry the idea short and sharp." His legal aim all along had been to lead the Supreme Court to rule that the mortgage was "in solido." But now the thought occurred to him that if the Court agreed about the mortgage, it might turn right around and "*lift* us" by holding that the individual bondholders were necessary parties with the plaintiff and the jurisdiction would therefore be gone. Could we get around "this ugly point," Russell inquired of his colleague in Michigan, by consenting on submission to the Court that if it held the mortgage to be "in solido" and the jurisdiction therefore lost, the individual defendants would consent to a decree carrying their interests in so much of the railway stock as should be subjected to the demands of South Dakota? But how could this be appropriately formulated? Russell, despite all his contemplation of the various possibilities, still clung to his belief that the Court would hold the mortgage to be "in severalty" and that, even so, a decree in favor of South Dakota alone would be a victory for his cause because North Carolina would be compelled to compromise with the other bondholders.[19]

[18] Russell to A. Abbott, May 22, 1902, *ibid*. The article referred to is Carman F. Randolph, "Notes on Suits between States," *Columbia Law Review*, II (May, 1902), 292-312.
[19] Russell to Alfred Russell, July 8, 1902, *ibid*.

As if such complicated legal points were not enough to harass him, Russell had to cope with the $555 estimated bill which the clerk of the Supreme Court submitted for having all of the depositions and other documents in the record printed. Russell requested Peckham, to whom the bill had gone nominally, to inquire around on his next visit to Washington and see if the clerk had not made an error or if he could not get the record printed more economically. The distinguished New York attorney replied that, while the clerk was no doubt liberal in both his estimates and charges, discussion of his bills was "rather rare." Yet Peckham really knew little about it: "With the liberality of a man handling the funds of another I have generally paid him whatever he asked without inquiry."[20]

Russell paid. Scraping together what he could, hammering away at Samuel Schafer for an advance, the hard-pressed former governor was determined to keep his case going. With the argument before the Supreme Court scheduled for April, 1903, he and Alfred Russell prepared their briefs for printing well in advance. Alfred Russell did not care to make an oral address to the Court; letting you and Peckham do that, he wrote Russell, "I will sit by, & smile." Peckham, still seeming less eager than the two Russells, admitted in mid-March, 1903, that he had been "exceedingly busy this winter" and had not been able to give any substantial attention to the preparation of his brief. He was at work on it but still much distracted "by lots of other things." He would deal with the whole question of jurisdiction, and the two Russells, making their briefs complete and independent of anything he might do, could carry the burden of the argument as to whether the plaintiff's relief should come by the mere sale of ten shares of stock per bond or by the sale of all the stock. As Governor Russell had argued, the ultimate object in the minds of those who donated the bonds to South Dakota had no relevance to the real question involved. If a conference of the

[20] Peckham to Russell, Jan. 31, 1903, *ibid.*

three lawyers should be desirable, let it be as soon as possible, Peckham urged, and since "I am between you both, the best place for it is this City."[21]

Both Russells urged Peckham on, specifically requesting that he also treat the point concerning how relief should be afforded to the plaintiff. "It is extremely desirable to obtain a sale of all the stock for the benefit of all the bonds," Alfred Russell again explained, "and I wish you would not only 'slightly touch' this point, but argue it as elaborately as you can find time to do." After such prodding, Peckham finally thought about the matter and concluded that their case was not like the "ten buggies case" which had haunted Russell. There the plaintiff's claim was for ten buggies, for 10/100 of 100 buggies. In "our case," Peckham argued, the claim was for an undivided share in the capital stock of the North Carolina Railroad. There was no such thing as a divided share of capital stock until a corporation was wound up and the capital stock divided; rather, a shareholder owned a mere interest in the concern as a whole and had only the right to have the corporate property and affairs managed in accordance with the charter and articles of agreement. With citations sprinkled throughout his letter, Peckham insisted, as the two Russells hoped, that such a thing as divided shares in a going corporation was unthinkable and it was impossible to distinguish any one share from another. Peckham had read Russell's printed brief, regarded it as "conclusive enough," and thought that all three of their briefs should be filed with the Supreme Court by April 6, 1903. If the counsel for North Carolina saw them for a few days before the argument, that would not really be of any consequence.[22]

Shepherd, Merrimon, and Rountree, the North Carolina counsel, were also ready and seemingly confident. Governor Aycock had informed the legislature, early in 1903, that the

[21] Alfred Russell to Russell, March 12, 1903; Peckham to Russell, March 11, 1903, *ibid.*
[22] Alfred Russell to Peckham, March 17, 1903; Peckham to Russell, March 23 and 26, 1903, *ibid.*

South Dakota suit was the first case of its character ever brought by one state against another, and North Carolina "confidently contended" that "no Court had jurisdiction to enforce public obligations in the hands of an assignee which could not be enforced by the assignor." Furthermore, Aycock declared, the principle involved in the suit was of the most serious importance, not only to North Carolina but to all the states; if the suit could be maintained it would be "a dangerous departure and one seriously infringing upon the sovereignty of the State."[23] Sharing Aycock's apparent confidence, George Rountree of Wilmington had even earlier asserted that, "I do not believe the courts have jurisdiction of an action of debt against a state. How can judgment be enforced?" Judge Shepherd, for his part, read Peckham's brief just before the argument began and admitted to Aycock that it was "the best that can be made on that side." Still Shepherd, on the eve of the big day, felt "greatly strengthened in my hope of success."[24]

With all the lawyers on both sides of the bond suit gathered in Washington, argument before the Supreme Court of the United States had finally come, two years after Russell had begun in earnest to arrange the suit. A recent and lively history of the Supreme Court pictures the turn-of-the-century Court as one that had more than regained "the institutional self-assurance" which had been shattered in the Civil War era. While using the Fourteenth Amendment to slash away at the states' attempts to regulate business activity, the Court in 1895 had asserted its dominance in the Federal sphere and its conservative, probusiness leanings in three famous decisions which upheld labor-leader Eugene Debs's prison sentence for contempt of court, emasculated the Sherman Antitrust act, and declared the Federal income tax unconstitu-

[23] Governor Aycock to the General Assembly of 1903, Governor's Letter Book, No. 109, p. 26. Also in the *News and Observer,* Jan. 9, 1903.
[24] Rountree to Theodore F. Davidson, October 22, 1902, in the Theodore F. Davidson Papers, North Carolina Department of Archives and History. Shepherd to Aycock, April 11, 1903, in the Governor's Papers, *ibid.*

tional. In its famous *Plessy* v. *Ferguson* decision in 1896, the Court had ruled that the states could segregate the races under the "separate but equal" doctrine, but freedom of contract was another matter—it was "the one kind of 'liberty' most jealously guarded by the Court under the Constitution."[25]

Chief Justice Melville W. Fuller had been a Chicago corporation lawyer and a Democrat when President Grover Cleveland named him to head the Court in 1888. Predictably probusiness, Fuller did not influence the Court as much as did some of the associate justices. Among the latter, John M. Harlan enjoyed seniority on the Court by virtue of his appointment by Rutherford B. Hayes in 1877. David J. Brewer had been appointed by Benjamin Harrison in 1889 and exercised a large influence on the thinking of the Court; he was to write the decision in the bond case. Henry B. Brown of Michigan had been named to the court by Harrison, in 1890, and, through Alfred Russell, was to play a small but nonetheless significant off-stage as well as on-stage part in the suit. Cleveland named Edward D. White and Rufus W. Peckham, Wheeler Peckham's brother, to the Court in 1894 and 1895, respectively; and Joseph McKenna received his appointment from William McKinley in 1898. In 1902 Theodore Roosevelt appointed the wise Boston Brahmin, Oliver W. Holmes, Jr., who soon became in the layman's mind "the perennial prototype of the genus Justice," and Roosevelt in 1903 also named William R. Day, who had been McKinley's secretary of state, to the Court.[26]

Since the Court usually relied heavily on the printed briefs, the ordinary limit for argument was four hours, with

[25] Fred Rodell, *Nine Men: A Political History of the Supreme Court from 1790 to 1955* (New York, 1955), pp. 169-173.

[26] Rodell, *Nine Men,* pp. 169-70; and Charles H. Butler, *A Century at the Bar of the Supreme Court of the United States* (New York, 1942), pp. 64-65. The latter volume, by a long-time reporter of decisions for the Court, furnishes an informal insight into the Court's workings and contains an interesting, although slightly erroneous, account of the bond suit (pp. 97-99). Willard L. King's *Melville Weston Fuller: Chief Justice of the United States, 1888-1910* (New York, 1950) is a detailed biography but does not deal with the bond suit.

each side using half of the time. But because the bond suit was a case of original jurisdiction the Court granted a total of five hours; subsequently, when the justices and lawyers had become involved in the several novel and significant features of the case, Chief Justice Fuller withdrew all limitation upon debate and informed counsel that they could have all the time desired. Only eight justices were present for the argument because Justice Day had not fully recovered from a bout with pneumonia.

An amusing incident marked the beginning of the proceedings. Chief Justice Fuller thought that Russell, Alfred Russell, and Marion Butler were appearing with counsel for North Carolina because they, as counsel for the second mortgage bondholders, were put down as defendants. When the chief justice was informed that Russell and his associates were with the plaintiff in reality, the Raleigh *Morning Post*'s correspondent noted that "a smile played around the court room."

Peckham led off in the argument before the august tribunal. The question which immediately seemed to arouse the greatest interest among the justices was the sale of North Carolina's railway stock as proposed by Peckham, counsel for South Dakota, and by Russell. Justice Harlan especially, but also other members of the court, asked numerous questions about the proposed mode of relief, indicating that the justices viewed with seriousness the idea of foreclosing on North Carolina's rail stock. When Justice Holmes asked questions about the identification of the shares of stock that were pledged as surety for the bonds, Peckham replied that there were no identified shares pledged and that all of the bondholders possessed an undivided interest in the stock. Justice White wanted to know if there were not a way to satisfy the claims of the individual bondholders without selling the stock; Peckham retorted that he knew of no way but would be glad for the Court to suggest a method.

George Rountree opened for North Carolina and dealt with the constitutional questions involved. The *Morning Post* correspondent reported that Rountree had such "complete mastery of his subject that he acquitted himself most creditably." Harlan asked him if a state repudiated a just debt would another state have cause for action, and Rountree replied that he thought not. He insisted that there was no precedent for the Court's taking jurisdiction in a suit brought by one state against another for debt. Furthermore, a claim which was noncollectible had no validity and did not obtain validity when transferred to a state for collection. When Rountree charged that the two individuals who represented the holders of the first and second mortgage bonds were the "tools of Schafer Brothers" and "used with South Dakota to obtain jurisdiction," Justice Brown asked for the evidence of such a scheme. Rountree pointed to the transfer of the ten bonds from Schafer Brothers to South Dakota, which action, he alleged, proved that the real purpose of the suit was to foreclose a mortgage for individuals who could not themselves sue. South Dakota, in other words, had been "hired by a gift of bonds" to foreclose the mortgage.[27]

Rountree's own version of his appearance before the Supreme Court differed interestingly from what the Raleigh newspapers reported. After his day in Court, he confessed to Governor Aycock that they had "listened patiently for a few minutes and then bombarded me with a fusilade of questions, which attempted to show that I was wrong in thinking the original Constitution did not give the Court jurisdiction over actions of debt against a state." But Rountree felt that Justices White, Brewer, and Harlan, at least, were with North Carolina on the contention that the individual bondholders were necessarily one with South Dakota in the action against another sovereign state. "I made a very unsatisfactory speech," Rountree judged, "because they were all on me at once, but think I succeeded in getting the point before them." There

[27] Special correspondence by Thomas J. Pence, *Morning Post,* April 13, 14, 1903.

was, finally, "some doubt about the result, but the chances are that we will win upon the ground that the suit is necessarily one on behalf of S. D. and individuals alike."[28]

Peckham and Russell, after surveying the drift of the justices' questions and conferring privately among themselves, must have shared Rountree's hunch about the chances of the suit. When Peckham reappeared before the Court to make his concluding argument he shifted his ground markedly and virtually dissociated his client's interests from those of the individual bondholders. He declared, in effect, that "The claims of the individuals can be dismissed for all we care. South Dakota is not a trustee for the second mortgage bondholders." The North Carolina counsel promptly interpreted this change of base to mean that Russell, Peckham, and their associates realized that it would be impossible to maintain a suit against North Carolina in which individuals were jointly interested. Rountree, Shepherd, and Merrimon now felt that their arguments had forced South Dakota to fall back upon her own case regardless of what might happen to the bondholders.

The financial difference to North Carolina in the shift from the broad to the more narrow request was the difference between around $700,000 and approximately $30,000. But Peckham's shift of position had been accompanied by "another game in contemplation" which Russell no doubt carefully arranged to have reported in the Raleigh press. If the Court rendered a judgment in favor of South Dakota, the precedent would then be safely established; South Dakota or some other state could, therefore, acquire all of the Schafer bonds if it were necessary or desirable and bring suit to collect the full amount of principal and interest on all the bonds. "This is the game in the event that Dakota wins." And Russell wished Raleigh Democrats to ponder well the "game" which had been foreshadowed.

[28] Rountree to Aycock, April [14?], 1903, Governors' Papers. Briefs of the Counsel for North Carolina are in the Governors' Papers, Boxes 307-308.

Meantime, James E. Shepherd, the former North Carolina chief justice, spoke strongly to the Court against the attempted fraud on the jurisdiction and about a sovereign state's right to control its own fiscal affairs. Justice White interrupted Shepherd to ask, hypothetically, what if North Carolina repudiated a debt owed to England and that nation made a demand upon the United States for settlement; did there not have to be a power whereby the whole could protect itself from the action of one of the parts? Shepherd replied that motive would have to be heavily considered; surely no country would go to war because its citizens purchased uncollectible bonds. Peckham spoke tellingly to this point by arguing that motive could not be attacked in such a transaction. Had it come to pass that the grant of judicial power over controversies between states had to be fought out on a question of motive? If so, every case brought into the Supreme Court would result in petty wrangles. "If South Dakota had no power to accept and own these bonds," Peckham concluded, "then the case cannot stand. If it did, then it cannot be ruled out of court by the charges of fraud and collusion." North Carolina had taken property which was pledged to bondholders, was living on the proceeds from the property, and then talked of fraud! In his "ringing" peroration, the distinguished New Yorker quoted no less an authority than John Marshall himself and referred to the necessity of the Court's preserving its jurisdiction over all possible controversies between states in order to preserve the peace and tranquillity of the Union.[29]

It was Peckham, polished veteran of Supreme Court practice, who most impressed the North Carolinians present in Washington, but the former governor of North Carolina drew blood, too. Russell's long, peppery brief included such phrases as the "turpitude of repudiation" and shamed North Carolina for having "descended to" such a level. That repudiation, Russell alleged, simply amounted to confiscation. After tracing the issue of the bonds and the state's treatment of them when

[29] Special correspondence by Pence, *Morning Post*, April 16, 1903.

the state declared itself bankrupt in 1879, Russell pointed to the fact that the pledged railway stock had since become worth enough on the market to pay not only the first mortgage but also the second one and still leave the state about $2,000,000. "And yet North Carolina retains the security . . . and is guilty of the monstrous wrong of collecting every six months the income of the stock and turning it into its own treasury, without paying anything upon principal or interest of the second mortgage bonds, although that income so collected every six months, in equity and in common honesty, is the property of the Complainant and the other second mortgage bond holders." There was, in short, no language too strong "to denounce the turpitude of this proceeding."[30]

Stung no doubt by the scalawag Russell's charges, the *News and Observer*'s editorial page launched into what had now become periodic rehearsals of the charge that the "South Dakota case is the abortive ending of a well-planned scheme." Men who had held high state office (Butler and Russell), high Southern Railway officials, and lawyers "who play toady to big officials" were the "conspirators" who had originally hoped to force the sale of the state's stock only to be thwarted by the exposure of Josephus Daniels' newspaper. The case being heard by the Supreme Court was "the most important one that has come before that court, so far as the South is concerned, since the attempt to make the Southern States pay the fraudulent debts contracted by the carpetbag's governments during reconstruction." Surely the Supreme Court would never allow such a preposterous fraud upon its jurisdiction, "such prostitution of one State's right to sue another." Its rival morning daily might sorrow but the *News and Observer* could only rejoice: "The Special Tax Bond ring with its high railroad officials, subsidized newspaper, and their legal toadies have not made the million or so they expected."

Fortunately for itself, the paper accused of being subsidized, the *Morning Post,* could give as much as it had to

<hr>

[30] *News and Observer,* April 15, 1903.

take in the hot journalistic feud. The *Post* first of all declared that no North Carolinian need feel any alarm about the now-famous case being argued in Washington. The *News and Observer*'s statement that a decision favorable to South Dakota would open the way for similar suits to compel payment of the special tax bonds was just "too silly for any consideration and was made upon the presumption that the readers of the paper making it are as ignorant as the party making the statement." That assumption might, of course, be true, the *Post* added, but meantime "intelligent people will not be alarmed or take to the woods, however the suit may end."[31]

With the argument before the Court ended and the Raleigh papers swapping insults about the possible outcome, the long wait for the decision had begun. Immediately after leaving the Supreme Court, Russell wrote optimistically to his old friend, B. N. Duke: "We *'wore out'* the other fellows. *They* believe they are *beat*. They are badly hacked. It looks our way; but nothing is certain till death."[32] And the uncertainty increased as the months passed and no decision came.

"The axles of time turn none too softly with me since you were here," Ricaud confessed to Russell, "and yet I fully expect to pull through my present difficulties and soon occupy a place of comparative independence." The financial sky might brighten regardless of the bond suit, but surely the "Court will not hunt for reasons to ignore the Justice and decency due our cause." Alfred Russell was apparently on tenterhooks throughout the summer and fall; Russell sent him encouraging gossip but that hardly satisfied. Unable to communicate orally with Peckham, Alfred Russell could only regret that the New Yorker, with his well-placed brother, "would not put in writing anything which he might have learned in a 'kitchen cabinet' way!" By October, 1903, Alfred Russell fervently hoped that the time was "near at hand when

[31] *News and Observer,* April 16, 19, 1903; *Morning Post,* April 15, 1903.
[32] Russell to Duke, April 16, 1903, B. N. Duke MSS.

we may expect a decision, a favorable one according to all" which Russell had heard and sent on.[33]

After the long, suspenseful wait, the Supreme Court's order on November 30, 1903, for a reargument of the bond case in January, 1904, came as both a great disappointment and a scare to Russell and his friends. The Raleigh *Morning Post*'s alert correspondent in Washington reported the widespread belief among informed Washingtonians that the Court was divided, and that this theory gained color from the fact that only eight members had heard the original argument. If the gossip were true, the *Post* continued, Justice Day would now become the arbitrator, for his restoration to health meant that a full Court would hear the reargument. The original briefs had been so elaborate and extensive that no one could imagine that the Court really desired further information. If it had, a rehearing would have been ordered months earlier. But when the Court adjourned in June for the summer, the South Dakota case was the only one of eleven cases argued in that term which the justices had left undecided. Just to complicate matters, another rumor discussed in Washington was that the Court was even more divided than half against half; this other view had it that three members felt that South Dakota was entitled to recover on its ten bonds, three others held that both South Dakota and the New York bondholders should recover, and the remaining two justices who had heard the argument had taken North Carolina's position.[34]

Poor Russell, sick with what he believed to be malarial fever and involved in an acutely embarrassing patronage scramble for the Wilmington post office, could only ask, What did it mean? He too felt that the Court probably was divided on questions regarding the individual bondholders and wanted a full bench. He suspected that the justices probably did not want a reargument of the jurisdiction question because there really was no more to be said on that point.

[33] Ricaud to Russell, Sept. 18, 1903; Alfred Russell to Russell, June 22, Oct. 8, 1903, Russell MSS.

[34] *Morning Post*, Dec. 1, 1903.

No, they had probably satisfied themselves that one state could sue another on a money question and that one state could create a controversy with another state by acquiring a demand against it. The real danger, Russell guessed, was that they faced the matter of not being able to administer the rights of South Dakota without substantially permitting individuals to sue a state "in the teeth" of the Eleventh Amendment. Why cannot we say to the Court, he asked Alfred Russell, that if it holds that individuals are not entitled to be paid off in this suit, then the private bondholders will consent to a decree in favor of South Dakota for 100 shares of stock and thus carry to the purchasers at the judicial sale all the rights and interests of the individuals in the 100 shares? A conference in Washington for at least a week before the reargument seemed highly important to the increasingly desperate former governor.[35]

Russell's plight sprang not only from illness but also from a worsening of his chronically poor financial situation. After earlier turning down a patronage job, he had written Ben Duke that he felt anxious to stay out of politics and tried hard to do it. "My whole object in this life is to make some money and pay my debts," Russell had declared. "And my prospects are good but I don't know that I can hang on long enough for prospects to realize—. . . ." When his personal situation became critical late in 1903, Russell again wrote to Duke, prefacing his letter with the admission that he was again distressed about money and it tore out his "very heart-strings to be compelled to annoy you after you have done so much for me." Russell then explained that he had paid all his debts left from the governorship in Raleigh during the past three years and had not speculated—"not a dollar"—in cotton, stocks, or anything. Besides working at law, he had lived frugally and worked hard as his own overseer on the

[35] Russell to Alfred Russell, Dec. 1, 1903, Russell MSS. The Wilmington post office imbroglio, where Russell put himself way out on a limb and got left there by President Roosevelt, may be followed in the *Morning Post* or *News and Observer* for Jan., 1904.

rice plantation. But now he found himself short $2,000 on his rice crop because of a shortage in yield and a decline in price. He had hoped for "big money in the big Bond Case," and if "I live a year and a half I believe I will get money enough out of this business to pay all my debts—including yours—and have a good sum left." But $1,500 was needed to make another rice crop. "To see my plantation go to ruin just as I have got it in good order makes me wretched. I have spent money to get it in good order; and this is another cause of my present trouble." He had paid interest promptly for four years on the $6,000 note which would fall due the next month, January, 1904, and the note, on which Duke had countersigned for $3,000, was secured by a deed of trust to land which ought to be worth more than the debt. Now, for an additional loan to get out of a crisis, although Russell admitted that he had no claim at all on his old friend and fellow Republican, he could give another 700-acre tract of land and a life insurance policy worth $1000 in cash. If he could only live to see his "big Bond Case" decided. . . .[36]

But the ever-helpful Ben Duke was now ill himself, and apparently there was no response, or an unsatisfactory one, to the plea. December's gloom broke only when the indefatigable Alfred Russell came through with an exciting tidbit. "I have ascertained, (don't ask me how,)," the Detroiter mysteriously commenced, "that the doubtful questions in the mind of the Court, were, first, whether justice could be administered without the presence of the prior encumbrancers; second, whether the power of suing another State could be exercised in the case of assigned credits, that is to say, in the case of debts originating in favor of individuals, and subsequently assigned to the plaintiff state; and the Court considered that the case turned upon these two points."

Hot on the heels of this timely news came three other excited communiqués in as many days from Alfred Russell. His information was "dead sure." In fact, his confidential in-

<hr />

[36] Russell to Duke, Jan. 29, 1902, and Dec. 7, 1903, B. N. Duke MSS.

formation was in writing and from a member of the Court, "so there is no mistake about it, but [we] must not speak of this to anybody, as the information is purely confidential." When the Court referred to the absence of the prior encumbrancers it apparently referred to the fact that Rothschilds, the representative for the first mortgage bondholders, had not been represented by counsel. Would it not obviate the objection of the Court if counsel now appeared for him and submitted an argument? As for the other matter about the complainant state's being an assignee and the lack of a controversy within the meaning of the Constitution, Alfred Russell had ideas there too; in her answer had not North Carolina stated that she had never had any agreement with South Dakota? "I note the despondent tone of your letter from Washington," Alfred Russell wrote his Wilmington colleague. "I do not think you need feel despondent in view of the information as to the points which trouble the Court."[37]

Emboldened and cheered by Alfred Russell's resourcefulness and buoyancy, Governor Russell bestirred himself, arranged to have counsel appear for the first mortgage bondholder (having the brother of the Supreme Court's clerk perform this routine role had certain advantages), and returned to the national capital for the reargument on January 8, 1904. Feverish and sicker than he let himself admit, Russell determined to push his bond case with whatever final energy he could summon. It had become, outside of his wife and rice plantation, his consuming concern and, one could almost say, his very reason for living.

The reargument on January 8, 1904, except for the additional elements which Alfred Russell's confidential tip inspired, brought a recapitulation of all of the major points which had been earlier argued so exhaustively. Justice Brown, who had heard the original argument, was now absent with eye trouble; but when Chief Justice Fuller asked if there were

[37] Alfred Russell to Russell, Dec. 14, 15, 16, 17, 1903, Russell MSS. Throughout much of 1903 and later when he was ill, Russell made no copies of his few outgoing letters.

any objections to Brown's sitting on the case, the counsel for both sides announced that there were none. Interest in the unprecedented case continued to run high in Washington, as elsewhere, and the members of North Carolina's congressional delegation, headed by Democratic Senators Furnifold M. Simmons and Lee S. Overman, crowded into the Court alongside Marion Butler and South Dakota's Senator Alfred B. Kittredge.

The justices, now familiar with the intricacies of the case, questioned and discussed quite freely, Justices White, Brewer, and Holmes leading in the number of questions. From the substance of the questions, as well as from the tone and demeanor of the questioners, the lawyers and reporters got their clues for the ever-fascinating game of guessing-the-Court. The *Morning Post* correspondent picked up an "expert" opinion that the Court was still equally divided with Justice Day, who had missed the original argument, the undecided pivot man. Justice Harlan, according to this source, appeared clearly against North Carolina, but Russell had long ago concluded this, since Harlan was the only justice still on the court who had held with New Hampshire and the bondholders in the earlier suit against Louisiana. Chief Justice Fuller and Justices White, Brewer, and McKenna gave indications of favoring North Carolina's contentions; Justice White especially, the Louisianian whom Cleveland had named to the Court and who was destined to become chief justice, tangled with Russell in several sharp exchanges.[38]

Alfred Russell also "guessed" the Court and felt encouraged. Or at least he told the sick Wilmingtonian, who had gone practically from the courtroom to the Johns Hopkins hospital, that he felt optimistic. Alfred Russell took consolation, first, from the fact that the "Court is a creditor's Court, and believes in people paying their debts." When it came to the individual justices, the Detroiter figured that Holmes,

[38] *Morning Post,* Jan. 9 and 12, 1904; *News and Observer,* Jan. 3, 9, 1904.

Brown, Harlan, and, if he voted, Peckham were surely against North Carolina. Day, from "his history and party politics," would be the same and that would mean a majority. If White were so strongly against South Dakota and the bondholders as Governor Russell believed, then that would mean that Fuller, Brewer, and McKenna would follow White's lead. Why, Alfred Russell reasoned, if Justice Peckham did not vote the Court might be equally divided and the case would be lost! The Detroiter asked a dozen questions about who said exactly what and how it might forecast the outcome on which so much effort and many hopes had been pinned.[39]

Governor Russell could write few if any letters responding to Alfred Russell's eager inquiries. The grossly overweight Russell had finally learned at the Johns Hopkins that what he thought was malarial fever was in reality caused by a serious kidney condition for which an operation, if his constitution should allow one, might or might not prove helpful. The newspapers would shortly be carrying bulletins predicting Russell's imminent death. But, meantime, as all the parties involved awaited the Supreme Court's decision, the *News and Observer* used the tense interlude to editorialize about the relative decency of the Reconstruction era's General Milton S. Littlefield when compared to the former Republican governor and Populist senator who had conspired to compel North Carolina to pay "outlawed bonds by resorting to a trick worthy only of free-booters and carpet-baggers." A "prominent" Tarheel was quoted as remarking: "I am now in favor of erecting a monument to Littlefield as in some way an atonement for believing him the worst man who ever put foot upon the soil of North Carolina. Since seeing Russell and Butler here in the Supreme Court trying to compel the State to pay some of the 1868-9 fraudulent bonds [*sic*], I wish to take back all I have said about Littlefield as the embodiment of meanness, and say that the honor belongs to Russell and Butler." Whatever the decision might be, the *News and Ob-*

[39] Alfred Russell to Russell, Jan. 28, 1904, Russell MSS.

server reiterated its belief that the Butler-Russell bond suit would always be "the blackest page in the history of conspiracies in North Carolina."[40]

[*chapter six*]

THE SUPREME COURT'S DECISION AND THE REPERCUSSIONS

THE LONG AWAITED decision finally came on February 1, 1904. The Supreme Court ruled, in a five to four decision, that North Carolina should pay to South Dakota on or before January 1, 1905, $27,400 for the ten bonds; in the event of North Carolina's failure to comply with this judgment the Court ordered the Marshal of the Supreme Court of the United States to sell one hundred shares of North Carolina's stock in the North Carolina Railroad after public advertisement of the sale for six consecutive weeks, "said sale to take place in front of the main entrance of the east front of the Capitol of the United States in Washington." The Court further ruled that Salter and Rothschilds, the individual representatives of the first and second mortgage bondholding classes, were not necessary parties and dismissed them from further consideration in the proceedings.

This majority opinion, which represented a defeat for North Carolina and something less than a full victory for Daniel L. Russell, was written by Justice Brewer and concurred in by Justices Brown, Harlan, Peckham, and Holmes. Justice White, joined by Chief Justice Fuller and Justices McKenna and Day, dissented on the grounds that the Court lacked the power to render a decree between the two states

[40] *News and Observer,* Jan. 20, 1904.

on the cause of action sued on, that is, on a state's bonds acquired as South Dakota had secured them from individuals who could not themselves sue; and that the Court lacked the power to render the decree which the majority had entered because of the absence of essential parties, that is the individual bondholders, whose presence would have ousted the jurisdiction under the Eleventh Amendment.[1]

Governor Russell, supposedly convalescing on his plantation but actually only temporarily out of the Baltimore hospital, undoubtedly felt a profound satisfaction even with the limited victory which he and his co-workers had won over the Democratic "enemy" in North Carolina. But if he wrote any letters at all, he scrawled them in pencil and no copies survive. Most of his associates, however, were jubilant and splendidly articulate. The news "flurried old man Schafer to such an extent that he was foolishly beside himself," Ricaud reported, "and fancied that he had to hide away from inquiries as the author of all this result. I was afraid that he would collapse, but he did not." As for himself, Ricaud's eternal financial crisis forced him to hope only for quick, tangible results: if Russell would now throw out his "line" to see what sort of compromise arrangement could be reached with Governor Aycock, which he would recommend to the North Carolina legislature, "then we can make these [New York] people advance us money enough to relieve us of the present tension in our affairs, and, God knows, we both need it." Ricaud, whose one great desire closely resembled Russell's own, wanted only "to get straight with the world once more and then I don't care."[2]

---

[1] 192 U. S. 286 (1904); *News and Observer* and *Morning Post,* Feb. 2, 1904. The *Post* printed a special section containing the decision and White's dissenting opinion on February 5, 1904. The record in the *United States Reports,* pp. 286-354, contains not only the opinion and the dissent but also, among other things, the relevant North Carolina and South Dakota statutes; the condensed arguments by counsel for both sides; and—as Russell had expected—Simon Schafer's philanthropic letter to Congressman Charles H. Burke.

[2] Ricaud to Russell, Feb. 2, 1904, Russell MSS.

Alfred Russell, bubbling more than ever, thrilled at the Detroit *Free Press*'s assertion that the decision was not only important but marked a "new departure in ordering the sale of property in dispute in case of failure to satisfy a judgment." The Detroiter saw no reason why such happy tidings did not cure his Wilmington friend's ailments and exulted in his belief that his "getting Peckham resulted (as I expected) in getting *his bro., & I got my old pupil, Brown. We could not have spared either one!*" Alfred Russell expressed respect for Justice White's dissent and regarded it as "much stronger" than the arguments of the lawyers for North Carolina. Since there apparently had been no public outcry protesting the decision in the South and since there already had been one rehearing, he believed that North Carolina would not be able to get another one from a Court that was "sick of the case." Yet when it came to monetary results, Alfred Russell had to confess, sadly: "It has been *all out-go & no in-come so far.* You think I am a rich man. *Far from it.* I am poor! The court's refusing the prayer of our client to order sale to satisfy *all the bonds,* has taken from us what promised better than anything! *Now,* so far as I can see, we can get pay only out of the $27,000, *if & when* collected, & out of other deals in *other bonds.* But, perhaps we have been drawing chestnuts out of the fire for *others!* A friend, a lawyer in Wall St. writes me: 'Your South Dakota case victory seems to have *stirred things up to a fever heat* in Wall St. Every one, who can, is looking up the defaulted State Bonds to find some quick assets among them!' "[3]

Wheeler Peckham, discreetly silent of course about the strange fraternal aspect of the decision, took the news in his calm, magisterial stride and judged that the first task was to get the decree "settled and properly entered." He thought it would be best to go slow on any further proceedings about the second mortgage or any other bonds; Henry Clews, of Southern bond fame, had rushed up on the platform of the elevated train to

[3] Alfred Russell to Russell, Feb. 2 and May 15, 1904, *ibid.*

offer warm congratulations but without even mentioning the Southern bonds in which he was known to have a large interest. Peckham, loftily putting the whole matter in proper historical perspective, regarded as "a very satisfactory feature" of the decision the fact that "it seems to have excited no particular comment; there is no rising of States or the people in hostility to the decision, as there was in early days when the decision was rendered in Chisholm against Georgia. Public opinion is now all with us. The tendency of the Court from the earliest days to the present has been one continual advance."[4]

It is true that the South in 1904-1905 basked in a nationalistic afterglow from the Spanish-American War and felt respect, perhaps tinged with fear, for the vigorous, toothy president who emphasized the nation and Federal power over any such abstraction as state sovereignty. No Southern state, and most certainly not North Carolina, entertained any notion of testing the strength of Theodore Roosevelt, who, after all, had a constitutional obligation to enforce the Supreme Court's decrees. And the Supreme Court itself earned the Democratic South's veneration at this time for the consistent manner in which the high tribunal upheld the ever rigidifying Jim Crow laws and bent backwards to allow the recent and spreading disfranchisement of the Negro. Still, Peckham overemphasized the degree of North Carolina's and the South's placidity in the face of a decision which marked a genuine triumph and extension of Federal judicial power; or perhaps the New Yorker simply did not see enough of the *News and Observer* and other papers like it. The *Charlotte Observer,* it was true, urged calm; the decision was "surprising, disappointing but not at all alarming." Perhaps some adjustment could be made with the holders of the other outstanding second mortgage bonds, Editor Joseph Caldwell of Charlotte suggested, but "North Carolina need not necessarily go bankrupt if she has to pay the face value of all of them, with interest." Also "in pallia-

[4] Peckham to Russell, Feb. 4, 1904; Peckham to Stewart, Feb. 8, 1904, *ibid.*

tion" of the situation were these factors, which other Democratic papers usually managed to overlook or distort: the bonds involved had been issued before the "reign of the carpetbaggers," they were sold for "good money" which presumably went for the purpose envisioned by the legislature, and they were the only bonds of the whole period which possessed a lien on state property. On second thought, and after seeking advice, even Editor Caldwell, however, asked "how would it do for the State to stand pat?" South Dakota had gotten her judgment—"how would it do to let her find means of enforcing it?" Even if suit were successfully brought against North Carolina on all of the outstanding second mortgage bonds, would not the creditors have to wait about fifteen years longer, because of the first mortgage, in order to get their principle and interest?[5]

The Raleigh *Morning Post* prided itself, with some justice, on having predicted as a strong probability from the first such a decision as the Court had rendered. Editor Robert Furman must have appalled Russell with the statement that the individual bondholders were not actually in any better position than before, even though the Court had upheld the validity of the bonds. *Post* editorials argued that the private holders could still take only the 25 per cent of the principal which North Carolina offered or give their remaining bonds to some state which, under the decision, could collect full principal and interest. Since 4 per cent state bonds would be issued to pay South Dakota's claim, the *Post* assumed, there was certainly no need for any alarm about the sale of a single share of the state's railway stock.

The *Post* set itself the task, in the days immediately following the sensational decision, of carefully reviewing the entire history of the second mortgage bonds. An evening paper, the Raleigh *Times,* drew on the Democratic mythology of Reconstruction and angrily snarled that there was "no doubt that these bonds were issued by wicked and dishonest

[5] *Charlotte Observer,* Feb. 3, 4, and 5, 1904.

men. . . . No honest, fair-minded man, who knows the history of these bonds, the character of the legislature that issued them, the reckless, the malevolent and unexampled manner in which they were gobbled up by carpetbag sharks for a song, can think other than that the whole transaction is a piece of rascality of the deepest dye." North Carolina's senior editor, Furman, merely pointed out again, as he had done earlier but apparently in vain, that the legislature of 1866-1867 had been composed of the state's "very best citizenship." He recalled the role of prominent men who had been involved in the bond issue, including the "honest Quaker governor," Jonathan Worth, and showed that too many important native, Democratic Tarheels had participated for questions about the bonds' origins even to be raised. As for the sale of the bonds, after the state officials had exchanged them for railway stock, Furman noted that a former state supreme court justice, A. C. Avery, had not only been the author and "urgent promoter" of the legislation authorizing the bonds but also a member of the firm of contractors who received them from the state and sold them to "innocent purchasers for valuable consideration." After Furman had penned his history-filled editorials, some other North Carolina editors reprinted them and one wryly commented, "There is no going behind the returns in this instance."[6]

The *Post* continued to analyze and consider various aspects of the decision in subsequent editorials, expressing admiration for Justice White's dissent and urging a petition for a rehearing in view of the close division on the Court. But its powerful rival, the *News and Observer,* eschewed analysis in favor of blood-and-thunder politics. When Butler and Russell "get the pieces of silver coming to them for the betrayal of the State that had chosen them to look after its affairs," the wrathful and righteous Democratic editor declared, "they ought to have the decency to follow the example of their predecessor and go and hang themselves." North Carolina

[6] *Morning Post,* Feb. 2, 3, 1904.

would "pay the pound of flesh denominated in the bond, but
it will not permit the shedding of one drop of blood beside."
(In a subsequent editorial, the Shylock allusion became even
clearer with a reference to North Carolina's not allowing the
bondholders to shed one drop of "Christian blood.") The
New York bondholders could apply for the 25 per cent from
North Carolina or "make a reputation as philanthropists"
and "rival Rockefeller in endowing State colleges."[7]

As the *News and Observer* began to gnaw at the bitter
bone of the decision, it found mingled cause for comfort and
alarm. Justice Brewer, in his majority opinion, had merely
skirted one of the most difficult aspects of the decision:
"Equity is satisfied by a decree for a foreclosure and sale of
the mortgaged property, leaving the question of a judgment
over for a deficiency, to be determined when, if ever, it arises."
The Court had ruled that South Dakota was entitled to have
100 shares of the state's railway stock sold at public auction
unless North Carolina paid $27,400 on or before January 1,
1905. The North Carolina Railroad stock then sold for about
$175 a share, meaning that the sum realized from a public
sale could hardly be more than $17,500 or almost $10,000
less than the sum the Court had found due. The Court had
avoided the troublesome and hitherto unanswered question
of how it could compel North Carolina to pay such a deficit,
if it occurred, and the *News and Observer* concluded that
merely to ask the question showed that "the decision of the
highest court" was wrong.

Furthermore, the 1879 adjustment which the North Carolina Democrats had made in the state's debt had been designed
by the "wisest and safest men" in the entire state. The financial
world, according to Daniels, had applauded North Carolina's
1879 action, which had been taken under the leadership of
such sterling Democratic Redeemers as Governors Zebulon B.
Vance and Thomas J. Jarvis; the whole transaction had been

[7] *News and Observer*, Feb. 2, 1904.

"one of the most creditable and honorable in the history of North Carolina."

Taken all in all, the *News and Observer* declared, the decision opened "a new door to dangerous encroachment upon the sovereignty of States that was never opened, even in the days of Reconstruction." As much as the decision was to be financially regretted by North Carolina, it was the Court's "new departure" which was a great deal more regrettable. It invited "base and covetous officials" to put their state's right to sue "on the block," for sale to any "gang of bond speculators" who saw money in doing through such a state what the Constitution expressly forbade them to do. "The decision, unless reversed—and it is sure to be reversed as [the] justices follow right precedent and the Constitution— will open a Pandora's box of evils that will breed the buying and selling of a State's right to sue." But if the new doctrine should be made permanent, "such buzzard-roost States as New Jersey and South Dakota" would be quoting the market price of the right to use the state to sue another state just as they had already "sold their character to persons wanting divorce or wanting stock jobbing and stock watering trusts organized to rob the public."

The *News and Observer* conceded one point which it had not earlier emphasized: the bonds involved were issued by "honest men" and the state's honor required that it "should pay every cent that it received from the men who purchased them." But the catch in this seemingly generous position was Daniels' insistence that North Carolina "is now, and has always been ready, to pay such sum." Anything more than the 25 per cent which the patriotic, wise men of 1879 had offered would represent "robbery," and before submitting to it, the state would require the bondholders "to give every one of the bonds to such States as are ready to sell their sovereign right to sue a sovereign State for the highest market price." This position about the 1879 debt adjustment, hammered home by the *News and Observer* among many Democrats, especially in the eastern part of the state, was about to become a party dogma and a powerful factor in the denouement of the South Dakota bond story.[8]

In truth, if North Carolinians were looking to their newspaper editors for guidance about the complex interstate lawsuit, they found more confusion and anger than dispassionate analysis. The *Charlotte News,* for example, a Democratic ally of the Raleigh *News and Observer*, announced bluntly that "there was suspicion enough to hang an egg-sucking dog" that the "precious pair," Butler and Russell, had concocted the whole scheme and chosen "the most disreputable commonwealth convenient," the "adventuress" South Dakota, to sue North Carolina, which belonged to "the aristocracy of States, the original thirteen." And then "the Supreme Court, five justices guessing one way, and four guessing the other, decide that the mortgage must be foreclosed." Despite such an angry arraignment of North Carolina's alleged antagonists, the Charlotte paper concluded that the state had to be "mindful of her honor" and if the Supreme Court had decided that these bonds ought to be paid, "let them be paid to the last dollar." The political moral from the whole affair? "The Democratic party is the only one which can be trusted in this commonwealth until at least a new generation arises with new traditions. With this stench in the nostrils of decent men, it would seem to be a good time for decent Republicans to bury their old clothes and put on a decent Democratic suit."[9]

While the newspapers stewed and disagreed about what, if anything, North Carolina should do, Governor Aycock limited his public remarks to an expression of surprise at the decision and a reassertion of his belief, for the sake of those who still believed the *News and Observer*'s charge of a Southern Railway "conspiracy," that not a share of the state's

[8] *Ibid.,* Feb. 3, 1904.
[9] *Charlotte News,* as quoted in *News and Observer,* Feb. 4, 1904. Many other smaller papers which agreed with and applauded Daniels in his newest crusade against the bondholders and their lawyers are reprinted in the *News and Observer.*

railway stock would be sold. He felt it inopportune for North Carolina to do anything, one way or the other, about the decision at that early juncture, that is, February, 1904.[10] Aycock, already in the last year of his term and ineligible under the state constitution to succeed himself, obviously wished that the bitter cup of the bond decision might somehow bypass him. Educational improvements had become his overriding concern, and his popularity and reputation as the state's "educational governor" were already large. Aycock had been elevated to political power, along with his party, by the fanatical white-supremacy crusades of 1898 and 1900, in which he had starred as about the most spine-tingling orator; once in office, however, he appears to have undergone the same sort of transformation or transmutation, on a smaller scale, as that which is familiar to students of Abraham Lincoln before and after his elevation to the presidency. Aycock himself sensed his change. He admitted it on a platform in Charleston, South Carolina, with President Theodore Roosevelt sitting close by and nodding his approval. To the Charleston audience the Democratic governor of North Carolina pointed out that it had taken the hot blood of the country four years to cool off in the 1860's, but it took "less than four years in office to cool the hot blood."[11]

With his cooler emotions and dedicated efforts to guarantee a four-month school term, among other things, Aycock understandably felt that he had not quite bargained for such a headache as that which his Republican predecessor had saddled him with in the bond suit. Charles Price, the Salisbury railroad lawyer and president of the state bar, confidentially wrote Aycock again, asking the governor's pardon because he had "no right to advise you at all." But, "I am proud of you,"

[10] *News and Observer,* Feb. 3, 1904.
[11] *Morning Post,* April 12, 1902; President Theodore Roosevelt to Aycock, April 17, 1902, in Aycock Scrapbook, Personal Collection 126.5, North Carolina Department of Archives and History. Oliver H. Orr, Jr., *Charles Brantley Aycock* (Chapel Hill, 1961), devotes only brief attention to the bond suit on pp. 281-285.

Price said, "and certainly want you to succeed." Price reminded the governor that three years or so earlier he, Price, had correctly predicted the outcome of the bond suit. The lawyer again emphasized that Colonel A. B. Andrews, vice-president of the Southern Railway, and other railway officials owned none of the bonds, had been opposed to his [Price's] becoming identified with the suit when the bondholders had first approached him about it, and "were sorry the matter had even been mentioned." Nevertheless, "as an humble man, and a poor lawyer," Price felt that "there may be serious trouble ahead, and the best way to get out of it, is to arrange some compromise with the parties." Price added that he knew none of the parties involved and cared "nothing for the whole crowd," so Aycock should not think him "guilty of presumption, but consider a moment what I have said."

In his confidential reply to Charles Price, Governor Aycock expressed himself a bit more fully than he had to the newspaper reporters. He explained that he would carefully investigate the Court's decision and the dissent before taking any public position because he simply had not anticipated such a decision. "I am confident now that the decision is wrong," Aycock added, and "I do not believe that the court can do anything to enforce its judgment." He mentioned that the state, in accordance with a Federal court's ruling in the earlier Swasey suit, held the railway stock in trust for the security of the first mortgage bondholders; any attempt to sell the stock under the Supreme Court's decree would give the purchaser nothing, the governor argued, and any attempt to help the purchaser get something would necessitate the making of the first mortgage bondholders parties to the suit already pending and thereby oust the jurisdiction. "I shall do nothing hastily," the governor again insisted. "I regard the decree as a very dangerous one; not to this State particularly, but to all States, and it may be the duty of the State to await the working out of results."[12]

[12] Price to Aycock, Feb. 4, 1904; Aycock to Price, Feb. 5, 1904, Governors' Papers.

Governor Aycock's privately expressed opinion, like that of the *News and Observer,* clearly reflected the influence of Walter Clark, chief justice of the state supreme court. Clark's view, which rather sharply conflicted with the United States Supreme Court's decision, pervaded a significant portion of the press and of the Democratic party, thereby becoming an important factor in the final working out of the South Dakota bond affair. Clark's notion, succinctly expressed to his brother-in-law and political confidant, Augustus W. Graham, was this: "The South Dakota decision is wrong in principle but [the] real plaintiffs are knocked out. Even So. Dak. gets only a right to subject equity of redemption in 1919 [when the first mortgage bonds matured]. This is worth *less* than the 25¢ offered by State statute & Schafer is not likely to give his $234,000 to South Dakota nor the latter to buy. The whole effort was to *frighten* the State into a bad compromise. . . . We are not one cent worse off by the So. Dak. decision. Schafer will now probably fund at the 25¢ all others have taken unless through the Corporation owned & subsidized papers they may think they can get the legislature to offer more."[13] Chief Justice Clark and his powerful allies, in other words, wished Aycock and the state to do nothing at all about the Supreme Court's decision, other than to let the state's one hundred shares of rail stock be foreclosed on and sold at auction on the steps of the national capitol. The *News and Observer* would eventually say as much publicly, although Governor Aycock refrained from identifying himself positively with this policy of inaction and drift.

Aycock played his cards close to his chest, but Governor Herreid of South Dakota was a veritable sphinx of the Western plains. In fact, when the Supreme Court's decision came, Herreid happened to be in the national capital on a short visit. He apparently said nothing for publication in Washington or Pierre, then or later. The South Dakota newspapers

[13] Clark to Graham, Feb. 8, 1904, in *The Papers of Walter Clark,* ed. by Aubrey L. Brooks and Hugh T. Lefler (2 vols.; Chapel Hill, 1950), II, 60-61.

carried brief news items about the decision, but one of the important dailies, the Sioux Falls *Argus-Leader,* saw nothing requiring editorial comment in the whole matter. The only official in South Dakota who publicly expressed his pleasure in the Supreme Court's ruling was the president of the struggling University of South Dakota. He confessed a "lack of knowledge regarding the whys and wherefores of the gift" from the "philanthropic New Yorkers" but nevertheless felt elated over the prospects of the university's receiving the $27,400; and he had written several letters in order to learn all about the early history of the gift—letters which probably got answered a bit ambiguously, if at all. As for just what would be done with the money, the president did not know, but surely, in view of the university's great need, the legislature would not act on the recently made suggestion that it cut the appropriation to the university to correspond with the bequest![14]

With confusion reigning in Carolina and delighted bewilderment in Dakota, it was not an opportune time for the architect of the bond suit to become ill. "Public opinion," especially in North Carolina, needed much attention. Yet Russell came dramatically close to dying in the two months after the Supreme Court spoke. In late February, 1904, the Johns Hopkins medical specialists decided to risk the operation which had earlier been avoided because of Russell's heart condition. In view of the heart complication, the doctors decided against administering an anesthetic. One of the doctors informed the *Morning Post* correspondent that Russell displayed "remarkable courage" and joked with the surgeons as they removed one of his kidneys, which had abscessed, and over a dozen kidney stones. Three of the Hopkins specialists, including the famed Dr. William Osler, attended the former governor. The Carolina newspapers announced in early March that his death was expected at any time, yet he was reported to be making a "remarkable fight for life." The most powerful

[14] *Daily Argus-Leader,* Feb. 2, 4, 8, 1904.

stimulants, such as nitroglycerine and brandy injections, were constantly being used, and Mrs. Russell and two nurses rendered all possible attention.

Russell, who had said that he wanted to live only to see his beloved lawsuit terminated and his debts paid, improved. Then in mid-March he suffered a relapse, from which someone at the Baltimore hospital said that he did not have one chance in a thousand of recovering. But he fooled them. He tenaciously hung on to life. And finally he left the hospital and returned to his plantation in late April, 1904.[15]

There is no record left in his papers of what his illness had cost him. Given the quality of his doctors, however, and the duration of his illness, the bills were undoubtedly large. Russell, moreover, appeared in public as a proud planter and former Republican governor of North Carolina. Only his immediate family, Ben Duke, and a very few other close associates knew that behind the pretensions was an omipresent financial crisis that constantly threatened abject poverty and public disgrace. When he had recovered sufficiently to resume some of his correspondence, Russell confessed how he felt to Duke: "But for the hope of getting so far restored to health as to be able to earn enough to pay my debts and take care of my friends I preferred to die & get out of it." And then, "If I can get my fees in the Bond case I will be able to pay my debts and this, with a little for plain comforts, is all I care for or hope for in the little while I have of this life."[16]

When Peckham and others were unable to lend him money to pay towards his medical bills, Marion Butler complied with a request for a loan of $300. Butler also tried to help arrange for Russell to visit New York, since "the little trip might do you good" and Wall Street's interest in Southern bonds had increased remarkably since the Supreme Court's decision. Concerning the newspapers' story in May, 1904, that he had made a fortune from oil leases on Indian lands,

---

[15] *Morning Post,* March 2, 6, 8, 19, April 23, 1904.
[16] Russell to Duke, July 3, 1904, B. N. Duke MSS.

Butler wrote his Wilmington friend and associate that there was "just a little truth" in the whole story. "I never deny anything now," the much vilified former senator declared.[17]

Alfred Russell apparently had no money to lend, even if he was approached about it, but he exuded good cheer and lusty hopefulness about the eventual outcome of the bond case. Through "an old and warm friend of mine, [who] succeeded me as President of the Society of the Sons of the Revolution," Alfred Russell tried to throw a little law practice in the way of his Wilmington friend. Alfred Russell's "old friend" in Detroit held much stock in a lumber company which had North Carolina interests; and incidentally, the friend was "a brother-in-law of Judge Brown, who gave us his vote in the South Dakota case" (and who, Daniel Russell now knew, had probably put Russell's side well on the inside track in the preparations for the rehearing which the Supreme Court had held in January, 1904). Alfred Russell came back from his Colorado vacation feeling like "a big sun-flower" after all the horseback riding and hiking. He even refused to be impressed by the number of stones removed from his sick friend's kidney, for Buffon, the French naturalist, "beat you on the *no.* of 'rocks', if not on *size!* He had 200 & upwards taken out! I wish we cd. get some of the *other kind* of 'rocks' out of the S. Dakota suit!!"[18]

It was precisely that "other kind of rocks" which Josephus Daniels and other key North Carolina Democrats were absolutely determined to prevent Russell, Butler, and their associates from getting. To complicate the already heated bond question, there were to be statewide as well as national elections in North Carolina in 1904. The political kettle began whistling early. Political storms had raged tumultuously in the 1890's and both of the major national parties were still deeply divided even among themselves. Under the circumstances of his time and place, it was by no means odd in

[17] Butler to Russell, April 12, 14, and May 16, 1904, Russell MSS.
[18] Alfred Russell to Russell, May 15, June 7, 23, and Oct. 15, 1904, *ibid.*

1904 that Marion Butler, who for eight years had served as national chairman of the Populist or People's party, was in the process of identifying himself, locally and nationally, with the Republican party. North Carolina Democrats then and later liked to sneer at Butler's political inconsistency. "As a rapid change artist on the political stage," the *Morning Post* commented, "ex-Senator Butler is the monumental success of the times." As Uncle Remus said of Brer Rabbit, Butler now made himself at home in the Republican household by "puttin' his foots on de sofy an' spittin' on de flo'."[19]

But despite the humorous use which Butler's political enemies made of his course, the real reasons for his joining the Republicans were quite simple: in North Carolina the bitter enemy that had fought and finally vanquished the now moribund Populists was the Democratic party; Butler, like some other former Populists, admired the energetic Theodore Roosevelt and applauded his strong reformist language and unabashed willingness to use the Federal government in a more positive fashion; and, finally, 1904 gave every indication of being a poor year for William Jennings Bryan, the old agrarian idol, who had had his two unavailing tries for the presidency and who had now to stand aside while the Democrats tried a more conservative, "safe" candidate in the person of New York's Judge Alton B. Parker. So Butler became a Republican. In South Dakota, where the circumstances had been and were quite different, former Senator Pettigrew, former Silver Republican, became chairman of the South Dakota delegation to the national Democratic convention, announcing however his intention to bolt the convention if Cleveland or any Democrat like him should be nominated. The *News and Observer*, horrified by The One True Party's acquisition of Butler's and Russell's South Dakota associate in the bond suit, announced piously that anyone who would bolt the Democratic party's regular and solemn convention

[19] *Morning Post*, July 5, 1904.

should simply not be permitted to take a seat in that convention.[20]

Wheels within wheels had been set to spinning merrily by the bond decision in such a politics-filled year. William Randolph Hearst aspired to the Democratic presidential nomination in 1904. In late March his New York *American* reported, quite correctly, that Wall Street had become intensely interested in repudiated Southern bonds as a result of the recent Supreme Court decision. But the New York paper, like many others across the nation, was not so correct in the remainder of its story. Counting principal and interest, the Hearst paper estimated that there were some $135,000,000 in unpaid Southern bonds and stated that Wall Street did not believe that it would be necessary to resort to Schafer's "clever methods" of establishing the validity of the bonds. "State pride, it is hoped, will make the south pay the bonds in full with interest," the *American* concluded, because such payment would improve the credit of the Southern states, whose bonds hundreds of financial institutions would not touch as long as the stigma of repudiation remained. Reprinting this item, the Raleigh *Morning Post,* still as fervently anti-Bryan as it was pro-Cleveland, deduced that the evident failure of the Hearst boom to materialize in North Carolina, unless it should slip in "under the quivering wings of the Bryan devotees," had obviously incensed "the yellow journal candidate." For revenge Hearst helped along "this silly rumor" about repudiated bonds which might just be regarded by "wool-gatherers and those who see ghosts and belong to kitchen cabinets as a dangerous thing."[21]

His kitchen cabinet allusion to Josephus Daniels' close relationship to Governor Aycock was one of Editor Furman's last sallies in the old feud between Raleigh's rival morning papers. Furman died in May, 1904. The *Morning Post* continued publication for another year and a half but without

[20] *News and Observer,* April 2, 1904.
[21] *Morning Post,* April 2, 1904, quoting New York *American* of March 31.

the editorial distinctiveness and independence which Furman had given the paper. And an interesting and important factor in the South Dakota bond story virtually disappeared with Furman's death.

His rival was very much alive and kicking—and laying the groundwork for the state Democratic convention which would be held in June, 1904. Through its nominations of the gubernatorial and other candidates, who had not yet in North Carolina been made subject to a nominating primary, and through its resolutions, the state convention could well have a decisive effect on the next legislature; and it increasingly appeared that the legislature convening in January, 1905, and the new governor taking office then would have to cope with the very hot potato that was the bond suit.

Events could hardly have been more propitious for the task which Josephus Daniels had set himself. Interest in the Supreme Court decision reached its peak throughout the nation, and especially the South and Northeast, in the spring of 1904. It is not surprising either that there existed a vast amount of confusion and ignorance about the rather special nature of North Carolina's second mortgage bonds, about the differences between them and the much larger mass of totally repudiated Southern bonds, and about precisely what the Supreme Court had and had not said in its recent decision.

Adding to the excitement about bonds in early April, one of the New York committees which had been organized to pool Southern bonds, though not the one in which Russell and Butler were interested, offered to give $10,000 worth of repudiated bonds to the District of Columbia, so that the District could bring suit for payment in the United States Supreme Court. The headline in the *News and Observer* trumpeted, "It Bears Fruit After Its Kind," and more bond worries descended on North Carolinians and other Southerners. The District officials promptly refused the offer, on the grounds that the District was not a state within the meaning of the Constitution and therefore the Supreme

Court would be without jurisdiction to entertain a suit by it against a sovereign state; but the incident served to kindle fresh fires.[22]

The *News and Observer* had no trouble at all in collecting useful opinions from other newspapers, opinions which were often based on erroneous interpretations and rumors or which merely reflected some unidentified individual's notion. From the Savannah *Morning News,* for example, "one of Georgia's ablest lawyers" was quoted as having declared that the South Dakota decision posed "the most important and far-reaching question that has come before the United States Supreme Court since the days of secession." If the treasurer of North Carolina should refuse to deliver the railway stock, "would the United States use the force of its army and navy to compel the recalcitrant State to disgorge the security?" "Could the Federal Government use force for the collection of a debt due another and against one of its sovereign members," the "Georgia lawyer" hypothesized, "just as one of the world powers sends a fragment of its navy to intimidate a weak nation into the payment of the claims held by some of its citizens?" These questions suggested why the South Dakota decision went to the "very root of governmental authority itself" and involved matters touching on "State sovereignty in its most essential form."

The Boston *Transcript,* reflecting a different outlook from that which dominated in Raleigh or Savannah, speculated that the decision might "give a fillip to the consciences of the defaulting States, and this spur, together with the renewed prosperity in the Southern States, may induce them to repudiate repudiation and redeem their good names in the markets of the world." The Boston paper also wondered if "a strong and courageous leader" might not arise in one or more of the Southern states, a leader who would "from motives either mercenary or moral, induce his State to pay its debts." The *News and Observer* added to these comments the explanation

[22] *News and Observer,* April 9, 1904; *Morning Post,* April 17, 1904.

that repudiated Southern bonds totaled perhaps $303,114,000 in principal alone, with Virginia and North Carolina heading the list; and many a Tarheel Democrat, especially the more unsophisticated agrarian ones who predominated numerically, must have shivered, cursed, and again rued the day that those Fusionists, Marion Butler and Daniel Russell, had begun all the trouble.[23]

The only safe course for North Carolina to pursue in the bond matter was "to refuse to re-open the question settled in 1879." This became the *News and Observer*'s theme song in May and June, 1904. The old charge about the bond suit's being merely one step in a long-developing conspiracy of the "Southern Railway crowd" now got one of its loudest and most dramatic airings. Certain deep-dyed villains "close to the Southern" were now alleged to be assiduously striving to secure control of the next legislature so that the second mortgage bonds could be compromised in a manner that would be "robbery" of the state and so that the North Carolina Railroad could be sold to the rapacious corporation for a song. "The South Dakota bond suit failed," Daniels editorialized, "provided the people send a Legislature here that will not take orders from 'HIGHER UP.' " There must be no reopening of what had been, once and for all, fairly and honorably, "settled in 1879."[24]

The *News and Observer* campaigned most successfully. The *Morning Post* suggested that it insulted North Carolina voters to "intimate that they can be hired, or bought, to send corrupt representatives to the legislature" and that it was a sad reflection on the legislators themselves to charge that they would be the "tools of corporations, or of any other influence whatever." Why did not the *News and Observer* name the man, the county, or the corporation where such monstrous guilt

[23] *News and Observer*, May 4, 1904.

[24] *Ibid.*, May 10, 11, 13, 18. A bold headline on May 19, 1904, proclaimed that Butler headed a bond-buying syndicate but the story which followed supplied no substance to warrant the headline.

might be specified and nailed down?[25] Such picayune caviling about the remarkable lack of hard facts in many of the *News and Observer*'s charges had little or no effect on the political game then being played out. Loyal Democrats of Granville County, in the north central "black belt" and home of Augustus W. Graham, who was Chief Justice Walter Clark's brother-in-law and confidant, were the first to supply Daniels with precisely what he wanted and had urged so fervently. Assailing the conspiracy which had so far failed in the courts and which now sought to capture the legislature, Granville Democrats solemnly pledged themselves to vote for no man for the legislature or for any state office who would not pledge himself to "oppose any movement at any time to re-open the compromise and settlement of the State debt made by our representatives in the General Assembly of 1879, and to prevent our people being saddled with the immense sums which would be required to pay the principal and nearly 40 years accrued interest, which would be entailed on us by re-opening the settlement of 1879."

Inviting the other counties to pass similar resolutions, Granville received the warmest plaudits of the *News and Observer*. The paper insisted that if only the other counties would now follow Granville's lead and see that none but "true men owing no obligations 'HIGHER UP' " were elected to the legislature, then the vast conspiracy and "scheme of plunder can be nipped in the bud."[26]

Other counties fell into line. The Raleigh editor's personal role in North Carolina politics reached something of a climax on the eve of the 1904 state convention. Governor Aycock, in addition to the bond headache, had stumbled into a true hornet's nest of trouble concerning the state-owned and state-operated Atlantic and North Carolina Railroad. The details of the tangled story need not be recounted here; suffice it to say that Josephus Daniels' attacks on the Federal judge,

[25] *Morning Post,* May 29, 1904.
[26] *News and Observer,* May 20, 1904.

among others, with whom Aycock had come into conflict became more and more feverish. Finally, after what he considered sufficient provocation and the wilful editor's refusal to heed warnings, the judge confined Josephus Daniels, in a room in Raleigh's leading hotel, on a contempt charge. Although a higher Federal judge promptly ordered the editor's release, the exicting drama furnished an heroic touch of martyrdom to the *News and Observer*'s editor. Under the circumstances, it is hardly strange that the state convention's work bore the unmistakable imprint of the colorful Daniels' policies.[27]

The *News and Observer*'s headlines in this period, like those of many papers of the era, were characterized by high drama and unintended humor. Reporting the 1904 national Republican platform, which contained, among many other things, the quadrennial and empty threat about reducing the South's congressional representation in proportion to the number of voters disfranchised in Dixie, the *News and Observer*'s headline proclaimed, "The Blow at the South Its One Notable Plank." But when North Carolina's Democrats assembled, the long heading achieved an almost poetic quality: "How the Dawn Broke over North Carolina. Those Who Sat Under the Black Shadow of Republicanism Saw in the East the Day Spring of Democracy and Rejoiced. . . . In Russell's Reign, that Period of Corruption and Misery Compared with the Conditions Now Obtaining When on All Lines of Progress the State is Pushing Forward, Every Wheel of Industry Humming, All State Institutions Prosperous under Efficient Management, and Over All the Broad Light Flowing that Comes From Universal Education."

Dazzled no doubt by the Light from the East, the "average delegate," according to the *News and Observer*'s own account, had to sit down with the morning paper after the nominations had been made and the convention adjourned in order to

[27] *Ibid.,* May 31, 1904. Josephus Daniels tells the story in his *Editor in Politics* (Chapel Hill, 1941), chap. xxxix.

ascertain the principles and resolutions to which he, "by his attendance and endorsement, has already been thoroughly committed." When the "average delegate" sat down quietly, he no doubt was interested to learn that the Democratic state convention had resolved, among other things: "The Democratic party of 1904 approves the settlement made in 1879 and will forever oppose any and all attempts from any quarter to set aside the settlement then made. It will abide the mandates of the courts but it will not consent to re-open the settlement that was alike creditable to the State and fair to the holders of its securities."

The Democratic state executive committee had tried in vain to have the platform considered early, before some of the more exciting matters on the agenda; but the recommendation had been ignored and the more dramatic business of nominations had been given precedence. Robert B. Glenn, who had shared oratorical honors with Aycock in the white-supremacy crusades, received the gubernatorial nomination because, as the *News and Observer* put it, "the country people have long memories." But when the spent delegates finally came to act on the report of the platform committee, there remained neither time nor energy nor inclination for much debate. The *Morning Post,* deploring the careless procedure about the platform, regarded the resolutions as good as far as they went but felt that they were the handiwork of a few, with probably less than one-third of the delegates knowing what had been resolved.

Certainly among the few in the know were the ten members of the platform committee, which included, in addition to Augustus W. Graham of Granville County's Democracy, the brother of Josephus Daniels, Frank A. Daniels of Wayne County. The committee had no trouble at all about the bond resolution; indeed, the only floor fight of the convention had been about an unsuccessful effort of many Democrats from the eastern part of the state to commit the party to a policy of dividing the public school expenditures between the white and Negro races in proportion to the amount each paid in taxes.[28] Not content with an already inequitable division of school funds between the races and with disfranchisement and Jim Crow, there were apparently quite a few Democrats (and white Republicans, too) in North Carolina, as elsewhere in the South, who saw no limits as to how far down the Negro should be pushed.

The meaninglessness of many political platforms is a sad fact of American history. The North Carolina Democrats' 1904 bond resolution was destined to remain very much alive and to play a role which probably few persons had foreseen. The resolution had been achieved, not by any conspiracy, but by the diligent and clever work of a powerful political editor who knew the temper of his Democratic followers and who, above all else, throve on making life as miserable as possible for all Republicans, especially Marion Butler and Daniel Russell.

The Democrats elected Glenn and an overwhelming Democratic legislature with little real trouble. Reading the contemporary Democratic newspapers, however, with their hysterical variations on the theme of Booker T. Washington's luncheon at the White House and the past crimes and present dangers of Radicalism (Southern Democrats kept Reconstruction terminology alive for a remarkably long period), one would be hard put to realize that North Carolina had already taken most of the essential steps towards one-party rule. In truth, as far as the Supreme Court's bond decision was concerned, Democratic officials were by no means as confident and defiant as the party's resolution might have suggested. Most important Democratic officials and newspapers, after all, had at least paid lip service to the idea of obeying the United States Supreme Court; and that Court had set January 1, 1905, as the deadline for North Carolina's payment to South Dakota, if the stock sale was to be avoided.

During the summer and early fall of 1904, Governor Ay-

[28] *News and Observer,* June 24, 25, 1904; *Morning Post,* June 26, 1904.

cock and the state's counsel were hoping to delay and play for time by petitioning the Supreme Court for another rehearing. Furthermore, Aycock and his advisers had decided that the matter's seriousness justified the hiring of an expensive but distinguished out-of-state lawyer. Avoiding publicity, for political as much as strategic reasons, Aycock first tried to secure the services of James C. Carter, a constitutional and business lawyer of New York and a former president of the American Bar Association. Carter had sailed for Europe and had virtually retired anyhow. Then the governor considered Elihu Root but, as George Rountree of Wilmington pointed out, Root engaged actively in Republican politics. North Carolina voters would be more apt to approve the retaining of Richard Olney, who had been President Cleveland's attorney-general and secretary of state. Aycock finally ended up, however, by getting John C. Carlisle, now of New York but formerly Cleveland's secretary of the treasury. After examining the records in the South Dakota case, Carlisle thought that "nothing practical" could be accomplished, but if North Carolina officials felt obligated to make a further effort he would prepare and file a petition for rehearing. Rountree expressed his as well as Judge Shepherd's lack of surprise at Carlisle's pessimism but understood why Aycock felt duty-bound to keep trying. Whatever might be done, Rountree cautioned Aycock's private secretary, had to be done quietly.[29] A noisy political campaign was in progress in North Carolina, and no good would come from publicity about the Democratic administration's engaging an expensive New York lawyer, who had been a blatant "goldbug" in the 1890's, to perform what might well be an unsuccessful mission anyhow.

Russell and his colleagues learned, somehow, of the "enemy's" plans. Marion Butler scouted around Washington

[29] Rountree to Aycock, July 22, 1904; P. M. Pearsall, Aycock's private secretary, to Carter and Ledyard, July 26, 1904; Rountree to Aycock, Aug. 3, 1904; Carlisle to Rountree, Sept. 16, 1904; Rountree to Pearsall, Sept. 19, 1904; and Pearsall to Carlisle, Sept. 21, 1904, Governors' Papers.

and learned from the clerk of the Supreme Court what to expect in the way of Supreme Court procedure on North Carolina's petition for a rehearing. Alfred Russell felt no anxiety. He thought "our five" would "stick," and none of them would vote for a rehearing, which at least one of them would have to do before the Court could grant North Carolina's petition. Alfred Russell admitted that the justices "die hard," and White's dissenting opinion was plausible enough, although, fortunately, "the five take no stock in it." Justice Harlan was not going to die or retire, no matter how much Tarheel Democrats might pray, and no Democrat was going to be elected president, either. "Up here, and indeed all over the country," the Detroiter judged, "there is very little interest shown in the political campaign, for the reason, I think, that it is evident to everybody that Roosevelt is certain of re-election. There is no 'ginger' whatever in the campaign."[30]

Alfred Russell proved to be quite correct about the immovability of the five concurring justices. Carlisle duly petitioned, emphasizing North Carolina's contention that the first mortgage bondholders were necessary parties to any action toward foreclosure of the mortgage on the stock in controversy. But on October 17, 1904, the Court denied North Carolina's motion. The Court's decision of February 1, 1904, was final.[31] Now what could North Carolina do to stave off the threatening unpleasantness? The Court had ruled that advertisements of a foreclosure sale, to take place on the Federal Capitol's steps, should begin on January 1, 1905, and run for six weeks before the sovereign state of North Carolina's humiliation should be finally consummated.

Governor Aycock played his next card by asking the Supreme Court in December for a postponement of the deadline, and consequently of the dreaded advertisements and sale, from January 1 to April 1, 1905. Russell and his associates,

[30] Butler to Russell, Sept. 30, 1904; Alfred Russell to Russell, Oct. 15, 1904, Russell MSS.

[31] Carlisle's petition may be found in the Governors' Papers, Box 308; *Morning Post*, Oct. 18, 1904.

naturally weary of a long-drawn contest which was about to
enter its fifth year, opposed any delay. But who were they to
tell a sovereign state what it could and could not do? Only
the United States Supreme Court could decide. Peckham, who
was in the best position to know, for more than one reason,
felt that the Court would grant North Carolina's request.
"They will be apt to say that what a State asks in good faith,
in a moderate way," he reasoned, "should be granted. At the
same time, they [North Carolina] might have made this
motion before, and they have given us no intimation that they
will pay if the time is granted to them; so that I think we have
a fair chance of successfully opposing it." He and the attorney-
general of South Dakota would oppose as vigorously as they
could.[32]

Lawyers and other informed persons in Washington
watched the Supreme Court's handling of the latest development in the bond suit with great interest. Never before in the
history of the Supreme Court had the marshal been called on
to execute a decree such as had been ordered in the *South
Dakota* v. *North Carolina* decision. Court officials, searching
the records, could find no precedent for a Court-ordered sale
of property from the Capitol steps. They had found, however,
a "humorous abstraction" in the form of a Federal statute
which forbade sale of goods or wares by itinerants, peddlers,
or others in or near the Capitol building! But anyhow, the
"best opinion" in Washington was that North Carolina would
eventually honor the judgment and escape the embarrassment
of a judicial sale.[33]

When Attorney-General Gilmer of North Carolina appeared before the Supreme Court to request the postponement, Chief Justice Fuller inquired if the state would agree
to meet the obligation if the deadline should be postponed.
Gilmer replied that he possessed no authority to speak for the
state since the legislature, meeting in its biennial session on

[32] Peckham to Russell, Nov. 23, 1904, Russell MSS.
[33] *Morning Post,* Dec. 13, 1904.

next January 5, would have its attention directed to the matter for final decision. Peckham and Stewart for South Dakota objected to the motion on the grounds that the effect would be to make the time "so much longer before the complainant could advertise the property for sale under the decree." Moreover, since the legislature would commence early in January and the decree ordered six weeks' advertisement of the place and time of sale, the North Carolina legislature would have sufficient time to take whatever action it thought best. "If the defendant's financial representatives should advise us of an earnest desire on their part to pay the sum decreed, and should ask for time in order to effect any particular action by the legislature," Peckham argued, "they would have no need to come to this court to ask for time. It would be a pleasure on the part of the complainant to grant whatever time was necessary for such purpose; but I have yet to hear of any tendency or desire upon the part of the defendant to pay the sum in the decree adjudged to be due, and the State of South Dakota therefore submits to this court that it would be unfair and inequitable to enlarge the time provided in the decree for the payment of the money even if under the settled practice in regard to foreclosures where a sale is adjudged, the court had power to do it, especially when the defendant at any time before sale can pay the amount due and so stop the sale."[34]

Even in the face of South Dakota's objection, the Supreme Court granted North Carolina's request for a delay until April 1. Actually, Russell, Peckham, and the others only half-heartedly opposed the delay anyhow, for they hoped against hope that North Carolina would not allow the state-owned stock to go on sale. That, as explained earlier, could not possibly bring in sufficient money to pay the $27,400 which the Supreme Court had ordered North Carolina to pay South Dakota, and there was absolutely no precedent, and great doubt and confusion, as to how the Supreme Court

[34] *News and Observer,* Dec. 7, 1904.

could compel North Carolina to pay any deficiency judgment that might have to be ordered. Alfred Russell, like his
associates, felt most worried about this point and fervently
prayed that North Carolina would "relieve us from an argument in the court upon that difficult subject" of making up
the deficiency if they should sell the stock. Even the United
States Supreme Court could not compel a state legislature to
levy taxes nor, according to most constitutional authorities
and all precedents, could the Court levy upon any state-owned
property which was used for public purposes. Altogether,
the matter of the deficiency judgment which would result
from any forced sale of the state-owned stock appeared to be
a quagmire best avoided.[35]

Well might the two Russells and Peckham have shied away
from the thorny subject of how the Supreme Court's judgment, as between sovereign states, could be carried into
effectual execution. It was, at that time, one of the great
unanswered questions in American constitutional history, having appeared as early as 1793 in the famed *Chisholm* v.
Georgia case, which had given rise to the Eleventh Amendment. The question had reappeared subsequently many times
prior to the South Dakota decision, but it had not been
answered and would not be until 1918. In that year the
Supreme Court, in the exhaustively litigated *Virginia* v. *West
Virginia* case, unanimously ruled that the Court's undoubted
constitutional right to pronounce a judgment necessarily
implied the right of the Court and the President to use appropriate means, or whatever means were at their disposal,
to enforce judgment against a state. The Supreme Court
further stated unequivocally that power existed in Congress
to provide for the execution of the Supreme Court's judg-
ments. Having answered the old question, with such affirma-
tive unanimity, the Court was spared the necessity of further
penetration into this supersensitive area of Federal-state relations when West Virginia finally yielded and came to an agree-

[35] Alfred Russell to Russell, Oct. 24 and Nov. 18, 1904, Russell MSS.

ment with Virginia for the payment of the judgment which the Court had ordered against West Virginia.[36]

Why did not Russell have the legal curiosity to want his own case to progress into the unprecedented realm where the Supreme Court in 1904-1905 might have felt called on to answer one of the great constitutional questions as it did in 1918? Russell loved the law and drew profound satisfaction from his mastery of many aspects of it and his contemplation and speculation about legal questions. His letters, especially those to Alfred Russell, clearly prove that aspect of his complex mind and temperament. But the reasons for his profound reluctance to see his bond case prolonged, regardless of what great constitutional questions might be involved, were simple: he desperately needed the money which he hoped to gain from the settlement and, with equal and related desperation, he wanted to live long enough to see the case settled.

At the very time when North Carolina was preparing to ask the Court for more time, Russell, who had returned briefly to the Johns Hopkins hospital in late August, 1904, was imploring the new New York bondholders, not to give, but to lend him at 6 per cent, a thousand dollars that would be paid back out of his share in the final recovery on the bonds. "I must have *funds* or I can not go on," he wrote. "The Bondholders ought to be immensely pleased with my achievement," the proud Southerner argued. "I speak of it as *my own* because Mr. Schafer certainly knows that I was the author of the whole scheme. I conceived it, and with the aid of those whom I associated with me, executed it. It is a success, unless our friends shall fail in the future to act on my advice." Russell went on to explain his optimism: "I think we should make a compromise with North Carolina, and my idea would be to take about fifty cents on the dollar for the total of our claim. This would be about thirteen hundred dollars for each one thousand dollar bond. It is not good policy for us *now* to offer anything. In the next four months the Legislature of North

[36] Charles Warren, *The Supreme Court and Sovereign States*, pp. 78-79.

Carolina must deal with the question and our future action must depend on what this Legislature does. We do not want to go to them. Let them come to us, and this in the long run they will have to do."

Russell then stated the truth when he declared that he had "spent a vast amount of labor on this case," and had spent his own money (such as the $600 cost of printing the record) "when I had not the money to spare." He believed, and again probably correctly, that but for his own "intense effort" the case would have been lost. "It was more than once in a most critical condition and I saved it by taking risks and resorting to radical measures which I can explain if I can see you all face to face." His health had finally improved and he was now "getting about very well."[37]

Russell got his loan, perhaps not as much as he had asked for, but enough to tide him over another of his recurring crises. He spoke so confidently of North Carolina's coming to a compromise with the private bondholders because he had hit on another of the "radical measures" for which he had given himself the credit. Aycock had successfully played his card and won a delay from the Supreme Court. In his final message to the North Carolina legislature in January, 1905, Governor Aycock, who now bequeathed the South Dakota bond problem to his successor, expressed his "entire sympathy with the able men who in 1879 undertook to settle and commute the State debt in North Carolina." Aycock expressed his certainty that what those earlier Democrats had done had been "honorable to the State and just to her creditors." The retiring governor continued: "I am equally certain that the jurisdiction of the United States [Supreme] Court over this matter has been secured by chicanery. It is certain also that the bonds have not been issued as provided in the act. All of these matters were, however, fully laid before the

---

[37] Russell to Gibson, Nov. 14, 1904, Russell MSS. Russell had written, in his own hand, other letters since his serious illness but this is one of the first carbon copies since before his sickness; this one is a typed carbon but some of the copies were made in ink and marked "copy."

Court and that eminent Tribunal has given judgment against the State. . . . " He then stated that he had reason to believe that the judgment against North Carolina could be settled for much less than $27,400, for the reason that even if the railway stock were sold for its full market value, unimpaired by the first mortgage, it could not bring more than $17,500 or two-thirds of the judgment. But as to what should be done with the bonds that remained outstanding, that is the Schafer bonds, Aycock merely declared that the legislators would have to give the matter their "gravest consideration." He doubted that the bondholders would feel disposed to transfer all of these bonds as a gift to any state that might be willing to lend herself to the bringing of a law suit against a sister state, so it seemed "safe to say therefore that the outstanding bonds may be settled at much less than their face value." Settling them "at a reasonable rate" ought to be "an easy matter"—for the legislature and the next administration. Then closing the bond passage of his last official message, Aycock played his own last high card with his declaration of complete accord with the Tarheel Democratic convention's resolution of June, 1904, which had "forever" opposed any reopening of the 1879 settlement even though the party felt the state should abide by the Supreme Court's mandate.[38] In other words, the popular retiring governor strongly hinted that North Carolina should seek a compromise with South Dakota and yield to the private bondholders not one cent more than the 1879 Redeemers had offered. The Democratic ace, in the struggle which would come during the legislative session, took the form of the party's solemn and binding resolution of 1904.

Russell, not to be outdone at this late stage of the game, believed strongly that he had a Republican trump which would yet take the trick. It called for bold, quick action on the

[38] Governor Aycock's Message to the General Assembly of 1905, Governor's Letterbook.

part of many persons, including the South Dakota legislators, but then Daniel L. Russell, even sick and aging and fat, was a past master at taking bold, quick action.

[*chapter seven*]

THE SETTLEMENT
APPROACHED

THE PACE of behind-the-scene negotiations about the bonds markedly quickened late in 1904. No one was more active than Daniel L. Russell. He had recovered his health sufficiently to write the same sort of long, detailed letters to his colleagues—they often resembled legal battle orders—which he had produced before his prolonged struggle against death earlier in the year.

Russell concerned himself with several fronts at once, but the most critical item on his battle plan was the preparation in South Dakota of what he hoped would be his final strategic coup. Working at first through Marion Butler in Washington, Russell demanded a great deal in the way of new legislation from his Dakota associates; but he had not learned about some significant new political conditions in the Western state, where a Progressive or "Insurgent" Republican group was emerging to battle and eventually triumph over the "Stalwart" Republicans. First, Russell wanted Stewart, the Pierre lawyer and powerful lobbyist, to get "his" legislature to authorize either the attorney-general or perhaps Stewart himself to compromise with North Carolina in the event that the Southern state offered a satisfactory settlement to all the bondholders. In other words, Russell desired the South Dakota legislature to put discretionary power to adjust the settlement in the hands of some friendly official; "of course, the wider the discretion, the better, if Stewart can control it." The reason for this, Russell explained, was that "if N. C. offers a reasonable settlement it is only fair that S. Dak. should come in with the other bond holders." Moreover, it would help in securing a "reasonable" offer from North Carolina; if the state officials should offer, say, 50¢ on the dollar of the bond-holders' total claim in principal and interest it would be about $1300 for each bond, but North Carolina might say that the Schafer counsel must "fix S. Dak." so that she did not receive twice that amount for each of her ten bonds.

Russell next suggested that the South Dakota legislature be prodded to authorize Stewart or some state official to attend the sale of North Carolina's 100 shares of stock, if the matter should come to a sale, and to bid on the stock if necessary to protect South Dakota's interests. Russell had other requests and suggestions concerning South Dakota's action, but the most crucial legislation he desired from the Western state was this: an act authorizing the state treasurer or the governor or any official that might be thought best, provided the power stayed in "friendly hands," to purchase some of the North Carolina second mortgage bonds. The authority could be hedged around with safeguards, such as a provision that no money should be used in the purchase of the bonds except that which might come into the state treasury from the initial judgment against North Carolina. In order for South Dakota to keep herself safe, Russell argued, "she need not risk one dollar beyond what she may hold as a simple gratuity." Surely "if our friends can hold the legislature to a friendly animus towards us, legislation of this kind can be obtained."

"We must prepare for the worst," Russell explained. "What is the worst? Possibly it would be for them to let the stock go to sale and buy it in. This would drive us to proceed to enforce the deficiency judgment." Since that would involve much trouble, expense, and time, "the enemy" might just pursue that course. Russell never doubted, he avowed, that the Supreme Court would eventually collect every dollar due from North Carolina, making "a precedent such as to cause the enemy to shudder for the future." But why run the risk of "more or less vexation" and more expense and delay? "If we can hold So[.] D[akota] to our course with a strong steady helm," Russell predicted, "we can bring these repudiators to our feet. But it will take time and labor and expense. What we want is a compromise, but let not this legislature of So. D. pass from us without getting our fortifications well erected." Butler, keeping Russell's letters to himself, should meet with Burke, Stewart, and Pettigrew and push hard for the essential new legislation.[1]

Conferences in Washington with the South Dakotans appeared highly desirable, but Russell claimed that he feared newspaper gossip about his representing South Dakota in the bond suit now that his clients were out of it. "Our best plan is for you and me to 'lay low'," he admonished Butler. "Neither of us should appear publicly in the matter for some time to come." With an overwhelmingly Democratic legislature in North Carolina about to convene and deal, one way or the other, with the bonds, Russell showed that his political antennae remained highly sensitive. But he probably did not have the money to go to Washington in any event.

Neither Stewart nor Burke could accept the Wilmingtonian's invitation to visit his plantation for a little quiet, unpublicized talk. Butler had still to act as intermediary with the South Dakotans, which had been his original role in the affair, and the younger North Carolinian disagreed somewhat with his older partner from Fusion days. Butler saw no reason why the bondholders could not get a better compromise out of North Carolina than the 50¢ on the dollar of the total claim, or about $1300 per bond, which Russell had mentioned as a possibility. "When the State sees that it must pay 260 [$2600 per bond] and Court costs in addition," Butler argued, "why should we compromise for

[1]Russell to Butler, Nov. 26, Dec. 12, 1904, Russell MSS.

130. If we compromise for 200 or anywhere about that figure, it would be very liberal and save the State a good deal of money." Butler did not believe that North Carolina would dare allow the stock to go to sale because the Democratic officials had good cause to fear the Supreme Court's process in collecting the deficiency judgment. If the Court should seek other property of North Carolina's besides the mortgaged railway stock, and the state did own other railway property, the action would merely blaze the way to collect bonds which were not secured by a mortgage, as the Schafer bonds were.

But Butler, as requested, conferred with Congressman Burke and reported to Russell that the South Dakotan felt "satisfied that there will be no trouble to get his legislature to authorize the investment of the amt. made out of this suit in more bonds, with the price left to be fixed by agreement between the Governor and the parties." The only limit which Burke suggested was that South Dakota should buy the bonds "at the best price possible and with a profit that will accrue to the State."

Now the different interests of three groups—the state officials of South Dakota, the negotiating lawyers, and, by no means least, Schafer and the other New York bondholders —began to grind and jar. Burke wished to know what the New Yorkers would take for their bonds. "I told him," Butler explained, "that I thought the State [South Dakota] ought to pay more for the bonds than the New York Parties would accept, in order that he, you and Pettigrew and myself may get a profit for ourselves for negotiating the transaction." This proposition struck Burke quite "favorably, and he said he thought there would be no trouble in arranging the same." But he still wanted to know what South Dakota ought to pay. Butler suggested 80 per cent of the value of the bonds, that is about $2,080 per bond, since Schafer would expect 60 per cent, which would be $1,560. "This would leave us a profit of 52 [$520 per bond] to be divided between us."

Burke expressed doubts about his ability to get South

Dakota to pay as high a price as Butler suggested, but the congressman still favored the plan and promised that a bill authorizing the purchase and one authorizing Stewart to be present at the stock sale would be introduced the first day of the legislature. "Of course," Butler reminded Russell, "we must prepare the bills."[2]

Russell gladly drew an eight-section bill and forwarded it to South Dakota. Entitled "An Act to protect the interest of the state in judgment recovered against North Carolina in the Supreme Court of the United States and to authorize the purchase of certain bonds, out of the net amounts received from the State of North Carolina," the bill would authorize those actions by South Dakota which Russell regarded as most important. Russell, actually less optimistic about North Carolina's docility than Butler appeared to be, kept up a bold front and pressed increasingly for "the pivotal point" of South Dakota's bond-buying legislation. Nor, oddly enough, did Russell concentrate as much as Butler did on the size of the immediate profits for the lawyers from Schafer's bond sales to the Western state. Without expressly disagreeing with Butler, Russell merely suggested that South Dakota pay only about $1300 per bond, since she could recover the full amount of over $2600. "See what a splendid investment," Russell argued. "Even if the State should fail to recover in another suit, it will have lost nothing except some money which it got gratuitously. But failure is impossible." Even if the personnel of the Supreme Court should change, Russell continued, "it is not probable that the present ruling would be reversed, because of the maxim 'Stare Decisis'. But this is even more. It is substantially *res adjudicata*." The concurring majority of the justices would be "bound to accept the present decision as binding in all future cases between the same parties on the same facts." Why, if South Dakota had to bring another suit on the Schafer bonds "we can railroad it through."

[2] Butler to Russell, Dec. 15, 21, 1904, *ibid.*

Warming to his subject, and inwardly fearful of Tarheel Democrats' perverse obstinacy, Russell marshaled other arguments in favor of South Dakota's further co-operation. "Not only should S. D. enrich her treasury by the purchase of these bonds but she should be proud to stand before the country as being the lofty instrument for correcting a monstrous wrong, for compelling a dishonest debtor to pay an honest debt." Furthermore, he continued, "a spirit of friendliness should be prevailing" in South Dakota towards the New York bondholders who had donated such a large sum to the state. Surely South Dakota would be willing to risk a part of the donation on a bond purchase when the risk was small and purchase would "benefit the State and be an accommodation to the bond holders."

The desired legislation in South Dakota loomed so large in Russell's plans that he urged Butler to plan a trip out to Pierre to be "on the spot" when their legislature convened early in 1905. "Don't you see what a powerful leverage this would give us at this end?" Russell implored. "The N. C. Legislature would see that we would sell at 130 [$1300 per bond] and therefore we will never take less, and the only question for them will be whether they will pay 130 for a lump settlement or pay 260 [$2600] at retail in the course of a year or so. And they will see that our talk about assigning to South Dakota is not bluff but that we are actually selling at 130 to a purchaser who will get 260. If this will not bring them to their senses, nothing will or can." And if the Democrats failed to compromise the bonds and had to pay the full "retail" price, Russell invited Butler to envision what a glorious field day the Republicans would have at the next North Carolina election. As for profit from the bond sales, Russell suggested that if "we can sell to South Dakota, there will be some ready, available cash for the lawyers, and, even if we fail to get a settlement for the whole thing this winter, we will in the long run realize all that we have hoped for."[3]

[3] Russell to Butler, Dec. 20, 1904, *ibid.* A copy of Russell's draft of the desired South Dakota legislation is on an undated memorandum, *ibid.*

Russell, like a commanding general, received intelligence reports which furnished a perspective that Butler did not have. There was, for example, Samuel Schafer to be dealt with. Ricaud, charged with the responsibility of handling Schafer, believed or hoped that the old gentleman would accept any settlement which Russell and Ricaud advised. "He never believed in the Bonds," Ricaud explained, and had "urged Simon to accept the 25%," that is, $250 per bond. Now, if he could get about $1400 per bond it would represent "a nice pick up" although he would "*fuss around like a monkey in a fit* and swear he ought to have all." And Ricaud, thinking along the same lines as Butler, warned that every dollar of reduction in what North Carolina paid for the bonds would hurt the lawyers more than the bondholders, since the latter group had "the 25% start" on the lawyers.[4]

Samuel Schafer did indeed "fuss around" when Fabius Busbee in Raleigh gloomily reported the situation as he saw it there. Busbee agreed with Russell in the opinion that North Carolina would not permit the railway stock to go on sale and that it would be best all around if the ten South Dakota bonds could be considered along with the others in a general adjustment. But the Raleigh lawyer feared that North Carolina would never pay the $1300 per bond which Russell envisioned. "I believe the Legislature might be induced to pay par, $255,000," Busbee opined to Russell, but even that "would be so strongly denounced by Daniels, Clark, and others, who are repudiationists by inclination and dishonest by nature (this is a privileged communication!) that I fear it will not go through." Busbee claimed to appreciate the difficulty that Russell would have in inducing Schafer to take $1300, "much less par, but I really believe it will be impossible to induce the Legislature to settle at more than par." And whether that Democratic body would even pay par, $1000 per bond, appeared debatable. Busbee could only pray that "reason and

[4] Ricaud to Russell, Feb. 7, 1904, *ibid.*

common sense would show that such an adjustment will be advantageous to the State."

On a visit to New York, Busbee, at Ricaud's urging, painted his pessimistic Raleigh picture for Samuel Schafer. "Schafer was evidently much disappointed at the tenor of this talk," Ricaud admitted, "and after Busbee left, rather indicated his indisposition to accept 50¢ [$1300 per bond]." Ricaud still felt that Schafer could be managed, but perhaps Russell wanted him, Ricaud, to be on the scene in Raleigh to "reenforce Busbee." If so, Russell should "write Schafer suggesting it, and incidentally advising him that it is worth expending the sum necessary to cover liberal expenses, for, frankly speaking, he is exceedingly close in dishing out cash."[5]

Only to his colleague in Detroit did Daniel Russell tell the stark truth as he saw it: if South Dakota could now be held fast "we will win out and get our money before we are due to die." To explain why he thought North Carolina would not resist the Supreme Court's order, the old Whig recounted a little history: "The time has passed when they can hang the Indian after the Court has ordered his discharge. This they did in Georgia, as you know. Old Jackson, being President, and commander-in-chief of the army and navy, said, 'John Marshall has given his judgment against the State of Georgia. Now, by God, let him execute it.' Some years afterwards the execution came along in the person of Mr. Sherman with a company of some one hundred thousand men with guns, singing, 'John Brown's soul is marching on', and trampelling [*sic*] that State of Georgia beneath their feet. This N. C. crowd has no thought of attempting any such unhealthy performance."

No, North Carolina would probably not openly defy the highest tribunal in the land. And if it chose to let the stock go to sale and to fight the deficiency judgment, choosing that course because it regarded it as "the hardest hit they could

---

[5] Busbee to Russell, Dec. 2, 1904; Ricaud to Russell, Dec. 21, 1904, *ibid*.

give us," the pending South Dakota legislation would still save the day. "It is the very trick that will sweep the table," Russell declared to Alfred Russell. Why could not the latter go himself to South Dakota to address a committee of the legislature? Could he not write Stewart and help push along the bills? And would he help stir up and awaken public sentiment? "The more noise we make," Russell calculated, "the better because we are in the right, and the other fellows are plastered by fraud and ought to be blistered by exposure."[6]

Manning the barricades of newspaper and public opinion took second place in Russell's strategic planning only to securing South Dakota's co-operation. Lamenting the death of Robert Furman, late editor of the Raleigh *Morning Post,* because he now had "no important newspaper to tell the truth for us," Russell turned half-heartedly to Butler's connection with the weekly *Caucasian.* "Intelligent men are so stupid about these bonds," Russell declared, "that something ought to be done to get some of the facts before the public." It would not do, he figured, for the *Caucasian* openly to advocate a settlement or "say anything in our favor," but "it might state facts for the information of its readers." The more talk around Raleigh about second mortgage bonds the better for getting a compromise settlement, Russell reasoned.[7]

The North Carolina front covered as well as possible under the difficult circumstances, Russell turned his attention to opinion in South Dakota. By doing so he probably hampered his own cause without realizing it. South Dakota's sleeping dogs might better have been left to drowse in peace. But Russell, now zealous in his determination to get the bond-

[6] Russell to Alfred Russell, Dec. 23, 1904, *ibid.* Russell himself submitted an article on the bond question to the *North American Review,* to answer Mark Sullivan's attack on the decision which had already appeared in the magazine; but the *Review* had accepted a prominent Southerner's article on why the Fourteenth Amendment should not be enforced and felt it could not use another Southern piece. O. A. Munro of the *Review* to John H. Gough, a Wilmington publisher, Dec. 27, 1904, *ibid.*
[7] Russell to Butler, Dec. 7, 1904; Butler to Russell, Dec. 9, 1904, *ibid.*

buying law and willing to forego all of his other requests of South Dakota, thought differently. He wrote urgently and at great length to Robert W. Stewart in Pierre to explain the necessity of the new legislative act. Along with the many arguments which he had already conveyed via Marion Butler, Russell now added a few new ones. If somebody asked why South Dakota should buy the bonds when it might get them again by donation, Stewart should quickly explain that there was no certainty at all of the state's getting another gift of bonds. Russell amplified: "There are many other states that would be more likely to get it if S. D. should act niggardly towards these bondholders who have made her a present of many thousands of dollars. Again, there are other states willing to buy but the bondholders prefer to stick to S. D. and will not make attempts to deal with other states if S. D. will stick to them."

Then, not knowing that he foreshadowed a most significant and for him altogether regrettable development, Russell moved to the subject of opinion in South Dakota. "I am, and always have been," he confessed, "more or less in fear that somebody will start up an agitation looking to the creation of a public sentiment against the acceptance by States of claims against other states, talking loudly about the fraternity and good fellowship of states, and about the discourtesy and impropriety of a sovereign state['s] lending itself to be a catspaw for the collection by individuals of claims against other states." Russell had seen in the newspapers that a Philadelphian had offered ten Southern bonds to the governor of Iowa, who had opposed acceptance of the bonds. "Are you afraid of any such opposition to our plans in S. D.?" Russell nervously asked Stewart.

The Wilmingtonian, remembering that attack is often the best defense, felt that the time had arrived when he and his associates should get newspapers in South Dakota and in New York to publicize the facts about the second mortgage bonds, especially as to how they differed from the sort of

Southern bonds which, Russell piously avowed, "we would
not touch if the holders would bring them to us by the barrel."
Russell sketched the complete history of the bonds for his
Pierre associate and then warned that if any considerable
sentiment against "our plans" should develop in South Dakota during the next couple of months he would "not be
greatly surprised to see an effort by the N. C. Legislature to
control S. D." Russell added this pungent characterization
of his fellow countrymen: "There is no limit to the assurance
of the high-minded and pious individual who poses as a
Southern Gentleman, when you get him in a corner. He has
unlimited faith in his own power to bamboozle and beat you,
to convince you that he is a persecuted victim while he is in
the act of assaulting and robbing you." Russell prophesied
that if the Tarheel Democrats discovered any tendency on the
part of South Dakota to desist from further action or to
apologize for what had already been done, then Stewart
"would see a delegation of visiting statesmen, appointed by
the N. C. Legislature, lobbying around your capitol and appealing to your legislature in the name of fraternity and good-
will and brotherly love." But "oh, what fun it would be for
us to skin them!" Russell chortled. "And this is the one
consideration which might hold them back."[8]

Carrying through the publicity plan which he had advocated to Stewart, Russell wrote out a newspaper interview for
Samuel Schafer to give out. Russell could "manage to get it
in all leading papers" over the country as well as scattered
throughout South Dakota and North Carolina, too.[9] Done
almost as soon as said, Schafer's be-Russelled words appeared
in the New York *Evening Post* and also the New York *Telegram* late in 1904. The New Yorker felt inspired to say,
among other things, that there was no truth in the frequently
made statement that the donation to South Dakota was part
of any scheme to collect millions from certain repudiating

    [8] Russell to Stewart, Dec. 23, 1904, *ibid.*
    [9] Russell to W. H. Gibson of Schafer Brothers, Dec. 23, 1904; Gibson
to Russell, Dec. 30, 1904, *ibid.*

Southern states (which was true only for Schafer himself, not for the author of his words). Schafer Brothers held no Southern bonds except the second mortgage ones; those it had bought "in good faith at a high price," in fact at prices ranging from 65¢ to 75¢ on the dollar. After explaining why he and his late brother had refused to accept North Carolina's 1879 offer of 25¢ on the principal and nothing on the coupons, Samuel Schafer lamented that North Carolina "has grown rich in the last ten years and is amply able to pay our debt, even if we had no security, but the security is sufficient to pay us in full and leave two millions in the State Treasury; and yet we cannot enforce our claim, because the defaulting debtor is what they call a 'sovereign.' " When the "Reporter" luckily asked if Schafer proposed to make other donations of his bonds to states, the New Yorker coolly explained that there would be no need of that; "since the highest Court of this Nation has decided that our bonds are valid and honest and free from any kind of fraud and that a State or a foreign power can collect them, we can find sale for them." Schafer remarked that North Carolina in her answer to the bill of complaint had made no defense on the merits of the case nor had she denied any of Schafer's facts. The nearest North Carolina had come to the merits of the case was her statement that the Schafers ought not to get more for their bonds than the other bondholders who had accepted the 1879-1880 compromise. But, Schafer concluded on a politic note, he and his brother had held faith in the recuperative powers of North Carolina, which had "grown to be a great State," and surely that proud Southern commonwealth would not be willing to live under the disgrace of repudiating an honest debt![10]

The Sioux Falls *Daily Press,* among other South Dakota papers, reprinted the Schafer interview, and in North Carolina the *Wilmington Messenger,* among others, carried the strategic item. The *News and Observer* carefully refrained

[10] A seven-page pamphlet which reprints the Schafer interview from the New York *Telegram* may be found among Aycock's papers, Governors' Papers, box no. 310.

from carrying the "cooked up" interview, as it correctly called the Schafer piece, and warned that it was "the opening gun" of the campaign that would be made to secure the recognition of the bonds by the North Carolina legislature. Large envelopes, postmarked from Wilmington and containing a copy of the Schafer interview, were received by every state senator, according to the *News and Observer*. Soon "so-called respectable men, with big fees from the Schafer crowd," would be crowded into Raleigh, lobbying to secure a compromise settlement. If the legislature should make the blunder of even considering the offers, Daniels warned, they would merely be opening "Pandora's box of ills that will give untold trouble." The Democratic convention of 1904 had taken the proper stance in its bond resolution, which the *News and Observer* carefully restated for the forgetful among its readers. "Every Democratic official in North Carolina is bound by this iron-clad instruction," the powerful party organ warned, "but that fact will not deter the lawyers and lobbyists who hope for big 'pickings' in case Schafer succeeds." Loyal Democrats could only do two things: beware of lobbyists who would descend on the legislature "like a flock of harpies" and admonish anyone who suggested reopening the matter to "Read the Democratic State platform."[11]

Josephus Daniels and his *News and Observer* had something of an advantage in means and a considerable head start in time over Russell in the struggle to "educate" Tarheel voters and politicians. The Raleigh editor renewed his long-standing campaign in December, 1904, and built it to a feverish intensity by the time the legislature convened in January, 1905. Grimly predicting that the South Dakota bond suit served as a "Trojan horse" designed to reopen the entire 1879 settlement, the *News and Observer* flailed out at the United States Supreme Court for granting the "Shylock demand of the pound of flesh nearest the heart." The paper

[11] Sioux Falls *Daily Press*, Jan. 14, 1905; *News and Observer*, Jan. 8, 1905.

insisted, however, that it remained to be seen whether North Carolina would permit "the shedding of one drop of Christian blood" by furthering the scheming designs of "the Shylocks who are behind this whole movement." Only temporarily allowing its old charge about the Southern Railway conspiracy to recede into the background, the *News and Observer* concentrated its fire on the " 'Trojan horse' in the talk of compromise."[12]

The bond affair late in 1904 became entangled with a new matter, the arbitration treaty which Secretary of State John Hay had negotiated with Great Britain and which President Roosevelt had submitted for ratification by the United States Senate. Not only did the repudiated-bond fears of Southern senators help kill the treaty, by amendments which altered it so drastically as to compel a mortified President and Secretary Hay to drop the whole matter of the treaties; but Josephus Daniels and his friends in North Carolina used the matter to add fuel to the fight against any reopening of time-hallowed settlements about Southern bonds.[13] The *News and Observer* took its cue in the matter from a large meeting of "patriotic Irishmen" in the Clan-Na-Gael in Philadelphia. The Irish speakers had bitterly assailed Hay's treaty as a covert alliance with Britain and adopted resolutions magnificently designed to attract Southern Democratic support for an all-out Senate fight. The Irish organization protested the ratification of any arbitration treaty which did not explicitly exclude from its operation all "financial or other claims against individual States or against the former existing association of States known as the Confederate States." It also, for good measure, deplored the "un-American action of South Dakota in prosecuting the State of North Carolina for the paltry sum of

[12] *News and Observer*, Dec. 7, 13, 1904.
[13] The Senate's emasculation of Hay's treaty, the one with Britain being merely one among a number that had either been already signed or were being negotiated, is described in Lionel M. M. Gelber, *The Rise of Anglo-American Friendship: A Study in World Politics, 1898-1906* (New York, 1938), pp. 180-183; and Alfred L. P. Dennis, *Adventures in American Diplomacy, 1896-1906* (New York, 1928), pp. 478-480.

$10,000 worth of 50-year old bonds, donated to South Dakota by New York bond dealers for the express purpose of reviving the question of the bonds repudiated or readjusted by the Southern States between 1876 and 1884." Speaking for "all patriotic citizens," the politically powerful Irish group declared its determination that "the Southern States shall not be made another Venezuela, and that arbitration treaties unless amended as above set forth will bring, not peace, but civil dissension, sectional hatred and increased taxation to every State of the United States."[14]

The *News and Observer* hardly needed to call the attention of North Carolina's Senators Simmons and Overman to this newest scare on the bond front. A Louisiana senator had already spoken out about the "Trojan horse" which lurked in the arbitration treaty and how wicked New York speculators had donated repudiated and fraudulent "Carpetbagger" bonds to South Dakota in order to rob a sister Southern state. The Raleigh paper did what it could to contribute to the Senate fight against the treaty. The opponents of the treaty succeeded despite the weak case of the fearful Southerners and the strong fight of the administration; but the alleged dangers of the arbitration treaty only added spice and immediacy to the *News and Observer's* main fight against North Carolina's doing anything even remotely resembling a departure from the 1879 settlement: "If the Legislatures of the South re-open the honorable settlements made after the hell of Reconstruction the harpies will rush down upon them, venal men will be bought, and Southern Legislatures will be harrassed or bought up."[15]

[14] *News and Observer,* Dec. 7, 1904. See also the long letter of one Dr. P. M. Cahey of Philadelphia to the Editor arguing, with an elaborate and misleading show of learning, that the "controlling motive" of the arbitration movement from its inception had been to annul or abrogate the Eleventh Amendment of the United States Constitution so that British and other European creditors could compel the Southern states through an international court to pay repudiated or readjusted bonds. *Ibid.,* Dec. 13, 1904.

[15] *Ibid.* Dec. 21, 1904. See also the issues of Dec. 28, 29, 1904, and Jan. 10, 26, 1905, for the outcome of the Senate fight about the treaty.

In the face of such dire warnings by the most powerful editor in the Tarheel Democratic party, it is no wonder that Governor Aycock and his successor, Robert B. Glenn, walked warily indeed around the bond question. Russell burned with curiosity, of course, as to what recommendations, if any, the outgoing governor would make in his message; J. C. L. Harris, Russell's long-time friend and political ally in Raleigh as well as a sometime journalist, picked up what inside information he could get. Harris learned that Augustus W. Graham, the Granville County state senator and Democratic stalwart, opposed doing anything at all about the bonds except whatever might be necessary to prevent the state's railway stock from being sold, a position that coincided with the plank of the Democratic state platform which Graham, Walter Clark, and Josephus Daniels had helped so much to formulate. "I think perhaps Ben. Lacy [state treasurer] knows exactly what Aycock will say in his message," Harris advised, "and I will see him to-morrow and get what he knows and write you."[16]

Even the friendly and astute Harris, however, could hardly be expected to ascertain what Governor Aycock himself did not yet know. For at the time Russell's agent inquired and listened around the state capital, Aycock's confidential agent, Judge Shepherd of the state's bond counsel, carried out his own most secret mission in New York. Shepherd, after meeting with Ricaud and first insisting that he had come to New York on personal business, finally admitted that he had come at the state's expense and with Aycock's sanction to find out how Schafer and his advisers felt about a settlement. The whole visit had to be kept quite secret, probably because the *News and Observer* would have exploded furiously at even the hint of a willingness on the state's part to negotiate with the "Butler-Russell" crowd.

Both Shepherd and Ricaud disclaimed any authority to speak for their respective clients, and each tried desperately to lead the other to make the first offer. Ricaud expressed his

[16] Harris to Russell, Dec. 25, 1904, Russell MSS.

belief that all parties concerned would prefer to give North Carolina the benefit of any concessions in order to obtain an immediate settlement rather than have Schafer sell bonds to other states, which would be done as a last resort. After considerable parleying and Russell's telegraphic advice to avoid making a definite offer at that time (December 29, 1904), Ricaud thought that Shepherd had agreed to recommend to Aycock the following settlement: $350,000 to Schafer for the bonds in his control (about $1500 per bond), the same proportionate amount for the eight bonds in Wilmington, and $17,400 to South Dakota, the bondholders conceding the extra $10,000 of the judgment if North Carolina could not effect a compromise with the Western state. Ricaud explained to Russell that he had not committed Schafer to this plan—and Schafer made it plain that the extra $10,000 to South Dakota would never come from his portion and that Ricaud's action there was "entirely personal" on his own part. Ricaud felt that "the enemy" had become "extremely anxious to settle, and Shepherd himself ambitious to accomplish it."[17]

Shepherd, however, after returning to Raleigh and conferring with Aycock, confidentially informed Russell that the propositions, which Russell had described as satisfactory in his own letter to Shepherd, had been suggested by Ricaud and were certainly not recommendations of his, Shepherd's. "They will be considered very fairly by the Governor," Shepherd assured the former governor, "and you will probably hear further soon. My connection with the matter was simply to ascertain the sentiment of the parties in respect to a settlement and this I have done." Russell could, "of course, appreciate the Governor's position just now. . . ." In other words, while Ricaud felt that he had not committed himself, Shepherd insisted that he most certainly had not; and Governor Aycock, as described at the end of the previous chapter, was perfectly

[17] Ricaud to Russell, Dec. 27, 31, 1904; Russell to Ricaud (telegram), Dec. 29, 1904, *ibid.*

free in his last message to urge the legislature to try settling with South Dakota for "much less" than $27,400 and with the private bondholders for "much less" than the face value of the bonds. As for himself, Aycock could only express his "entire sympathy" with the Democrats of 1879 and his complete accord with the Democratic state platform of 1904.[18]

"The incoming governor cannot be as well informed with reference to the needs of the state as the outgoing governor," Robert B. Glenn informed a reporter in December, 1904, "and it is entirely unfortunate that there should be a change in administration upon the eve of the legislature."[19] Grumble though he did, understandably enough, Governor Glenn had to handle the bond affair—to keep the "Trojan horse" safely out while sitting on the lid of "Pandora's box" without "shedding a drop of Christian blood." It threatened to be quite a chore.

Robust and commanding in appearance, "Bob" Glenn of Winston-Salem came to the governorship after dedicated service to the "White Man's Party." As recently as 1902 he had used his stentorian voice to thrill and horrify a Greensboro audience with his description of what he had seen with his own eyes on a Northern trip—"white men walking with negro women, black men with white women, . . . no law to keep a white man from marrying a negro woman and no law to keep a white woman from marrying a negro man." Theodore Roosevelt could dine with a Negro if he pleased, Glenn had declared, but the "humblest white man" in Guilford County was too good to do so. "North Carolina gives the negro his rights, we want the world to understand that; but God made us the master and him the servant and we are not going to break the divine arrangement."[20] Glenn was clearly all right on the racial question, which Democrats long con-

[18] Russell to Shepherd, Jan. 1, 1905; Shepherd to Russell, Jan. 3, 1905, *ibid*.
[19] Washington correspondence of Thomas Pence in *Morning Post*, Dec. 15, 1904.
[20] *News and Observer*, Oct. 10, 1902. A few days earlier, on Oct. 4, the paper reported a minor Federal officeholding change under the headline, "Nigger Goes Out and Pop[ulist] Comes In."

tinued to use after the Negro had been stripped of whatever political power the race had earlier held. Glenn's economic background as a lawyer who had served the Southern Railway and other corporations, as had so many fee-starved Tarheel lawyers when they could land the more lucrative clients, made him sensitive to loose charges which the *News and Observer* and many others tossed around in the Populist afterglow. While still a state senator, Glenn had retorted to an attack on "railroad lawyers" by insisting that some of the "ablest and most honorable lawyers" in the state served the railways and that it was "outrageous that members of the legal profession who have business dealings with railroads or other corporations or individuals should be subjected to such slurs."[21]

Still Josephus Daniels recalled many years later that on the evening of Glenn's inaugural reception the new governor whispered to the Raleigh editor: "You opposed my nomination because you thought I would be influenced by Andrews [vice president of the Southern Railway]. You will see that, as Governor of North Carolina, I have no strings tied to me." Nobody in short, including probably Glenn himself, knew how he would handle the South Dakota bond affair. The state treasurer, Ben Lacy, had confided to Russell's confidential agent that "wise and conservative counsels of the party will prevail against the hot heads like Gus. Graham and others." Lacy also believed that the legislature would appoint a commission, probably with himself as chairman, to compromise the "whole batch of bonds."[22] But despite such gossip, Russell, who knew from long experience how tangled and ambiguous politics could be, well understood that something bordering on massive confusion reigned in Raleigh as the new state administration took over, and as the days slipped away towards the April 1 deadline set by the Supreme Court.

[21] *Morning Post*, Feb. 19, 1903.
[22] Daniels, *Editor in Politics*, p. 483; Harris to Russell, Dec. 29, 1904, Russell MSS.

Amid so many uncertainties, Russell took fresh hope in January, 1905, from a letter of Alfred Russell's; but Daniel Russell's hope proved to be based on a misunderstanding. "Your letter has the *old ring* to it," the Detroiter declared to his friend, "and I judge that your physical part is about well. Your intellectual part never could be anything else." As for himself, Alfred Russell felt saddened by recent suicides among several of his acquaintances and seemed "to hear pistols cracking all around me." He rejoiced at the Wilmingtonian's plans for South Dakota and at his belief that the North Carolina governor wanted a compromise—"because you and I and the rest of us have done a lot of work, and I am getting desirous to see that some money comes before I die"—but "I always regretted that you could not wait a little so as to use the State of Michigan, which I could handle so conveniently and readily, instead of the State of South Dakota. . . ."

Russell, delighted at what he considered this unexpected prospect of a Michigan bond-buying law to provide the "best possible leverage for lifting North Carolina to the right place," urged his friend in Detroit to get the law passed "by all means and do it quick." He explained, "My South Dakota men say they will get an Act through. . . , but it will greatly help things to get Michigan into it also." Alfred Russell would have to hurry, since the North Carolina legislature would adjourn on March 1. As for fees, they would start coming in whenever Schafer sold a second mortgage bond for over $250, so suppose Alfred Russell tried to get Michigan to pay about $2,000 for each bond on which a state could quickly receive $2,740. If the bond-buying law scared North Carolina into the compromise settlement which Russell wanted, it would mean at least $10,000 for Alfred Russell and the same for Peckham. "I have got out a lot of promises contingent which will cut us deep but it could not be avoided," Russell explained. "The thing came near going to pieces and would have smashed but for my resorting to extreme measures." And yes, to answer the Detroiter's anxious query, Russell was holding off on the North American Trust Company's repudiated bond pool until after the second mortgage case had been closed.

Alfred Russell, no doubt embarrassed by his friend's falsely based enthusiasm, quickly shot back the explanation that when he said he could "handle" Michigan he meant that he could have done so in 1901, at the time of the donation. At that time the governor and other officials, as well as leading members of the legislature, had been his "warm friends." Now he not only had never before seen the new attorney-general who had just taken office but "our new Governor coming into office at the same time is a farmer of limited intelligence, and I could not expect to do anything with either of them, I am sorry to say." The not-so-intelligent "farmer" to whom Alfred Russell referred was Fred M. Warner, a successful businessman turned politician. A political reformer in the Progressive Republican mold, Warner, despite Alfred Russell's denigration—which reveals more about Alfred Russell than about the new governor—would be the first Michigan chief executive to serve three terms. Progressivism, sweeping into Michigan as into South Dakota, boded no good for the type of political manipulation which the bond suit required.[23]

Russell renewed his pleas and proddings for action in South Dakota. And he was not nearly so confident in actuality about "my South Dakota men" as he had pretended to Alfred Russell. Storm clouds, small at first but unmistakable, were appearing in the West. Neither Stewart nor Pettigrew cared especially for the type of publicity about the bonds, such as the Schafer interview, which had suddenly begun to appear in South Dakota, where blissful ignorance had reigned conveniently for so long. Pettigrew visited Butler on his Sampson County plantation on New Year's Eve, 1905. A Sampson

[23] Alfred Russell to Russell, Jan. 4, 16, 1905; Russell to Alfred Russell, Jan. 11, 1905, Russell MSS. M. M. Quaife and S. Glazer, *Michigan: From Primitive Wilderness to Industrial Commonwealth* (New York, 1948), chap. on "Beginning of Reform," pp. 277-285.

County correspondent of the *News and Observer* shiveringly reported the mysterious conferences of "these plotters," and the paper editorially warned that the villains were clearly getting ready to "ask the Legislature to pay the two North Carolina conspirators for their treachery." The Raleigh paper now boldly advocated doing nothing about either the ten Dakota bonds or the Schafer bonds except to let the hundred shares of railway stock be sold under the Supreme Court's decree. "But it will be a cold day in July when any member of the North Carolina Legislature votes a dollar to pay them [Butler and Russell] for their base conduct."[24]

Russell soon joined Butler, Pettigrew, and probably Burke for a conference in Washington. There, presumably, whatever differences there had been were patched over, quite temporarily as it turned out, and Russell continued to pin his hopes on South Dakota for scaring North Carolina. No news came of the South Dakota legislature's action. Russell sweated. He assured Butler, as he probably had the Dakotans themselves, that Schafer would sell his bonds for about $1600 per bond and that they need not worry that the price would be raised when South Dakota appeared to purchase. Still no news. "If they are about to flunk, I want to know it," Russell finally declared on January 23 to Butler. "They should be made to understand that they are 'not the only pebble on the beach'. I can work Michigan. I have already got the donation and assignment law passed there and can get the matter in friendly hands. There are possibilities also in Nevada." Then, resorting to the psychology he knew so instinctively and well, Russell dangled the promise of bigger things to come in front of his friend's, and indirectly the South Dakotans', eyes: he wanted so much to settle the second mortgage bonds before the Tarheel legislature left Raleigh. Then "wider and more fertile fields" could be opened. Butler should urge the North American Trust Company to seek out more of the old Mississippi bonds and to get into touch with the Council of Foreign

[24] *News and Observer*, Jan. 1, 10, 1905.

Bondholders in London. As soon as he received Russell's masterful mixture of threat and promise, intimidation and cajolery, Butler sent the welcome news that the bill had been introduced into the South Dakota lower house. He had requested copies and urged early passage.[25]

South Dakota legislators might have begun to act, but in North Carolina confused debate, on and off the record, and the *News and Observer*'s angry suspicions and threats dominated the scene. On January 18, 1905, a member of the North Carolina house finally summoned his courage, with much prompting from others it may be assumed, and introduced a resolution authorizing a commission to seek information about the South Dakota bonds. The legislator explained that members were receiving marked copies of newspapers, circulars urging payment, and other such material, and he merely desired full and accurate information. The *News and Observer*, staunchly opposed to doing anything at all about bonds, insisted that the legislator merely sought the "light that all good legislators should desire" and would be "found fighting the lobby now organizing to make a raid on the treasury, for he is the sort of man who cannot be influenced by the newspaper, circular or lobby propaganda emanating from Wilmington and elsewhere." Resuming the use of its pet symbol for corporate malevolence, the *News and Observer* warned, "Watch out for the lobby that runs on the Southern Railway track."[26]

Those who opposed Josephus Daniels' and his friends' idea that North Carolina should sit still and allow the stock to be sold were more numerous than the editor would admit. On January 21 a state senator also introduced a bill authorizing the appointment of a commission to investigate the bond matter, with two members to be named by the president of the state senate, two by the speaker of the house, and one by Governor Glenn. The senator stated that he had discussed the

[25] Russell to Butler, Jan. 23, 1905; Butler to Russell, Jan. 26, 1905, Russell MSS.
[26] *News and Observer*, Jan. 18, 1905.

matter with Governor Glenn, who favored the action. When a *News and Observer* reporter sought out the chief executive, however, Glenn explained that he had not committed himself on the matter. He would not advise the legislature as to what course it should follow unless he were specifically asked to do so; and he did not like the idea of having the governor name one member of the commission, the responsibility for which should be laid wholly on either the legislature or the governor. In addition to finding the governor in such an interestingly cautious frame of mind, the same reporter conveniently discovered a "prominent gentleman" who wondered, in view of the 1904 Democratic platform, why the legislators needed to waste their time considering any compromise on the bonds unless they were going to deal exclusively with the ten held by South Dakota.[27]

Raleigh political circles buzzed. The commission had been proposed, and Daniels, Clark, Graham, and their various allies strongly opposed it. Were the Democrats headed for a rip-roaring family fight, the kind that could happen with relative safety to the party now that the Populists had gone under and the Republicans had been devastated by disfranchisement? Russell had all along hoped for a commission and had done all that he could, which was not much under the circumstances, to encourage it. "Answering your enquiry as to what alliances I have made to fix the Legislature," he had earlier snapped at Ricaud, "I have not made any, and do not know how to make any. Do you?" But the astute Russell had put his friend J. C. L. Harris to work, charging him on more than one occasion, "Talk this as much as you can in the right places."[28]

The truth was that Russell, forced to remain on his plantation by the political logic of the situation as well as by what the newspapers would say if he came to Raleigh, sadly lacked much-needed channels of communication. The hand-

[27] *Ibid.*, Jan. 21, 1905.
[28] Russell to Ricaud, Dec. 17 [or 7?], 1904; Russell to Harris, Jan. 13, 1905, Russell MSS.

ful of Republicans in the legislature, including especially George Butler, Marion Butler's able younger brother, stayed scrupulously away from the whole bond question and left it to the Democrats to settle among themselves. Fabius Busbee remained one of Russell's chief links with Raleigh, and Busbee held most pessimistic views about the possible outcome. Busbee, for example, still insisted that North Carolina would not give more than $1250 per bond, if it gave that, for he figured that the entire amount which even a state could recover would be $1740. He felt certain, in other words, that the Supreme Court would not, and probably could not if it would, collect a deficiency judgment after the sale of the railway stock. Busbee realized how difficult it would be to convince Schafer that his "troubles are by no means over" and that so much remained to be done before he could hope to collect anything. Perhaps it would help out in Raleigh if Ricaud would send, as he had promised, an exact statement of how much Schafer had originally paid for the second mortgage bonds which he had purchased before the "virtual repudiation" of 1879. Or at least Ricaud could send "the figures of the most favorable transaction, which might be used to illustrate the whole."[29]

Busbee never got the complete statement of all the purchase prices, probably because too many of them were below the relatively high figures of 65¢ to 75¢ on the dollar which Schafer had mentioned in his interview but possibly also because there was no record for all of the transactions of long ago. Russell specifically instructed Ricaud to "Get figures from Mr. Schafer and send them to Busbee *if they look well.*" Instead of the itemized statement, Busbee got Ricaud himself. Explaining to Samuel Schafer why Ricaud's expenses in Raleigh would be more than justified, Russell mentioned that his former law partner knew "nearly all" members of the legislature, who recognized him as a Democrat and former Wilmingtonian. Busbee, while faithful and loyal, had always

[29] Busbee to Russell, Jan. 7, 14, 1905, *ibid.*

been "weak" on the bond case; Russell explained that despite the Raleigh attorney's abilities, "somehow he is not enthusiastic, being controlled entirely by his own judgment, which is generally correct, but which is this time, I hope and believe, erroneous." Of course, Russell would use Busbee to "advantage and he knows the more we get, the more we, (Ricaud and myself), will allow to him."[30]

Ricaud arrived in Raleigh on January 19, 1905, just as the legislature first openly broached the idea of setting up a bond commission. He found that the Schafer interview and other statements had stirred up much public interest in the bonds; but if there existed any "concrete sentiment," outside of the *News and Observer,* he had not found it. That paper, under a front-page heading on "The South Dakota Bond Conspiracy," reported that the former Wilmingtonian and present attorney for Schafer had arrived to ask the legislature to violate the 1904 platform, to head a lobby "which had or was to come with green adornments peeping from the corners of its pockets and with devious promises to ensnare the State into the payment of a debt which it had solemnly decided it did not owe." Ricaud, according to the story in Daniels' paper, came as "a gentleman of address, of suave ways, and delightful personality" whom "it is a pleasure to meet, the grasp of whose hand is a token of a superior fellowship, who is utterly frank." Unassuming and deprecatory, Ricaud wore clothes which had the "habit of the city upon them; they are new, with the exquisite air of age about them which denotes a wardrobe."

When questioned by the *News and Observer* reporter about his mission in Raleigh, Ricaud assumed "that ultimate finesse which tells the truth." He had come as Schafer's lawyer. Was it true that he had offered a compromise? No, that was incorrect. But what about the reported figure of $350,-000? "You are partly right and partly wrong," Ricaud in-

[30] Russell to Ricaud, Jan. 13, 1905; Russell to Schafer, Jan. 14, 1905, *ibid.*

formed the reporter. "Acting really upon my own responsibility, I did make an intimation that my clients would accept the figure you name as a compromise. Of course, I could not have mentioned it before I ascertained that you had obtained the figures."

The Ricaud interview concluded with the editorial observation that the "hour has struck" when the legislature had to decide about the bonds. Ricaud had been frank, but "what of the facts which can be but guessed at but which peep from the veil of the mystery surrounding this whole transaction?" There was, surely, "a fatality of direction about these bonds which leads always" to the Southern Railway.[31]

Ricaud's mission to Raleigh proved highly frustrating and apparently fruitless. He felt that Governor Glenn, who teased him about his "colossal magnitude as a lobbyist," wanted a settlement. Sizing up the legislative situation for Russell, Ricaud judged that "we have the Senate" and that Josephus Daniels, who was making "a personal canvass among the members," had the house. Ricaud confessed himself "greatly astonished at Daniels' influence with the country members." The editor's "fuss about the 8 Bonds has created a lot of talk and they would raise hell if they knew who owned them."

A few days after his arrival, Ricaud reported, Glenn had stopped Busbee and begun talking bonds. The governor stated that it would be utterly useless to submit an offer of $350,000 or anything like it, for he would strongly recommend against it to the legislature. Glenn had heard gossip that Chief Justice Fuller believed that the South Dakota judgment could not be collected, and Judge Shepherd had told him that Schafer could never find purchasers for his bonds. In short, Ricaud now felt that Walter Clark, Augustus W. Graham, and Josephus Daniels had strongly influenced Governor Glenn against a settlement. When Busbee went back to see the governor, Glenn had been a little more rational and suggested another meeting, but Ricaud judged that "they are dealing

[31] *News and Observer,* Jan. 21, 22, 1905.

with the State's name and credit as a lawyer would with his client[']s lawsuit in trying to effect the best settlement possible."[32]

Busbee expressed himself even more pessimistically than Ricaud. Explaining that he and Ricaud had made it a point not to solicit the legislators personally, Busbee believed that whatever "the Grahams, under the instructions of Judge Clark, can do to defeat any settlement, will be done." Moreover, he charged that "whatever the *News and Observer* can accomplish by appeals, by falsehoods, and by any kind of chicanery, will certainly be done." Busbee thought that most of the "conservative" legislators desired a settlement without appreciating the danger of further litigation or the evil that would be done to North Carolina by "blazoning forth" its continued repudiation of honest debts. Still convinced that Russell's hopes were too high, Busbee avowed that the state would undoubtedly reject the figure of $350,-000 which Russell had mentioned.[33]

The two attorneys, Ricaud and Busbee, tried one last time to do business with Glenn by offering to submit Samuel Schafer's rock-bottom price if Glenn, after conferring with his advisers, would agree to recommend the settlement to the legislature. "He stated emphatically that he would not commit himself in advance," Ricaud reported, "and seemed to think it was a piece of effrontery upon our part to make such a request, characterizing it as an attempt upon the part of the bond-holders to dictate to the Governor." Convinced that "the state is playing a great game of bluff," Ricaud, joined by Busbee, now wrote a long, formal letter to Glenn; it set forth many facts about the bonds and explained why they had not submitted a formal proposition to the state for the settlement. Schafer Brothers, in their own right, owned 112 of the second mortgage bonds (122 before the donation to South Dakota) and controlled for others an

[32] Ricaud to Russell, Jan. 21, 23, 26, 1905, Russell MSS.
[33] Busbee to Russell, Jan. 27 [or 28?], 1905, *ibid.*

additional 130, making a total of 242 bonds. Most of their own 112 were purchased before the state's default in interest and the price paid for the entire lot, including some bought at 60 after the default in interest, averaged 66¢ on the dollar. The firm had no record of the prices paid by other owners but did have the original bill of sale for about forty-five of the bonds which any North Carolina official could inspect.

After reviewing the 1879 adjustment, the 1901 petition to the legislature which had been ignored, and the South Dakota suit, Ricaud and Busbee got down to figures. Schafer Brothers had paid for each bond on an average of $660, which with simple interest for thirty-seven years meant that each bond had cost them $2,125; therefore, they had thought that a settlement on the basis of about 57 per cent of the amount actually due on the bonds would be reasonable, and one of their counsel (Russell) had so stated in a letter to one of the state's counsel (Shepherd). In informal conferences in Raleigh, however, the governor and other officials indicated that such a proposal would not be approved, so one of the bondholders' counsel (Ricaud) left Raleigh to confer with his client (Schafer) and urged him to make additional concessions and to submit to a larger personal loss so that a proposition could be made "which every man who values the financial credit of the State would be obliged to approve."

Ricaud prevailed on Schafer, the letter to Glenn continued, to make the final proposition which embodied "every conceivable concession which the holders of the bonds, in common fairness, could be asked to make": $302,500 or $1250 for each of the 242 bonds, that being 46 per cent of the debt as adjudged by the Supreme Court, 57 per cent of the actual cost of the bonds to Schafer Brothers, 71 per cent of the actual value of the security pledged for the bonds, and 77 per cent of the amount already collected by the state as dividends on the stock. Having made "so liberal and just a proposition," the bondholders were naturally unwilling to submit the proposition to the legislature if the governor was going to recommend that it not be accepted, and Glenn had stated that the bondholders had "no right to expect from the Executive Department any indication of its approval or disapproval" of their offer. Thus Ricaud and Busbee felt it would be "utterly useless" to repeat efforts made in 1901 and, having failed to reach any understanding with the governor, to approach the legislature again.[34]

Governor Glenn, after requesting that Ricaud and Busbee hold off a day or two in publishing their letter to him, soon replied formally that since they had made no formal proposal for him to transmit to the legislature, "I consider that there is nothing before me requiring any further action on my part." The offer of 1879 still stood.[35] Ricaud clung to his hunch that Glenn had planned his "game to force us to submit our offer and then knife us and force a settlement at par or less." Why should not he, Ricaud, go on back to New York? "They are all damned cowards & it will place full responsibility on them to publish our willingness to accept a settlement but our indisposition to be made a fool of." Glenn wanted to settle, Ricaud still believed, and so did others in Raleigh, but the governor was "playing for the U. S. Senate." Aycock had urged Ricaud to send in an offer of $200,000, which the latter had refused to do. "We will get the $1250 per bond in my opinion," Ricaud concluded, "and it is best for me to go to N. Y. and let the activity come from them." Anyhow he was thoroughly fed up with "too much pot-house politics from the 'Statesman' of the Capitol."[36]

[34] Ricaud and Busbee to His Excellency, The Governor of North Carolina, Jan. 30, 1905, *ibid.* To counteract the Schafer claim about the relatively high prices paid for the bonds, one old-time Democrat pointed out that at the time the bonds were sold the chief circulating medium had been "Greenbacks," worth considerably less than their nominal value. *News and Observer*, Jan. 28, 1905.

[35] Glenn to Ricaud and Busbee, Feb. 1, 1905, Russell MSS.

[36] Ricaud to Russell, Jan. 30, 31, Feb. 1, 3, 1905, *ibid.*

Ricaud had gone to Raleigh not to bribe legislators—
Russell had stated to Schafer that Ricaud's total expenses
would "hardly exceed $250"—but to negotiate a compromise
with the state authorities. But with Governor Glenn playing
a dodge game and the legislature confused and leaderless,
there turned out to be no one with whom he could negotiate.
The *News and Observer* unloaded all of its biggest guns:
"There is deserved injury to a political party that, after election on a given platform, repudiates its platform and does
exactly what it declares it will not do." "The people have
long memories—particularly the country folks." There was
a "high moral question" involved and political death for the
faithless. Where did Schafer Brothers get their bonds anyhow? In law perhaps that question was immaterial, but "as
a point in the history of an infamy against the State, as the
key of a suspected conspiracy of men who were elevated
by political fortune to places in which they came into possession of facts which enabled them to map out a plan of
campaign by which they sought to enrich themselves at the
expense of the people who had honored them, the question
is one that serves to point both a lesson and a duty." [This
charge that Butler and Russell had somehow put the bonds
into Schafer's hands, which any number of widely available
records showed to be false, had never been made before.]
What about the eight bonds which had been sent from New
York by "the gentleman with the Jew name" and which
Russell had tampered with while still governor?[37]

The outcome of all the *News and Observer's* charges and
agitation, Governor Glenn's cautious public silence and private elusiveness, and the legislature's bafflement was that the
joint committee on claims of the North Carolina house and
senate, a cumbersome body of about fifty members, angrily
debated whether it or a special commission should handle
the bond question. The backers of the commission plan
pointed out, at length, that the full committee was too large

[37] *News and Observer*, Jan. 22, 24, 1905.

a body to deal with such a technical, delicate matter and that the governor himself had approved the plan for a commission, which could act more quickly and intelligently in recommending a solution to the legislature. Senator Augustus W. Graham and Representative William A. Graham vigorously opposed the commission plan, the latter declaring that the full committee should "thoroughly investigate the matters which had been set out in the *News and Observer* before anything else was done." Supporters of the full committee's handling the question, which included many who really did not want it handled at all, won out. But on January 30, with about one more month of its session to go and with two more months before the United States marshal would presumably appear, the state senate tabled a resolution directing the claims committee to investigate South Dakota's claims against North Carolina.

Satisfied and happy, the *News and Observer* repeated that the legislature alone could decide the matter, and if Glenn should "so far forget himself" as to permit Schafer's attorneys to learn his position in advance "the people would have no respect for him." The paper pointed out that South Dakota would get whatever the stock brought at sale, provided the Supreme Court really ordered it sold. Of course, if the Court were called on actually to order the stock sold the justices in a rehearing might not hold to its five-to-four decision. But was it not really wisest for North Carolina to "sit steady in the boat" and " 'abide the mandates of the court' with that dignity and wisdom that should characterize the conduct of a great state, conscious that it has dealt honorably and fairly with all its creditors?"[38]

The *Morning Post,* now edited by Robert M. Phillips and rarely at war with Josephus Daniels since Furman's death, finally spoke up to assert the need for "the sober and calm thought of the statesman, the application of the practical ideas of the careful and prudent businessman, rather than an

[38] *News and Observer,* Jan. 25, 31, Feb. 1, 2, 1905.

attempt to flippantly toss the whole matter aside." A state senator had declared that there existed no need for any legislative action on North Carolina's part because the Federal marshal might not be able to find anything to levy on to satisfy the Supreme Court's judgment; the *Post* replied that surely no Tarheel "seriously contemplates the state treasurer['s] hiding from the marshal, or in any other way evading the decree of the court." To buttress its case in support of the proposition that the state's situation was "a grave and serious one" calling for treatment in a "serious, business-like way," the *Post* now reprinted one of Furman's comprehensive and careful editorials which had been written a year earlier when the Supreme Court delivered its decision.

As for the 1879 compromise settlement, which the *News and Observer* now treated as the ark of the covenant, the *Post* pointed out that nobody claimed that it had not been an honorable action. But as a matter of common sense, the paper continued, a compromise could hardly be binding on those who had not been a party to it and who had refused to accept it, as had been the case with the Schafers. The *Post* believed that the Democratic legislature would yet save North Carolina the embarrassment of having any part of its railway stock put on the block and "if there is any 'light' behind all this business which the public has not seen it is time to turn it on and stop all the vague insinuations that have been from time to time made." As for the *News and Observer*'s charge that "every step in the transaction" had been on a par with Russell's "treasonable action" in the matter of the eight bonds, the *Post* inquired if the United States Supreme Court in making its decision had been "guilty of 'treasonable action,' or something on a par with it?" Were the Democrats in the legislature who favored investigation of the matter, such as J. Crawford Biggs of Durham, guilty of "treasonable action?"

Finally the *Post* delivered a little lecture on journalistic ethics to its old rival: no paper dealing with an important public question, such as the South Dakota bond matter, should "strike in the dark, or make statements calculated to cloud an issue or befuddle facts without offering direct proof as to the source and reliability of its information." The *Post* entertained strong suspicion for its part that the "source" of the *News and Observer*'s constant charge about the Southern Railway's connection with the bond matter was none other than Josephus Daniels himself. "It has long been the custom of the *News and Observer* to entertain wild suspicions and dignify them as if they were facts." The *Post* pled, "Let us be fair, and just, and reasonable."[39]

Emboldened perhaps by the *Post*'s willingness to speak out, other newspapers also ventured to criticize the legislature's paralysis. The Lumberton *Argus* and the Raleigh *Times*, for example, both Democratic papers, indirectly joined the *Post;* the former declared that if "might makes right, then North Carolina is right—but only then," for the Lumberton paper felt that the state owed the debt and could no longer plead bankruptcy as it had in 1879. The Raleigh evening paper expressed its surprise, as well it might in view of the circumstances, that so few men in the state even yet understood the true nature and origin of the second mortgage bonds. The influential *Charlotte Observer,* remarking that the legislature was well into the last half of its session with its most important work yet undone, insisted that "of course the state does not intend to permit this stock to go to sale." The Winston-Salem *Union Republican,* one of that party's few newspapers, wryly commented that if the Democratic editors throughout the state could ever get it clear and straight that the bonds in question had been issued by a "Democratic legislature," then the word "fraudulent" would of course be at

[39] *Morning Post*, Jan. 31, Feb. 2, 5, 1905. Fabius Busbee again wrote a public letter to the *News and Observer* declaring that Southern Railway officials had nothing to do with the bond suit nor did they own any of the bonds; in a signed comment of his own, Josephus Daniels asserted that Busbee's denial only showed that he knew nothing of the scheme and did not belong to the "inner circle." *News and Observer,* Feb. 3, 1905.

once "banished from the transaction."[40] There were strong indications, in short, that many persons in North Carolina, including perhaps a cautious governor, were not happy with the do-nothing policy which promised to put North Carolina in an embarrassing new position on April 1, 1905.

[chapter eight]

THE "TAKE" DIVIDED

RUSSELL took heart from the rising chorus of protest which came from those who disliked the idea of North Carolina's doing nothing at all about the bond matter. He again pressed Butler to "move with vigor and celerity" in securing the South Dakota bond-buying act. In early February, 1905, Russell thought there appeared to be no danger of the North Carolina legislature's trying to "monkey with So. Dak." He figured that the idea of launching a public counterattack in South Dakota had never occurred to them, that there was not enough time for them to organize such a move, and that the Tarheel legislators would have to appropriate money while still believing that they could not weaken South Dakota. "We should quit this bush whacking and come out into the open, and appeal to the morality, and sense of honor and justice of that State," Russell declaimed, "and then get what we want: and that is for that State to buy our bonds." The Dakotans had been assailed by "the States' Rights repudiating crowd" so why did they not hit back? "I know we can save this thing if the So. Dak. end is well managed," Russell asserted. "If it miscarries, the fault will not be mine."[1]

Inwardly sickened by the prospect of further intermin-

[40] *Morning Post,* Feb. 7, 9, 11, 1905.

---

[1] Russell to Butler, Feb. 4, 1905, Russell MSS.

able delay, Russell also pressed Busbee into greater action. Could the Raleigh lawyer get his and Ricaud's "airtight" review of the bonds' history, as contained in their letter to Glenn, into the *Charlotte Observer* and *Morning Post*? It might also be well for Busbee "to let it leak" that South Dakota was in the process of passing a bond-purchasing act and that she would bid on the railway stock, if it went to sale, up to its full value. Furthermore, Russell suggested, the chances of a compromise settlement would be infinitely better with a three-man commission appointed by Governor Glenn; there had been just such a commission which had adjusted the first mortgage bonds back in the 1880's, furnishing a precisely similar precedent to the present case. The "taking points" of the plan, as Russell saw it, were that it shifted the responsibility from the legislature and "lets them out." It would make "some spoils" and give Glenn a chance to pay off some of his political debts or at least "to help along his crowd." Busbee should think it over; he knew "when and where and how to lodge it."

Busbee did indeed consider Russell's timely suggestion, which grew out of the former governor's increasing anxiety. The Raleigh attorney promptly conveyed the idea, precedent and all, in a letter to Glenn, who wanted to look into the matter and then confer with Busbee. Russell expressed surprise that Busbee had considered it "good policy" to have the commission idea come so openly from himself. "I thought it better to let the Grand Army of Fools look at it as coming from the Governor, or somebody in the legislature," Russell commented. Busbee, for his part, insisted that "it might be possible to play the game rather too finely," and therefore he had acted openly. For many reasons, he continued to be pessimistic. Now, in addition to all of the earlier reasons he had given for his gloomy view, he felt that too many of the Democratic lawyers in Raleigh, including Judge Shepherd, hoped that "if litigation follows they may be 'it', and will hardly do anything which might interfere with their future retainers."[2]

The Washington correspondent of the *Morning Post,* Thomas Pence, supplied, whether knowingly or not, an important element in Russell's broad-scaled maneuver. In what appears to have been a story which Pence checked out with Congressman Burke and probably Butler, and one which the *Post* headlined on the front page, the *Post* correspondent declared that lawyers in the national capital "do not doubt for a moment that the Supreme Court of the United States will enforce its judgment if such an issue is presented." If a deficiency judgment should be necessary, the Federal marshal would be authorized to levy on any of North Carolina's property, such as state-owned stock, which was not used for governmental purposes. The correspondent also mentioned that one member of the Tarheel congressional delegation, who did "not want to appear in the attitude of advising the legislature," had nevertheless privately written several letters strongly urging compliance with the Court's judgment because it would be "disgraceful" for the state not to do so.

The companion story from Washington on the *Post's* front page contained even more dynamite-laden news. Representative Burke from South Dakota had given Pence the history and "full significance" of the bond-buying law which the South Dakota senate had already passed and which the house was expected to pass momentarily. By a "unique and original" plan, which "so far as is known has never occurred to any one" in North Carolina, South Dakota would authorize her governor to use the money to be derived from the original suit to purchase additional bonds from Schafer Brothers; this would set up an "endless chain" whereby South Dakota purchased bonds for "something like $400,000" and easily recovered on them $600,000 or more. South Dakotans insisted that future litigation would not be costly or time-

---

[2] Russell to Busbee, Feb. 1, 2, 6, 1905; Busbee to Russell, Feb. 5, 10, 1905, *ibid.*

consuming because the precedent had already been established in one of the Supreme Court's most "elaborate opinions
ever handed down." Even the Tarheel congressmen who knew
the seriousness of the proposition, the *Post* correspondent
concluded, admitted that the plan was "cleverly conceived"
and adroit.[3]

Russell's various maneuvers, coinciding with the pressure
from the *Post* and *Charlotte Observer* and other papers,
brought action. On February 11, 1905, Governor Glenn
drafted a special message to the legislature. He urged that
the South Dakota judgment be compromised or paid and
declared that unless the legislature took prompt steps the 100
shares of state-owned stock would be sold. Glenn also transmitted the commission proposal from Ricaud and Busbee;
while the governor did not recommend that the legislature
accept the terms that Schafer's attorneys had offered, he did
strongly recommend that the whole matter be adjusted if the
bondholders would meet the state in a "fair settlement" and
take what was "just." As soon as the legislators heard the
governor's recommendation, and undoubtedly as Glenn and
his advisers had planned, legislative leaders went into action
and secured authorization for a committee composed of the
governor and five legislators to investigate the matter and
recommend all steps necessary to protect the interests of North
Carolina in the bond matter.

Glenn, animated partly by his own judgment in the matter but clearly nudged forward also by the subtle pushes
which Daniel Russell had arranged, had finally acted on the
bonds. He also had taken the most elaborate, and beautifully
transparent, care to cover his *News and Observer* flank. Governor Glenn wrote a public letter to Josephus Daniels warmly
congratulating the editor on the announcement that his paper
had passed the 10,000 mark in circulation, thereby setting a
record for that time in North Carolina. With all of the editor's great power and his genuine love for the state, the gov-

[3] *Morning Post,* Feb. 11, 12, 1905.

ernor soothingly concluded, surely Daniels would "concede
the same devotion to others, though they may differ with
your views," so that the *News and Observer,* with charity as
well as patriotism, could always be a mighty "power for
usefulness."

The editor, apparently supremely happy with the governor's tribute to his newspaper's role in the state's life, suddenly became strangely uninterested in bonds and wrote not
a single editorial dealing with Glenn's proposal for a commission. Rather, Josephus Daniels, on the same page that
carried the news of the governor's message to the legislature as
well as his billet doux to the editor, declared again that the
News and Observer was an "independent and fearless Democratic paper." It did not wait for the party to formulate its
policies; it fought to secure what it deemed "right and wise,
and usually the Democratic platform and the *News and Observer's* editorials are as alike as twin brothers." One paper
at least certainly stood by its principles and "fights every day
in every year for Democratic supremacy."[4]

In the light of these developments, Russell believed that
the end, at last, had come into sight. He had labored too long
and too tirelessly to allow wild hopes now to enter his mind
and spoil or prolong the approaching negotiations. Moreover, Samuel Schafer would also have to bring himself to
face grim realities even though he might not appreciate the
tangled threads of Tarheel politics. Russell advised him that
the "enemy" would probably give par, that is $1,000, for each
of the 242 bonds in the Schafer block. Russell hoped for
and would try for a bit more, say $1100, and would "never
go under $1000 to the bond," for the matter had absolutely

---

[4] *News and Observer,* Feb. 12, 1905. It might also be mentioned that
Daniels at that time took great interest in a further extension of North
Carolina's movement toward state-wide prohibition; although many Democrats insisted that the 1904 platform had not called for it and that the
measure discriminated against rural and small-town Tarheels, the Ward
bill would forbid the liquor traffic in all communities other than in-
corporated places of at least 1,000 inhabitants (there were then only
eighty such towns in the state).

to be settled. "But you must understand that if we fail to settle, we are lost," he admitted to the New York bondholders. As he had already explained, "it will be expensive, and irritating and difficult to work the South Dakota end." Furthermore: "Who is going to make more donations? Who is going to pay out more money? Who is going to bear the expenses of another suit? To say nothing of the expenses of getting ready for a suit." (And, although Russell did not say this he might well have, who would live long enough to see the thing termiated?) If a settlement should fail and Samuel Schafer be responsible for that sad outcome, "the other bondholders would feel very ugly."[5]

Russell must have sensed the impending disaster to his plans. The news of South Dakota's final action on the bond-buying bill, so necessary for scaring the Tarheel Democrats into a settlement favorable to the bondholders, had never come. Russell had pled for it with every trick and argument he could think of since late in 1904. On February 16 Butler finally wrote that "there is some trouble developed in the S. D. House," but "we are doing all we can to overcome it." On the very same day, Governor Glenn somewhat tardily but quite effectively began to play the "public opinion" gambit which for so long had been Russell's (and the *News and Observer's*) specialty.

Glenn dispatched a sizzling public letter to Senators Simmons and Overman. It described the efforts of the private bondholders to force North Carolina to "pay 'the pound of flesh', regardless of its effect upon our people" and declared that the report of South Dakota's pending bond-buying bill sounded "so monstrous and foreign to what appears to me to be good faith in the comity between States, that I cannot believe it, and am satisfied that [the rumor] is being circulated for effect." But if it should be true, then "it is high time that in the Council Halls of the

[5] Russell to Schafer, Feb. 12, 1905; Russell to W. H. Gibson, Feb. 13, 1905, Russell MSS.

Nation, a ringing resolution should be introduced, denouncing in no uncertain, but in most scathing terms a State that thus allows itself to be used as a catspaw by individuals to annoy and harass another sister State." Surely, Glenn continued, the Constitution never contemplated a state's becoming "a bond broker, or a second hand junk shop, where persons holding depreciated or fraudulent bonds, or bonds bought for much less than their face value, could sell the same, and through the sovereign accomplish indirectly what the Constitution prohibits." Would the senators ascertain the facts from their South Dakota colleagues, and, if the rumor of a bond-buying law be true, confer with the Carolina delegation in the House in order "that such a scheme to injure a sister State" could be exposed and properly condemned? If the bondholders still refused to meet North Carolina in an honorable settlement, Governor Glenn felt sure that the United States Supreme Court would refuse to allow the state's stock to be sold to pay a judgment thus "obtained by collusion between individuals and a sovereign State."[6]

"The enemy" had made a master stroke, one worthy of Russell himself. It had taken the Tarheel Democrats four years to think of an open, dramatic appeal and threat aimed directly at South Dakota. But Glenn, possibly nudged first from Simmons and Overman in Washington, had pulled his coup at what for him was the exactly right moment. The bond-buying bill had not sped through both South Dakota houses and the governor's office, as the 1901 donation act had done, simply because by 1905 the "Insurgent" or Progressive Republicans in the Western state were threatening the more conservative Stalwart Republicans with whom Congressman Burke and Lawyer-lobbyist Stewart had enjoyed such warm rapport. Moreover, Governor Samuel H. Elrod had replaced the more bond-minded, or at least more pliable, Governor Herreid after the 1904 election.

[6] Glenn to Simmons and Overman, Feb. 16, 1905, Governors' Papers; *Morning Post* and *News and Observer*, Feb. 17, 1905.

Russell, already blocked in Michigan by a similar political upheaval, now found his last, best hope exploded when
South Dakota's passage of the desired legislation became out
of the question. A member of the South Dakota house of
representatives and of its judiciary committee wrote South
Dakota's Senator Robert J. Gamble that the bond-buying bill
had come into the hands of the committee, and "there is no
question but what it will remain there to the end of the session." The Pierre legislator explained that as soon as the
"real condition of this affair" became known "there was a
very determined stand against it," and if "any further action
than to suppress the legislation that has already been proposed
should be necessary to put our State in the proper light, I
would be very glad to further it as much as possible."[7]

South Dakota newspapers publicized Glenn's letter, and
even the newspaper which had long been quite friendly to
ex-Senator Pettigrew, the Sioux Falls *Daily Press,* sarcastically
assured Governor Glenn that "while the legislature of South
Dakota has proved itself capable of almost any act of deep
dyed villainy that may be initiated at the center of power,
it has not yet precipitated itself into the plot suggested by him
[Glenn]."

The Sioux Falls newspaper also reported that South Dakota's congressional delegation daily received offers of repudiated state bonds but that the letters now went into the
trashbasket "on the ground that any negotiations of that sort
would be a violation of state courtesy." As for South Dakota's
earlier acceptance of bonds, the *Daily Press* sardonically
commented that the University of South Dakota "secured its
little donation from North Carolina before this fine point in
interstate etiquette was discovered." An interesting and possibly related item also appeared in the South Dakota papers:
publication of the statement that some anonymous donor
(Pettigrew, Burke, or Schafer?) wanted to give $25,000 to

[7] John Holman to Senator Robert J. Gamble, Feb. 21, 1905, enclosed
in Gamble to Overman, Feb. 25, 1905; both printed in *News and Observer,*
March 8, 1905.

the University had been premature; the gift was conditional and the conditions could not now be met in the short time remaining before adjournment of the Dakota legislature.[8] The Sioux Falls *Daily Argus-Leader* and other papers in South Dakota joined in the chorus of disapproval for further bond activities on the state's part.

After reading Pence's bond-buying story in the *Post,* the Tarheel congressmen hastened to ascertain the facts. Senators Kittredge and Gamble from South Dakota assured their North Carolina colleagues that the bond-purchasing bill would never be passed and that the donation act would probably be repealed. Senator Overman, explaining a bit wildly that the donation act itself had been "the outcome of the unhappy Populist days," telegraphed the good news to Governor Glenn and to the *News and Observer.* That paper had never informed its readers of the possibility of the Dakota bond-purchasing law, but it now crowed that the " 'goblins will get you if you don't watch out' story, industriously circulated to scare the legislature into a compromise unjust to the State, turns out to have been a canard" as the telegrams proved. The *News and Observer's* Washington correspondent, moreover, finally got his hands on the Sioux Falls *Argus-Leader* and jubilantly reported that Republican paper's strong conviction that South Dakota should not and would not think of buying a sister state's bonds for the purpose of making a profit out of them. The *News and Observer,* still calmed and soothed by Governor Glenn's sweet words and rejoicing in Russell's South Dakota failure, now declared merely that North Carolina would "pay what is right." The editor's memory had, no doubt, become temporarily fuzzy about the fact that the Democratic convention of 1904, resting on the shoulders of the Redeemers of 1879, had proclaimed the eternal "right."[9]

[8] Sioux Falls *Daily Press,* Feb. 19, 21, March 11, 1905.
[9] *News and Observer,* Feb. 18, 19, 24, 1905. The *Morning Post's* Pence reported also that the Tarheel delegation in a cloakroom conference had agreed that there was now no need for any congressional action, which would not have done North Carolina's reputation any great good anyhow,

Daniel Russell's fury and anxiety knew no bounds. Marion Butler, on seeing Glenn's letter in the *Washington Post,* remarked cautiously that it was hard to tell yet what effect it would have, but he thought it "wise to employ some more counsel." Would Russell contribute $10,000 for that purpose? Twenty-four hours later Butler admitted that the South Dakota senators had already conveyed their apprehension about the bond-buying bill to their Governor Elrod and that Glenn's public letter had merely hardened their opposition to the plan. "It is now certain that the bill cannot be passed," Butler finally confessed, "though our friends trust" that the earlier donation act could still be saved. What could Russell do in Michigan?

Ignoring the unwelcome queries about the $10,000 which he did not begin to have and about Michigan's availability, Russell grimly prophesied that failure in South Dakota meant that "the commission might refuse to give us even the disgraceful shave which the Governor offers." Glenn had mentioned $250 for each bond, the sacred 25 per cent of 1879, plus 6 per cent for 25 years on the same, making a total of $625 per bond. The prospect of such a settlement so disgusted and horrified Russell that he clutched for straws. If neither Pettigrew nor Butler would go to South Dakota, what about Schafer's sending Ricaud? In order to answer Glenn's publicity splash, why did not Ricaud make himself famous by giving out a statement to the New York papers, which Schafer could pay for if necessary, pointing up the irony of Glenn's offering $625 per bond (one-third of the value of the security and about one-fifth of the amount of the debt which the Supreme Court declared to be lawful and honest) for bonds which the governor himself admitted to be honest?

under the circumstances. Chief Justice Walter Clark of the state supreme court had earlier suggested the advisability of a congressional prohibition of execution of a judgment against a state. "Such action by congress was regarded as impossible," Pence added, "the belief being that that branch of the government would never consent to legislative action" which would nullify a Supreme Court decision. *Morning Post,* Feb. 19, 1905.

"In your writings make your sentences short and sharp," Russell instructed Ricaud. "Don't spread. Leave that style to such humbugs as Roosevelt and Cleveland."[10]

In spite of Russell's last frantic efforts, the game had slipped rather completely from his control. Ricaud reported that Pettigrew disapproved of Ricaud's going out to South Dakota and that the former Silver Republican senator had blamed Russell for awakening "the opposition to the proposed legislation" by his "deluge of communications to every body in South Dakota, from the Governor down." The angry infighting and snarling, thinly veiled for so long, now began in earnest. Ricaud snapped that Pettigrew "is like all populists I have ever seen, damn small and mean." Ricaud just simply did not "like him, or his ways, especially as he made efforts to hurt you [Russell] with Schafer in my opinion." As for the publicity counter-offensive which Russell had urged, Ricaud sadly admitted that there just was not any money for "a newspaper war on the MOUNTAIN STEER" who advertised himself as the governor of North Carolina. Ricaud felt, in short, that there was nothing that could now be done except to "accept the inevitable" and let matters develop as they would.[11]

Philosophic resignation had never been Russell's cup of tea. He knew the game was about to end in a defeat, possibly approaching a rout for his side. But he would go down swinging and "cussing." He dispatched a hot letter to Pettigrew. First of all he inquired why the South Dakotan had reportedly made certain statements about Russell's deluging South Dakota with communications when Russell insisted that he had never written to anyone out there except Stewart. Russell had left it to Butler to keep Pettigrew informed. Russell admitted that he had insisted on South Dakota's coming "out from behind the bushes" and facing the world "like an honest State." If his plans for new legislation had been adopted

---

[10] Butler to Russell, Feb. 17, 18, 1905; Russell to Butler, Feb. 17, 1905; Russell to Ricaud, Feb. 18, 1905, Russell MSS.
[11] Ricaud to Russell, Feb. 20, 21, 1905, *ibid.*

"we should now have a healthy and prevailing sentiment in our favor," but Pettigrew and Stewart "refused to adopt this policy and the result is not calculated to arouse your pride or inspire confidence in your judgment."[12] Russell had warmly opened a correspondence with his associate that would promptly grow sizzling hot. But there was hardly time yet for personal feuding. The North Carolina bond committee and the Schafer lawyers would have to act with great dispatch if they were to settle before the early March adjournment of the legislature and thereby escape the Federal advertisements which were scheduled to begin on April 1.

On the final, hurried round of negotiations there were disagreements, and one which nearly prevented the settlement; but on the whole and as far as Daniel Russell was concerned, the climax of the settlement came quickly. Fabius Busbee played a leading semi-public part for Russell's side. Ricaud hated the idea of returning to Raleigh, where he declared he had avoided "a personal encounter" only by a "force of will-power, born of necessity." In his room on the night before his departure, he had been compelled to demand a retraction from the city editor of the *News and Observer,* and only the newsman's compliance had prevented bloodshed. Not knowing that Josephus Daniels would undergo a marvelous, albeit temporary, change of heart about the bond matter, Ricaud feared another journalistic attack: "This dirty sheet is so rantankerously [*sic*] opposed to you and Butler, that it would not hesitate to say anything to prejudice the Legislature and perhaps include me in its personal slaughter."

But neither Schafer nor Ricaud fully trusted Busbee, whom they suspected, probably unfairly, of "running with the hare, and playing with the hound." Busbee thought it might be well for Samuel Schafer himself to come down, if "the utterance of any unwise sentiments" could be prevented; but Ricaud found that the aged financier, "with all of his previous blow about going down to Raleigh, is now reluctant

[12] Russell to Pettigrew, Feb. 23, 1905, *ibid.*

to go." So Ricaud himself finally returned for the last show-down.[13]

Before Ricaud left New York he obtained, as a condition precedent to his mission, Samuel Schafer's permission to accept par or $1000 per bond. Yet on the eve of the bond committee's meeting with the lawyers, Busbee learned that Glenn would recommend only something like $800 per bond. Busbee had one last hope for retrieving a bad situation: "In my opinion $500 could be well expended, certainly contingently, in getting the cooperation of Gov. Jarvis, who has already taken ground in favor of an adjustment. He might appear as an *amicus republicae*. He was Governor when the Act of 1879 was enacted and could give valuable testimony concerning the adjustment of that year."

Russell jumped at this proposal from Busbee. But the cynical Republican expressed himself in such language that he apparently scared the horrified Busbee away from the whole idea. "If you can get that old fraud on a $500 contingent," Russell advised, "get him." Possibly Busbee could arrange for Glenn "to invite Jarvis to appear as *amicus patriae*, concealing from Glenn and the committee the fact of our having fixed him." Why not also get Glenn to invite Aycock? "Of course you see that I mean that Aycock, if he appeared as *amicus*," Russell amplified, "would not take [a] fee." But Busbee rightly suggested "that Jarvis would." In fact, Russell declared that "J[arvis] has done it."

Busbee returned the original of Russell's shockingly candid letter, as the ex-governor had requested if a copy were not made and sent to him. But the dignified Raleigh lawyer, who, for all his McKinleyite ideas and votes, regarded himself as a good Democrat, could not accept Russell's aspersion on Thomas J. Jarvis, the Tarheel Redeemer who, after all, ranked second in Democratic hagiography only to Zeb Vance. "I did not mean to reflect on Gov. J.," Busbee scribbled, not

[13] Ricaud to Russell, Feb. 15, 23, 24, 1905; Busbee to Ricaud, Feb. 22, 1905, *ibid.*

once but twice, on the distastefully cynical letter which he promptly returned to Wilmington.[14]

Busbee and Ricaud, unsupported by Jarvis, now tangled again with Governor Glenn and the committee from the legislature. No reporters were allowed to attend the conferences, and no *News and Observer* charges complicated the procedure. Glenn now had all the high cards and knew it. After Ricaud indicated that Schafer regarded par as the absolute, unshakable minimum, Governor Glenn responded with an offer of $250 per bond—in accordance with the 1879 and 1904 Democratic positions—plus 6 per cent interest for thirty-eight years, in accordance with such latter-day realities as the bare possibility of more bond donations to sovereigns. This would mean that North Carolina would pay about $818.18 per bond, or $198,000 for the 242 bonds, and would itself pay the South Dakota judgment.

Ricaud refused to accept this offer not only because of his understanding with Schafer about par but also because the North Carolina legislature expected to adjourn shortly, leaving insufficient time, Ricaud felt, to pass the necessary bill which would be constitutionally required to have three separate readings in each house of the legislature. Governor Glenn assured Ricaud that if he accepted the proposal, the necessary legislation would be passed in an hour, but Ricaud reminded Glenn and the others about the three separate readings on different days. Ricaud, reporting all the details to Russell, concluded that "this kills our chances of getting a settlement at this session," and the only thing left to do was to try to make a deal with South Dakota, Nevada, or Michigan whereby the state accepted the bonds and gave Russell *et al.*, the job of collecting on them on the basis of a percentage which would enable the lawyers to pay over to Schafer as much, or more, than they would realize from what North Carolina offered. Or perhaps Russell had thought up some better scheme?

[14] Busbee to Russell, Feb. 24, 1905; Russell to Busbee, Feb. 25, 1905, *ibid.*

Anyhow, even Busbee now resented "Glenn's insincerity" and went around "cussing" the governor. The two lawyers had written another formal letter to "His Excellency" which said, along with much else, that they pledged their professional word that since the bondholders had made such extreme and repeated concessions, no further reduction was possible and counterpropositions of less than par could not be entertained nor would they be transmitted to Samuel Schafer.[15]

During the meeting with Glenn and the committee, Busbee had understood the feature of the 6 per cent interest for thirty-eight years as a "subterfuge" necessary for sensitive politicians who knew that most of their constituents would never dream of sitting down and laboriously checking on the arithmetic of Governor Glenn and the other Democratic officials. Busbee made a memorandum, and handed it to Attorney-General Gilmer during the meeting, showing that if the offer were made of compound interest at 4 per cent or even interest on the coupons for twenty-seven and a half years, then the bondholders would accept. Either of the Raleigh lawyer's methods of computing the face-saving interest would have meant par for the bonds. But the North Carolina offer stood at almost $200 less than par. Busbee and Ricaud decided to abandon the negotiations.

Not so Daniel Russell. He wanted a settlement. Quickly. When Busbee telephoned him at Wilmington, Russell urged the Raleigh lawyer absolutely not to allow the legislature to adjourn without having the matter settled, even if the offer were less than par and regardless of what Samuel Schafer had said. Busbee thereupon "made a fresh calculation" and concluded that the state's committee would not possibly go beyond a bond issue of $250,000 for both the South Dakota judgment and the 242 bonds. The end of the session loomed closer and closer; one of the vehement legislative members of

[15] Ricaud to Russell, Feb. 28, 1905; Ricaud and Busbee to Glenn, Feb. 28, 1905, *ibid.*

the committee had declared that he would fight any settlement
at par and would use all possible parliamentary tactics to
defeat it. And Russell demanded a settlement "in the strongest possible manner."

Busbee put all the pieces together and calculated a way,
he later reported, whereby the Democrats could actually evade
their platform while appearing to be loyal to it: they could
add to the $250 per bond the interest for twenty-four years and
about four months together with interest on the deferred coupons. This procedure would mean about $892 per bond and a
total bond issue of $250,000 to settle the whole matter.
Busbee's second memorandum turned the trick. The committee made the $892 proposition in writing. Russell, in-
formed by telegram of the offer, wired back: "Assure Committee that we, the lawyers, will compel Schafer to agree.
I know how to do it." Poor Schafer, bombarded with frantic
telegrams from the South, agreed. Only the formalities remained for the public portion of the South Dakota bond
suit to become history as far as North Carolina was concerned.[16]

Governor Glenn promptly reported to the legislature that
he and the legislative committee had easily agreed that the
South Dakota judgment should be left to the chief executive.
The counsel for Schafer had proposed $242,000 or par for
their bonds, this being a substantial reduction from the $395,-
000, then $350,000, and then (in writing) the $302,000
which they had earlier mentioned. When the committee rejected the par proposal and the attorneys refused the committee's counterproposal of almost $200 less than par, the
committee had offered $892 for each of the 242 bonds, a
total of $215,864. Glenn urged the legislature promptly to
enact a law allowing the state treasurer to issue bonds in the

---

[16] Busbee to Russell, two telegrams, March 1, 1905; Russell to Busbee
and Ricaud, telegram, March 1, 1905; Schafer to Russell, telegram, March
1, 1905; and Busbee to Schafer, March 2, 1905, *ibid*. The last citation is to
the long letter where compound interest is so skilfully blended with Tarheel
Democratic politics.

amount of $250,000 to pay off both the judgment and the bondholders. The difference between the $10,000 a year interest on the $250,000 worth of bonds and the $30,940 which the state received in dividends from its railway stock was $20,940; and that sum would easily pay off the new state bonds in less than twenty years, the governor figured.

Glenn declared that in view of the Supreme Court's decision and the "temper" of the Court as revealed therein and since the principal and interest on the Schafer bonds amounted to $663,080, it "would be folly to run the risk of a suit and judgment" for over $660,000. He and the committee had saved North Carolina $447,216. Moreover, the settlement strictly accorded with "the instructions that we have received from the Democratic platform."

Then Governor Glenn explained that in order for the measure to have required readings it would be necessary for the legislature to remain in session until March 6. Since the per diem pay stopped on March 4 Glenn admitted that it would "take both patriotism and personal sacrifice to remain over, but true North Carolinians have never shirked a duty, and therefore with confidence, I appeal to your State love, and ask that you remain and properly ratify the work of your committee." He urged again, in conclusion, that the legislature act quickly so "that this dark cloud that has for years been overhanging and casting a shadow over our beloved State, may at once be swept away."[17]

The legislature complied. In the face of the governor's eloquent leadership and the unanimous sentiment of the newspapers—the *News and Observer* still remained in its quiescent, one could almost say drugged, condition—how could the members have done otherwise? On one of the readings the house passed the urgent measure by a vote of 101 to 1, with a lone Republican from mountainous Swain County having the temerity to differ. On the last, and unpaid, day

[17] Governor Glenn to the General Assembly, March 2, 1905, Governors' Papers.

of the legislature, the Tarheel solons apparently felt little sadness as they performed their constitutionally required chore. After the members had sung several hymns and popular songs, they called on the crowd of visiting ladies in the gallery to sing. The fair ladies obliged with several numbers, finally plunging into the "beautiful sextette chorus from Floradora." The honorable members below (now clearly carried away and quite beside themselves) responded with "Tell me, pretty maiden, are there any more at home like you?" After tremendous applause all around, the gallery girls hit on "Goodby, My Lover, Goodby," the effect of which they immediately spoiled by closing with "Teasing, teasing, I was only teasing you."[18]

Altogether, the Tarheel legislative song-fest, with its flirtatious Gibson girls and its sentimental politicians, furnished a totally incongruous ending for North Carolina's settlement of the South Dakota bond suit. Unfortunately for them, neither Daniel Russell nor any of the many persons associated with him in the affair felt the least bit inclined to sing about anything. They had dreamed great dreams of their lucrative contingent fees. Now, after over four years of herculean labor, especially on Russell's part, sacrifice, and patience, the lawyers' pay promised to be a sad pittance, a thin bone all too well suited for fighting over.

Busbee had a nice gift for understandment. "It is a most discouraging thing to treat for the adjustment of any claim," he informed Samuel Schafer, "when the debtor cannot be sued in any tribunal and when the creditor is utterly powerless to do anything more than to accept whatever the debtor offers, or to wait." The Raleigh attorney now further unburdened himself with the remark to Russell that he anticipated "differences of opinion" in arranging compensation for the various lawyers in the case. He figured that there would be about $43,142 coming to the lawyers for the 224

[18] *Morning Post*, March 2, 3, 7, 1905. Copies of North Carolina House Bill 1841 and Senate Bill 1605 are in the Russell MSS.

bonds controlled by Schafer. Surely, since South Dakota would receive $2,740 for each of her ten bonds for which she paid nothing, she should pay most of the fees of her counsel. But what about a part of Busbee's own fee plus a part of Peckham's and Alfred Russell's being deducted from the $43,142 before the balance was divided on the basis of 20 per cent each to Butler and Pettigrew and 30 per cent each to Ricaud and Russell? Busbee also felt that since he had represented the eight bonds held in Wilmington and the ten by Ricaud in New York, they too should be considered in fixing his fee. Would Russell write his confidential views?[19]

Ricaud, now back in New York, insisted that he had not yet concluded that Russell and Busbee had not "cut us out" of $26,000, "nor am I exulting over the settlement." Ricaud urgently wanted an advance from Schafer for a Mexican business venture but had "not spoken to him on the subject as yet, for the reason that he is extremely sensitive on the N. C. bond question, and the integrity of the Legislature." Schafer received the *News and Observer* regularly, Ricaud reported, and probably would not do anything about an advance until his own money was virtually in hand. It was not, however, the still apprehensive Schafer but Richard F. Pettigrew who threw Ricaud into real fits of worry.

Pettigrew, glossing over the earlier dispute about Russell's alleged letter writing to South Dakota, admitted that he had experienced "some difficulty even in saving" the original donation act. He felt that North Carolina was settling the bonds "in the most contemptible manner," and he, for one, would certainly not have accepted their proposition. When would Russell be in New York? He would certainly come, wouldn't he, when the settlement was made, so that it could be "adjusted to the satisfaction of everyone?" Russell promptly replied that it would be some time, perhaps several months, before the new North Carolina bonds could be engraved and sold. Pettigrew should send an itemized

[19] Busbee to Russell, March 2, 1905, Russell MSS.

statement of his expenses because so many expenses, including Peckham's and Alfred Russell's fees, would have to be
paid—"all before there will be anything to divide."[20]

Pettigrew, fearful about the fees, called on Ricaud and
for the first time showed him the September, 1901, agreement between Russell, Butler, and Pettigrew. Ricaud immediately wrote his old partner in Wilmington that he was
surprised at Russell's leaving him out of the larger plan for
repudiated Southern bonds except for a contingent that de-
pended entirely on Russell's own "generosity and longevity."
He was even more surprised at that part of the contract which
promised Pettigrew that in the event of "recovery" in favor
of the private holders of the second mortgage bonds, Pettigrew should receive, in addition to his 20 per cent of what
was left after expenses, $10,000 "to satisfy the claims of
Robert Stewart and Charles Burke for assisting in securing
a settlement of said bonds." That clause, Ricaud asserted,
"to my mind means a dangerous lawsuit to us." He had never
in his life had a serious dispute with Russell, and "will not
engage in one, but I will die in the last ditch before permitting Stewart or Burke to harvest a feast when we are distressed with a famine. . . ." Ricaud hoped that the word "recovery" might save the situation, but in any event, as against
any exorbitant demands that Pettigrew and Butler might
make, he would contend that his own contract with Schafer
still existed and that the agreement Russell had made in September, 1901, was unauthorized and even unseen by himself until 1905. "As between you and myself," Ricaud loyally
averred to Russell, "I shall not permit any disappointment of
feeling that you would have entered into such an agreement,
without at least permitting me to see it, influence me, and
we will finally adjust, as between us, as always heretofore.
I know no friendship, or sense of friendship, superior to
what I believe governs ours, and by this [I] shall abide."

[20] Ricaud to Russell, March 4, 6, 1905; Pettigrew to Russell, March
6, 1905, and Russell to Pettigrew, March 13, 1905, *ibid.*

Russell, in his turn, quickly mollified his former partner by explaining the terms and circumstances of the 1901 agreement and by his assurances that he would share everything with Ricaud on the same 60-40 per cent basis as that agreed on for the Schafer bonds. Furthermore, as for Pettigrew's claim, Russell swore that, "I will never pay them more than $4000."[21]

Russell's mailbox must have overflowed suddenly in the spring of 1905. Alfred Russell bombarded his friend with eager inquiries. Marion Butler confessed that he felt as unhappy about "the weakness shown by the S. D. parties" as Russell did, but he realized that when the senators from out there opposed the new bill "it was impossible for Burke & Stewart to pass it." And as for Russell's expressing surprise that Senator William M. Stewart of Nevada needed paying, Butler lectured sternly: "You seem to think it a very small matter to get a U. S. Senator to put the Sovereignty of his state behind us. Of course we must settle with him." To have anything left for the lawyers, as Butler saw it, "we must get Schafer to come to our assistance." Samuel Schafer, for his part, wasted few words: "About feeling happy, the boot is on the other leg. The State of N. C. should feel happy."[22]

Russell directed his own fury and frustration at the "South Dakota crowd." He certainly did not agree, he told Butler, that it had been impossible for Burke, Stewart, and Pettigrew to get the purchasing act passed. "On the contrary I believe that if they had acted vigorously and boldly, if they [had] gone to the legislature and addressed it or its committees, if they had openly and manfully appealed to the moral sense of that state and to its material interests, I believe the measure could have been passed and we could have gotten nearly double what we did get. They were so intent on their hide and seek

[21] Ricaud to Russell, March 13, 1905; Russell to Ricaud, March 17, 1905, *ibid.*
[22] Butler to Russell, March 16, 1905; Schafer to Russell, March 20, 1905, *ibid.*

game that I could not get them to scatter literature showing the tremendous strength of our case." Russell, either uninformed or not caring about the political changes which had occurred in South Dakota since 1901, set out to revenge himself on the "South Dakota crowd" by trying to reduce the amount of money which that state would get.

Governor Glenn and Attorney-General Gilmer hoped to compromise with South Dakota for less than the $27,400 ordered by the Supreme Court, to settle in fact for the $17,-000 or so which the hundred shares of railway stock were worth. Glenn and Gilmer visited New York to confer about a compromise with Peckham, whom they believed to be the proper authority to represent South Dakota. Russell sent word to Glenn via J. C. L. Harris that Peckham had no authority in the matter and never would get any from South Dakota. Russell wanted to help Glenn save what he could for North Carolina but could see only one way to do it, "and that is for him to let the stock go to sale and bid on it." Russell believed that "the South Dakota crowd are wanting in legal knowledge and brains sufficient to take proceedings to collect a deficiency judgment." Glenn would not, of course, want the stock to be sold because of the notoriety, but "he could have it announced that all the bonds had been settled and that the sale was a matter of form." Glenn did not feel inclined to try Russell's slippery game, and South Dakota's constitution forbade any compromise of such a claim of the state's. North Carolina finally paid South Dakota the full amount of the judgment, $27,400. Russell's revengeful plan came to nothing, but his own dealings with "the South Dakota crowd" were by no means ended. Pettigrew had a lawsuit on his mind.[23]

[23] Russell to Butler, March 20, 1905; Russell to Harris, March 17, 1905; and Harris to Russell, March 21, 1905; *ibid.* See *Morning Post,* April 2, 1905, for Attorney-General Gilmer's last-minute arrival in Washington to settle the judgment. Chief Justice Fuller directed the North Carolina official to the home of Justice Brewer, who had written the opinion, and Brewer assured Gilmer that it would be entirely satisfactory to the Court for him to deposit North Carolina's check with the clerk of the Court

Wheeler Peckham by this time felt thoroughly confused about the bond developments. "I only know," he wrote Russell, "that thus far I have not only not received any compensation for services, but am quite a little out of pocket for disbursements." His ideas of compensation for himself were "not extravagant," for his great interest in the case "was on the point of the principle involved." Still, it was not saying too much that "the services I rendered contributed very decidedly to the result attained." The distinguished New York lawyer, who was now ill, relied on the two Russells to see that he received "reasonable compensation."[24]

As the day for North Carolina's payment to Schafer neared, quite a few legal minds scattered over America, from Wilmington to Pierre, turned, like aroused radar pieces, toward New York and Russell's probable arrival there. Ricaud reminded his old associate of the many matters that would have to be settled. He fully realized that "a controversy with Pettigrew here, would be infinitely more dangerous and annoying, than in N. C., but believe the settlement can be made, the funds received and your return to N. C. accomplished, before they are any wiser. . . ." Russell agreed and cautioned Ricaud not to let anybody know anything about the settlement, when it came, and to use the telegraph to inform him. Russell had arranged to be informed from Raleigh when Treasurer Ben Lacy mailed the check north and would telegraph Ricaud to get him a room. "Don't care where it is nor how disreputable it is," Russell instructed, "provided it is clean and has a good bed." He could not stop at his usual Fifth Avenue hotel "for obvious" (Pettigrew) reasons.

---

with the understanding that it should not be turned over to South Dakota until the ten bonds were surrendered. The *Post* correspondent reported also that the Federal marshal and other officials were pleased and relieved that no foreclosure proceedings would be needed.

[24] Russell to Peckham, March 16, 1905, urging him to be careful not to intimate to Glenn and Gilmer that Peckham had any connection with the individual bondholders and was to be paid by them; Peckham to Russell, March 21, 1905, Russell MSS.

"Neither will you tell it that I am coming unless your mouth gets away with your head."[25]

The $250,000 worth of North Carolina 4 per cent bonds sold above par, for 106.176, thereby relieving the fears of some Tarheels who had felt that the South Dakota bond affair might impair North Carolina's credit. Ben Lacy informed Russell in mid-May that if the bondholders would pay the expenses of Governor Glenn and himself they would go up on May 21 to pay for the bonds on the next day. If the bondholders refused to pay the North Carolina governor's and treasurer's expenses, payment would be made in Raleigh on May 17. Lacy preferred Raleigh himself; it was impossible for Glenn to go to New York before May 21 and "if I go, he desires to go also." Russell telegraphed Schafer that he had better pay for Glenn's jaunt unless, as Russell cracked, the financier had decided to keep his bonds "30 years longer as an investment." When Schafer agreed to pay, Russell requested Busbee, who just thought he would go to New York too, to ask Glenn and Lacy not to tell the newspapers anything about their New York trip until the moment they left Raleigh. "I will be there," Russell explained, "but I hope to get about in N. Y. without being bothered by certain hungry citizens."

Well might Russell be careful, for Ricaud warned that Pettigrew and Butler were "keenly on the scent" and would probably be haunting Schafer's office. As if his troubles were not already mountainous enough, Ricaud swore that Schafer had grown "plumb crazy." He had asked Ricaud if the secret agreement between Schafer Brothers and Ricaud-Russell did not provide that no attorneys' fees were to be paid on his 112 bonds. Ricaud told him that if he could produce such a memorandum Schafer "could have all my fees." "We have trouble ahead and plenty of it," Ricaud warned, and Russell had better head north at once. Meantime, Marion Butler

[25] Ricaud to Russell, April 25, 1905; Russell to Ricaud, April 28, May 6, 1905, *ibid.*

had delayed a trip to the West in order to confer in person with his old Fusion partner. "When are you coming here?" Butler wanted to know. Why did not Russell plan to stop at Butler's hotel on Fifth Avenue? But Ricaud, himself nervous and adequately cautioned by the lawsuit-wary Russell, met the former governor in New Jersey to hide him away, after preliminary matters had been settled, to await the exactly right moment for the hurried dash across the Hudson and down to Wall Street.[26]

The Raleigh papers reported in late May, 1905, that the secrecy surrounding the real purpose of Glenn's and Lacy's trip to New York had been deliberate. Former Governor Russell and other attorneys for Schafer Brothers had wished to "safeguard against the possibility of any legal interference with the transaction." There had been a report that some holders of the repudiated special tax bonds might try to get an injunction or in some way hold up North Carolina's payment to Schafer Brothers. Samuel Schafer had taken "a great fancy to Governor Glenn and made the party's visit very pleasant." Schafer seemed greatly relieved at having the matter finally disposed of and during the formalities of the settlement remarked that his brother, Simon, in his will, "which was spoken into a phonograph, gave as a last request never to compromise those bonds." But they had been, at long last, compromised and, as the *News and Observer* put it, the "Schafer bonds have at last come home to roost for once and all."[27] Josephus Daniels did not say, only because he did not know, that the bond chickens really had not all safely roosted. Pettigrew threatened to become a veritable Western fighting cock.

The New York encounters between Russell and his associates must have been in great contrast to the sentimental, smiling ceremony in which Samuel Schafer and the North

[26] *Morning Post*, May 11, 1905. Lacy to Russell, May 13, 1905; Russell to Ricaud, May 13, 1905; Russell to Busbee, May 14, 1905; Ricaud to Russell, May 15, 1905; and Butler to Russell, May 23, 1905, Russell MSS.
[27] *Morning Post*, May 25, 27, 1905; *News and Observer*, May 28, 1905.

Carolina officials participated. Russell's stealthy sally across the Hudson and down into Wall Street did not escape the vigilant watch of Pettigrew. There were quarrels, not only about the September, 1901, agreement but also about the theretofore secret agreement between Schafer and Russell-Ricaud whereby the latter agreed to remit 3⅓ per cent of the lawyers' total share as a commission or "special consideration" for Schafer Brothers; in other words, Pettigrew, and presumably Butler, fought back strongly but in vain when they learned that the whole company of lawyers were to receive only 30 per cent, rather than 33⅓ per cent of the excess above $250 collected on each of the 224 Schafer bonds.

Russell had long ago explained to Alfred Russell about the many persons, not all of them lawyers, who had claims on any profits that might be won from the bond suit. The "division is long," Russell had written, and he never spoke more truly. There are several undated memoranda in Russell's papers, one on New York hotel stationery and one on Washington's "Ebbitt House" paper as well as one or two on plain sheets; clearly it was a fitting matter for a battery of electronic computers, if there had been such machines then, and a whole tribunal of Olympian judges. Russell formally and officially received from Schafer Brothers a check for $47,936; but after the secret 'kickback' of $4,793.60 and expenses totaling $2,320.81 were paid to Schafer, only $40,-821.59 remained to be divided. Considering the number and the size of the appetites involved, there really were not many fishes and loaves to go around.

Just before Russell left New York in late May, 1905, he wrote to Butler that it was quite plain that Butler and Pettigrew were on one side with Ricaud and Russell on the other as to the distribution of the fund. After thinking it over, Russell had concluded that there was nothing to be gained by his remaining in New York for arguments over a matter about which an agreement was "obviously impossible." Besides, Pettigrew acted like a man "contemplating a lawsuit" and Russell proposed to face any litigation, if it came, in North Carolina. "I shall not consent to pay any $10,000 to Senator Pettigrew for Messrs. Burke and Stewart," Russell declared flatly. "I deny that I contracted to pay them on the facts and circumstances of the case as they have resulted." Stewart, who received 10 per cent of the Dakota judgment, or $2,740, as his fee, had already received "more than he earned," and Burke should be satisfied with $1,000. Russell felt strongly that Alfred Russell and Peckham should each have $5,000 but if Butler believed, as he had stated, that he could induce Peckham to accept only $2,000 that "would materially increase the margin for concessions." Busbee had asked for $5,000 and there were a large number of smaller obligations which Russell had incurred in North Carolina. "I shall be very sorry to have any misunderstanding with you," Russell declared to Marion Butler, "and I hope that on further reflection our differences may be reconciled."[28]

No open, angry break did occur between the two former Fusion chieftains. Russell must have either handed the above letter to Butler or perhaps told him the substance of it as the two men rode the train to Washington, for on the same day that Russell wrote the New York letter the two signed a written agreement in Butler's Washington law office. They had apparently conferred in the Ebbitt House, where Russell habitually stayed when in the capital, and decided that the available $40,821.59 should be divided approximately as follows: $15,132.93 for Russell and Ricaud together; $5,-044.31 each for Butler and Pettigrew; $5,000 each for Peckham and Alfred Russell; $2,500 for Busbee; $1,000 for Congressman Burke; $500 for Senator Stewart of Nevada (for preparing usable but unused "sovereignty"); and the remaining $1,600 for miscellaneous payments, especially to the various North Carolinians such as J. C. L. Harris, Marshall D. Haywood, W. H. Worth, and Baylus Cade who had helped Russell in one way or another in the long legal struggle.

[28] Russell to Butler, May 27, 1905, Russell MSS.

After coming to their informal agreement, Butler and Russell may have gone to the former's law office. At any rate, there is a formal, signed document in the Russell papers, dated Washington, May 27, 1905, wherein Butler states that Russell had paid $12,088.62 in full settlement of all claims of Pettigrew, Butler, Burke, Stewart of Pierre, and former Senator Stewart of Nevada. Attached telegrams from Pettigrew and Burke authorized Butler to act for them. But Pettigrew certainly did not intend to let the matter rest at that.

Enclosing a paper designed to dissolve the partnership agreement of September, 1901, Pettigrew demanded that Russell sign and return same. "Of course the partnership heretofore existing can no longer exist," the South Dakotan declared, "you having violated the provisions of that contract in such a manner as to make it impossible for me to associate with you in any business transaction whatever. The reasons which induced me to enter into that agreement with you were based upon the supposition that you were financially and morally competent to associate with honest men; but subsequent developments have shown that you are far more bankrupt in character and integrity than you are financially, and unless I can get the dissolution of the partnership by your signing the enclosed paper, I shall commence an action against you. . . ."

The former Republican governor of North Carolina was not one for turning the other cheek: "Sir: To insult me was evidently the only purpose of your letter, unless you were so drunk and so stupid as to be in a condition of maudlin imbecility. I never had any partnership with you. Among, perhaps, many misfortunes, I at least have escaped the disgrace of that. The paper you refer to did not constitute a partnership and would not be so regarded by any intelligent layman or by any lawyer except one who does not know enough law to distinguish a legal partnership from a So. Dakota hay stack. You must not seek to achieve some degree of respectability by claiming to have been a partner of mine."

After this blast at the Silver Republican-turned-Democrat, the proud old Tarheel Whig-Republican went on to insist that Pettigrew's "malevolence" sprang from his "failure to put up a rascally job" on Russell. Pettigrew had thought to "steal" $10,000 "under the fraudulent pretense that it was for certain alleged beneficiaries." The agreement had contemplated a full recovery on the bonds, Russell argued, but there had been no such recovery because by Pettigrew's "mismanagement and stupidity and imbecility and cowardice the case was wrecked and I was driven to accept a disgusting compromise." After various other hits at the South Dakotan, Russell concluded: "You say that you will commence a suit against me. . . . Come on and try it."[29]

Pettigrew never took legal action against Russell, obviously because of the unwanted publicity, but he was not the only person who disagreed sharply with the manner in which Russell divided the "take." As soon as he returned to Wilmington, Russell wrote to Peckham and Alfred Russell explaining about his trouble with "the South Dakota crowd" and enclosing checks for $3,000 with a promise of more to come when it became certain that certain claimants could not "swamp the fund." Russell thought Peckham and Alfred Russell would "admit that I ought to have more than the rest for manifold reasons." Peckham, sick at home and scratching out his reply in longhand, responded that he did not know what Alfred Russell admitted but "I don't admit anything of the kind." Peckham insisted that he should have "at least ten thousand dollars," and "I don't care how the rest is divided." Senator Pettigrew himself had stated in the office of Peckham, Miller, and King that the senior member of the firm would receive $10,000 as his fee from the bond case. "If you think this to be a fair deal I do not," Peckham concluded. "Without me in the case it was dead sure lost & you

[29] Pettigrew to Russell, June 10, 1905; Russell to Pettigrew, June 16, 1905, *ibid.* See also Pettigrew to Russell, June 28, 1905, where the feud continues and Pettigrew states that only Marion Butler's persuasion kept him from taking legal action in New York against Russell.

coolly send me this nominal sum & say you hope to send me more. I hope so too & I think I am entitled to it."[30]

Russell did send more, but certainly not more than the $5,000 which he, after all, had staunchly insisted on as a minimum sum for both Peckham and Alfred Russell. Pettigrew and Butler had wanted to allot them much less than that, with Russell tackling the job of persuading Samuel Schafer to put up extra money to pay Alfred Russell and Peckham. Russell and Ricaud knew from long experience that the prospect of Schafer's volunteering extra sums for hungry lawyers was not bright. Russell insisted that his share of the fee from the Schafer bonds amounted only to about $7,000 and that even then there were unsettled claims, some of them of an "exceedingly confidential and secret character," which might reduce his own profit. What he did not discuss with his angry fellow lawyers was the fact that he either owned outright, or had a large interest in, eight of the second mortgage bonds, the eight which had afforded "the enemy" such a field day in their attack on Russell's conduct as governor. Moreover, Ricaud either owned, or had a large interest in, ten of the bonds, and he and Russell were supposed to divide everything on a 60-40 basis. Assuming that Russell and Ricaud paid as little as, say, $300 per bond for the eighteen on which they too received $892 per bond when North Carolina settled, then Russell's personal return from the eighteen bonds may have amounted to something in the neighborhood of $5,000, after paying interest on the money borrowed to buy the bonds. That sum added to the $7,000 he claimed to have received from the Schafer bonds meant that Russell's total income from his "scheme" may have come to about $12,000. It was a good bit of money for the planter-politician whose governorship had financially ruined him and whose annual rice crop called for more and more red ink each year. Russell had frankly stated his claims

[30] Russell to Peckham, Alfred Russell, and Busbee, May 29, 1905; Peckham to Russell, June 2, 1905, *ibid.*

for "more than the rest for manifold reasons." He boldly and bossily handled the disbursement so that he received more. He had, in truth, invested more—in ideas, time, and brain-numbing labor—than any two others combined. And he took no chances on not getting what he judged that he deserved.

While they too hoped that additional cash would come their way, Busbee, J. C. L. Harris, Alfred Russell, and others understood Russell's dilemma in dividing a sum that had turned out to be so much smaller than any had dreamed. But Russell's most satisfying personal relationship now proved to be with none other than Samuel Schafer. Russell admitted to the financier that the compromise with North Carolina had not been for the large amount they had planned and would have gotten if South Dakota had stayed in line; still they had "nevertheless succeeded in making something out of nothing" when North Carolina paid almost $140,000 more than the $60,000 which she had offered for so long. Russell graciously thanked Schafer for his "excellent management" of the matter and expressed the hope that the other New York bondholders realized how instrumental Schafer had been in procuring benefits to them. "We have had sharp differences in the course of this business drama," Russell ventured, "but I am pleased that the conclusion is so satisfactory and pleasant to both of us and that the curtain falls upon us greeting each other as friends." So much for the past. For the future: "Don't you feel like taking a shy now at other repudiated state bonds? I think you said that you had some of them. . . ." Russell admitted his interest in North American Trust Company's pool but explained that he was "at liberty to make a bargain . . . and I could take care of you."

Schafer replied to Russell by declaring that he too felt pleased that "matters have so shaped themselves that we may greet each other as friends. . . ." But the New Yorker did not, at present, care to take up the matter of other Southern bonds because "this last matter has bothered me more than you know of, and I think a little rest is due me."[31]

Why Russell did not feel that a "little rest" was also due him is one of the mysteries in the old rascal's complex make-up. But the North Carolina settlement had made him the "Southern man of the hour" in the repudiated-bond field. His hopes were destined to flare again, but briefly, before sickness and then death claimed him, leaving others to dream of vast fortunes to be made among the "hundred millions" and to cope with the reverberating echoes of the South Dakota bond suit.

[*chapter nine*]

REVERBERATING ECHOES OF THE SOUTH DAKOTA BOND AFFAIR

JUST AS the Supreme Court's decision in early 1904 had sparked a flurry of interest in all repudiated Southern bonds, the North Carolina legislature's final settlement with Schafer Brothers in 1905 made financial news and set off a revival of interest in the old securities that would last for many years. Russell himself, having deferred the matter of the "hundred millions" after the South Dakota case began to consume most of his attention and energy, basked in the fleeting fame which he had acquired in certain Wall Street circles. A scant three days after the North Carolina legislature had settled the bond matter and adjourned, he renewed his efforts in the vast field of all repudiated Southern bonds.

Russell reminded Henry Clews that the financier had

[31] Russell to Schafer, June 23, 1905; Schafer to Russell, June 24, 1905, *ibid.*

promised, several years earlier, to use his influence to have the former Tarheel governor retained for the holders of repudiated Georgia bonds if the South Dakota suit succeeded. "I have succeeded," Russell declared. The Supreme Court had sustained his "unpatented invention," and the matter had concluded with North Carolina's settling with the private bondholders at about 90 per cent of the principal of the bonds. "It is now in order for me to follow the fate of other inventors," Russell complained, "by looking serenely from icy shores, at other lawyers profiting by my discoveries and endeavors." But, the far-from-serene lawyer continued, "I want to say with becoming modesty, that not one of them in all this land knows as much about this bond question as I do and not one of them is as well equipped for handling it." Russell believed that the Georgia bonds had merit, that their repudiation represented "robbery," and that something could certainly be accomplished with them if Clews would do his part and arrange to pay Russell the necessary retainer plus a contingent fee.[1]

Ricaud, still serving as Russell's Wall Street contact man, went after Clews. The bond dealer first claimed that nothing could be done because of the illness of Russell Sage, the millionaire railroad leader and financier, who, with other bondholders, had held annual meetings with Clews for years about the repudiated Georgia securities. Ricaud kept trying. But Henry Clews remained as elusive as he had been four or so years earlier, and Ricaud finally gave up with the disgusted conclusion that Henry Clews was nothing but an "old hypocrite" hiding behind "rotten subterfuge."[2]

Despite the renewed hope given to the holders of all repudiated bonds by the outcome of the South Dakota case, the subsequent efforts were doomed to failure. For one thing, the special nature of the second mortgage bonds, with their specific lien on valuable state property, put them in a class

[1] Russell to Henry Clews, March 9, 1905, Russell MSS.
[2] Ricaud to Russell, April 6, 7, 11, 1905, *ibid.*

apart from the "hundred millions." But aside from that factor, which many poorly informed persons at the time only
dimly perceived, if at all, another reason why the lawyers and
bondholders repeatedly failed with the "Carpetbag" bonds
was the very vastness of the field and the rivalry of many
competing groups and interests. Russell's task with the second mortgage bonds, he now came to understand, had been
immensely simplified by the fact that he had dealt only with
Schafer Brothers on Wall Street; no competing financial
house had held any of the bonds.

In addition to the strategic yet evasive Henry Clews, at
least one other committee, and perhaps others, had organized
to compete in Southern bonds with the Coler Company—
North American Trust Company committee which Butler,
Pettigrew, and Russell had helped to set up in 1901. John
G. Carlisle, the lawyer whom North Carolina had retained
in her futile effort to get a second rehearing of the South
Dakota case, headed the rival committee. It had Edward
L. Andrews as counsel and another New York trust company
as the depository for the bonds. Russell, the "man of the hour"
in Southern bonds, also approached Carlisle, via Ricaud,
about the possibility of becoming associated with the Carlisle group; but here too Russell found himself left on the
"icy shores" to contemplate other lawyers profiting from his
"unpatented invention."

The Carlisle-Andrews committee in late March and early
April, 1905, went on a well-publicized offensive. Large advertisements in the *New York Times,* the *Tribune,* and other
metropolitan papers proclaimed the committee's proposed
collection of "North Carolina Special Tax Bonds." The committee magnanimously intended to surrender all claims for
accumulated interest and "to accept a Settlement Bond for
the principal, to carry two Per Cent. (2%) until 1910,"
when all of North Carolina's debt would probably be funded
into bonds paying 3 per cent, "the rate paid by other Southern States of restored credit." The newspaper advertisements

and circulars concluded with the assertion that the South
Dakota suit had enabled bondholders "to subject North Carolina to heavy burdens by donations of any proportion of the
Bonds to such States," but the Southern state might avoid
such a result by settling with the present holders "upon a
lower basis than the amount of the prospective donations."[3]

This threat from a rival quarter inspired Marion Butler
to take a rash step which he shortly afterward, and for the
remainder of his life, deeply regretted. Butler had become
zealous about the "hundred millions" after North Carolina
settled; in fact, he claimed to be much disappointed that Governor Glenn had not let the state's stock be sold, so that the
Supreme Court could have gone after the deficiency judgment.
"It would have blazed clearly the way for the collection of
all bonds not secured by mortgage," Butler believed. When
Russell wanted "all the learning obtainable" from the State
Department in Washington about the relatively new practice
whereby sovereign nations took up the property claims of
their private citizens against other and usually smaller nations, Butler ran the necessary errands and dispatched the
desired information. The former Populist, like Russell himself, hoped for and diligently worked towards some harmonizing of interest among Henry Clews and the two rival bond
committees. When the Carlisle-Andrews group made its public splash, however, Butler felt that he should act with the
boldness and celerity which Daniel Russell had often urged.[4]

Immediately upon seeing the Carlisle committee's effort
to "reap the reward" of the Russell-Butler group's effort and
expenditures, Butler dashed up to New York from his Washington office. After conferring with Peckham, who was sick
in bed, and with one or two others, Butler, together with representatives from Coler and Company and the North Amer-

[3] Carlisle-Andrews committee's circular, March 29, 1905, *ibid.* The
Morning Post, April 8, 1905, and *News and Observer,* April 19, 1905, reprinted and commented on the advertisements in the New York papers.
[4] Butler to Russell, April 2, 4, 5, 8, 1905; Butler to Russell, April 2,
1905, Russell MSS.

ican Trust Company, prepared a counter-advertisement and circular. This document, destined to become the most famous advertisement in North Carolina's recent political history, bore the names of Russell, Butler, Pettigrew, and Coler and Company and proudly announced that this same committee had pooled the second mortgage bonds and originated the successful South Dakota suit. The committee now proclaimed its readiness to proceed "with the collection of all other repudiated bonds of every class, of each State." It had no connection with any other bond committee, and, moreover, it felt certain "that it alone is now in a position to avail itself of the benefits of the above-mentioned decision." Any who desired to enforce collection of their Southern bonds would bring them to the North American Trust Company and receive receipts and a contractual agreement.[5]

Russell had misgivings about the signed notice as soon as he saw it and admitted frankly to Butler that he would have advised against putting his own and Butler's names to it. It would mean more bitter attacks on the two Tarheel Republicans, create "an ugly stir" about special tax bonds, and since North Carolina had not yet actually laid down the cash for the Schafer settlement, Russell felt that it would have been more prudent to avoid doing anything to make Glenn and his fellow Democrats "feel ugly to us." Russell alleged that his own plan all along had been to "let N. C. alone for a while" and to concentrate on bonds of Georgia, Mississippi, and Louisiana. But since Butler had issued the advertisement in good faith, he would go along but thought it best for him promptly to issue a clarifying statement to the North Carolina newspapers.

Russell's statement, after establishing the completely separate identity of the Carlisle committee, explained that he, Butler, and the others associated with them were mostly interested in bonds from states other than North Carolina.

[5] Butler to Russell, April 28, 1905; circular dated April 26, 1905, *ibid.* The *News and Observer,* April 30, 1905, reprints the advertisement from the New York *Evening Post.* See also New York *Sun,* April 28, 1905.

"So far as I am concerned," the former governor publicly explained, "I shall not seek to enforce against North Carolina any bonds that were not honestly issued, nor will I attempt to collect from the State the proceeds of bonds that were fraudulently disposed of by State or Railroad officials, except to the extent of such amounts as went into the treasuries of the State or of the railroad companies, and were used for the benefit of the State in railroad construction, or other use." Russell added that he felt sure that he spoke also for ex-Senator Butler.

Butler had suggested by letter and telegram that Russell not issue any statement, because it was "time enough to cross a bridge when you get to it." The North Carolina papers had not noticed his advertisement, Butler mistakenly argued, and "now they will not, and I will have the next advertisement changed so that our names will not appear." Russell's interview would only be "advertising just what you want to suppress at present." Nevertheless, when Russell's statement appeared in the newspapers, Butler too decided that he would go along and issue his own statement endorsing what Russell had said.[6]

Butler, who was always pictured by his political enemies as the "sly fox of Sampson County," proved less astute and farsighted than Russell in the matter of affixing their names to the bond advertisement. Just as Russell had predicted, Tarheel Democrats did indeed again "get ugly" towards the two bond-collecting Republicans. Nothing prevented Governor Glenn from settling with Schafer Brothers, but the *News and Observer* resumed the old attacks on the two former Fusionists and their bond plans. Shaking off the unnatural calm which had suddenly and temporarily descended on him and his paper in February, 1905, Josephus Daniels in May of the same year restored his war-paint. The *News and Observer*

[6] Russell to Butler, April 30, 1905; Butler to Russell, May 1, 5, 1905; undated memorandum of Russell's statement with Butler's notations, Russell MSS. *Morning Post,* May 2, 1905, and *News and Observer,* May 3, 1905.

declared, repeatedly and with dramatic variations on the theme, that the Butler-Russell statements about not wanting to enforce fraudulently issued North Carolina bonds came from "two traitors" and "two ignominious enemies to the State that paid them money to look after its interest while they were conspiring to injure it." Butler's and Russell's gang were probably secretly in partnership with the Carlisle committee, but anyhow the tender solicitude of Butler and Russell for their native state equaled exactly "the love the snake has for the frog he is preparing to swallow." Since the *News and Observer* soon revived its charges about the Southern Railway conspiracy and the "real men" who were "HIGHER UP" behind Butler and Russell, the attacks which Russell had predicted became even angrier than he had expected.[7]

Aside from the revival of the *News and Observer*'s attacks, many Southern Democrats, especially in North Carolina, were extremely nervous and wary about repudiated bonds by 1905. The matter had been much agitated for several decades but never more so than in the months after the Supreme Court decision and the final settlement resulting from that decision. New Hampshire had reportedly approached South Carolina about the payment of $30,000 worth of repudiated bonds which had been willed to the New England state for educational purposes. The Carlisle committee had fastened a cold and beady eye exclusively on North Carolina's famous special tax bonds; it had publicly presented an elaborate argument about North Carolina's "rapid and substantial development" in the industrial field, her "almost phenomenal" progress even since 1900, and her exceptional situation with respect to state-owned railway stock. That stock, because it was not "dedicated to public uses," was presumably easily within the reach of the United States Supreme Court. The Carlisle committee capped the climax early in June, 1905, by the highly publicized announcement that the New York legislature had just enacted a law whereby that state undertook to accept

[7] *News and Observer,* May 3, 4, 7, 1905.

donations of defaulted obligations of other states in order to enforce them by New York's sovereign authority.

Governor Glenn by now knew exactly how to proceed. He had finally learned the proper defensive technique in his public counterblasts directed at South Dakota. Glenn himself on several occasions, as well as his successors, had to repeat the procedure in order to stave off the acceptance by other states of North Carolina's repudiated bonds. This technique of Governor Glenn's, probably more than anything else, contributed to the failure of the many efforts to cash in on the "hundred millions." The Southern bond question, quite aside from the intrinsic strength or weakness of the Southern states' arguments, was simply too controversial and complicated for Northern or Western states to become involved with when the publicity klieg lights had been turned on. Russell's success in South Dakota proved the point, for his troubles began in the Western state in direct proportion to the degree of publicity and popular awareness there about the bond question. It should be remembered also that the Southern Democratic version of Reconstruction enjoyed a virtually unrivaled hold over the entire nation's mind in the early years of the twentieth century. This had disastrous implications for Russell's more unusual Whig-Republican view of the matter.

Governor Glenn, upon learning of the Carlisle committee's threat to work through New York state, addressed a ringing appeal to New York's Governor Frank W. Higgins. After giving the "true character" of the special tax bonds and explaining why North Carolina had enacted a constitutional prohibition against their payment, Glenn requested the New York governor "to treat me and my state as I would you and yours under similar conditions, and consult me before allowing this syndicate to induce you to take these bonds."[8]

[8] Glenn to Governor Higgins, July 3, 1905, Governors' Papers; Carlisle committee's circular of June 5, 1905, and copy of New York's donation act (Chapter 388 of 1905 laws) in Russell MSS. When a Raleigh banker addressed the New York State Bankers' Association on the subject of

Other North Carolinians helped Glenn succeed in warning New York officials against the Carlisle committee. Samuel A. Ashe, former editor of the *News and Observer* and faithful Democratic writer and historian, addressed an indignant, lengthy public letter to Carlisle giving the history of the special tax bonds. The *Morning Post* declared that the efforts of "slick artists" to scare a bond compromise out of North Carolina on the grounds that the state was now able to pay compared with an individual's opening a damage suit merely because some other person had the ability to pay. "That condition is the illegitimate progeny of populism in this and other states," the conservative Democratic paper insisted, "and it has been reared, clothed and educated by some of our so-called Democratic newspapers." There had to be an end to all such "slimy and ill-smelling relics."[9]

Glenn's next bond-fighting mission came in 1906 when the Carlisle-Andrews group approached Michigan about a possible bond donation. This had come about in an amusing way. Alfred Russell, despite his and Governor Russell's illnesses in the late summer of 1905, still hoped that "a handsome thing" could be made out of the repudiated bonds. With their own North American Trust Company committee paralyzed by the Russell-Pettigrew feud, among other factors, Alfred Russell bemoaned the fact that the Carlisle-Andrews committee made all the headlines. In November, 1905, a new development came when the Carlisle committee addressed a letter to President Roosevelt, who showed great interest in having the Latin-American nations pay their debts, and requested that the President act as intermediary with the South-

repudiated bonds and New York's recent law, an Albany banker wrote the Tarheel speaker the following note: "I myself had the [donation] bill drawn and secured its passage through the legislature. My bank holds some warrants on the treasurer of Colorado, which were bought at par, and we are having trouble in collecting them. Hence we had the law you cited enacted in order to facilitate the collection of these warrants and without any reference whatever to southern bonds." *Morning Post,* July 22, 1905.

[9] *Morning Post,* June 22, July 1, 2, 25, 1905. Ashe also published his history of the special tax bonds in the *New York Financier,* July 24, 1905.

ern states before the committee donated its North Carolina special tax bonds to Venezuela. Daniel Russell sneered at this application to one whom he called the "great National and International Meddler at Washington" but admitted that the idea was "not bad as an excuse for Roosevelt to gratify his passions for meddling." Why did not Alfred Russell write E. L. Andrews emphasizing Daniel Russell's unique familiarity with the subject and his role in the South Dakota suit? Marion Butler had become "skittish about being connected with a suit against North Carolina," because he wanted to get back into politics and feared "the odium resulting from such a suit." But Alfred Russell could surely explain to Andrews and Carlisle that the two Russells were "not squeamish about an action against North Carolina any more than any other State."[10]

Alfred Russell, reanimated by the prospect of his and his Wilmington friend's making *"each* out of this business a sum the annual interest of which at 5% would give a living income," acted with dispatch. Why shouldn't he write to Andrews explaining that there was no need even of trying to work through Venezuela because Michigan had a donation law exactly like South Dakota's and Alfred Russell "would run the thing here"? After receiving Daniel Russell's proposed draft of the letter to Andrews and exchanging ideas back and forth between Detroit and Wilmington, Alfred Russell sent off the overture to the Carlisle group, enclosing a copy of Michigan's donation act. He received a prompt, courteous, and totally noncommittal reply from E. L. Andrews. Then no further word came. The two Russells had apparently failed to interest the Carlisle-Andrews group either in themselves or in the Michigan possibilities.[11]

[10] Alfred Russell to Russell, Nov. 2, 4, 9, 11, 17, 1905; Russell to Alfred Russell, Nov. 7, 28, 1904, Russell MSS. For the Carlisle committee's Venezuela gambit, see the *Morning Post,* Nov. 4, 1905; *New York Times,* Nov. 1; and *Detroit Journal,* Oct. 31, 1905.

[11] Alfred Russell to Russell, Nov. 22, 1905; E. L. Andrews to Alfred Russell, Nov. 21, 1905, Russell MSS.

Alfred Russell exploded with anger when he learned in March, 1906, that Andrews had made overtures to Michigan but without seeking any help at all from either of the Russells. The bond committee asked Michigan's Governor Frederick M. Warner to whom they could deliver the North Carolina bonds which they proposed to donate. Governor Warner immediately requested Governor Glenn to furnish information about the bonds, so that the Michigan chief executive could reply to the New Yorker's letter. Governor Glenn went through his well-rehearsed recital. When Governor Warner then declined to involve Michigan in litigation with another state, Alfred Russell gleefully reported to Wilmington: "But you will see, by the enclosed clipping, that Brother Andrews has been doing something; viz., making a precious fool of himself by coming into my own State and going behind my back! He thought he could 'paddle his own canoe' but he quickly found he could not. . . . He evidently does not know anything about human nature or how to manage men." Could not Daniel Russell "put on paper the hearty laugh in which you will indulge?"[12]

It was just as well that the two Russells got at least one good laugh out of the activities of the Wall Street group who would not take them in. Daniel Russell made one last elaborate appeal to John G. Carlisle himself; but even Russell's pleasure in recalling his and Carlisle's association in the United States House of Representatives and "our controversies when you represented the Southern Railway and I the people of North Carolina as their Governor," failed to win Russell a place in the operations of the active committee. As for Alfred Russell, death came suddenly on May 8, 1906.

[12] Committee of North Carolina Bondholders to Governor Warner, March 10, 1906; Warner to Glenn, March 16, 1906; and Glenn to Warner, March 20, 1906, Governors' Letterbook. Alfred Russell to Russell, March 24, 1906, Russell MSS. The clipping from a Detroit paper of March 26, 1906, mentions at the end of its account that the former state senator who was said to have introduced the 1901 donation act remembered very little about it and said that if he did introduce the measure, it was by request and "must have been drafted before he had it in charge."

Wheeler Peckham had died, unreconciled to the size of his fee in the South Dakota suit, on September 27, 1905. Daniel Russell's own recurring illnesses and repeated trips to the Johns Hopkins hospital suggested to him that his days were numbered.

Russell cheered himself in his last days by reflecting on the legal coup he had masterminded in the South Dakota suit—and the dismay he had caused North Carolina Democrats. In addition to his own candidly immodest statements, the fact that he so carefully saved every scrap of paper about the bonds, including many letters that more timid souls would have burned, shows his pride in the matter. He never seemed to understand the political changes which had occurred in such states as South Dakota and Michigan and quite failed to appreciate the weaknesses in his own ardent argument in defense of many (not all) repudiated bonds; therefore it annoyed him no end when even South Dakota gave every indication that she might repent and make amends for the recent lawsuit against North Carolina.

Governor Samuel H. Elrod of South Dakota, in his last message to the legislature in January, 1907, declared that he would "rather have South Dakota right, fair and just in all her transactions with her sister states than to have millions of tainted money in her treasury." Elrod mentioned that he had refused an offer of more North Carolina bonds (the Carlisle committee literally made the rounds seeking a sovereign donee) only the year before, 1906, on the ground that acceptance of such bonds for purposes of interstate litigation would be "against public policy and good conscience." The retiring governor then urged the legislature to repeal the donation act under which the first bonds had been accepted, and to refund every penny of money which he believed that South Dakota had improperly secured.[13]

South Dakota's most important Republican newspaper, the Sioux Falls *Argus-Leader,* stoutly endorsed Elrod's sug-

[13] Sioux Falls *Daily Argus-Leader,* Jan. 8, 1907.

gestion. The paper argued that the "plain people of the state did not understand that the [1901] gift was made by speculators who were thus seeking to establish the validity" of "carpetbag" bonds. Real North Carolinians had had nothing to do with issuing the bonds, the Sioux Falls paper insisted, and all the cash return from them was "stolen by carpetbaggers."[14]

Now, in 1907, South Dakotans began for the first time to hear a great deal about the second mortgage bonds, of which North Carolina had heard so much since the turn of the century. It was odd that the bond question entered South Dakota politics after it had become history, albeit of the "hot" and still controversial sort, in North Carolina. It was also ironic that the newspapers and public figures of South Dakota now made the same mistakes about the origin and nature of the bonds that North Carolina Democrats made so persistently in the face of repeated proof to the contrary.

It does perhaps shed some indirect light on South Dakota's penitence about its action against North Carolina to note that in these very same years Senator "Pitchfork Ben" Tillman of South Carolina addressed packed audiences in Dakota schoolhouses and delivered his diatribe against Reconstruction and his violent "protest against negro domination in the south and against the social and political equality of the black man with the white." The colored steward at the Sioux Falls Elks Club dared, in a letter to the editor, to appeal to the memories of the Grand Army of the Republic and to deplore Tillman's crude approach to the race question. But who was a steward to pit against one of the South's loudest, most newsworthy senators? The same Dakotans who filled Tillman's lecture halls also spent large sums, just as millions of other Americans were doing, to see the Reverend Mr. Thomas Dixon's widely discussed theatrical spectacle, *The Clansman,* which would later become even more famous in its cinematic incarnation as *The Birth of a Nation.*

[14] *Ibid.*

A night or two before the elaborately publicized *Clansman* company reached Sioux Falls, the "ladies aid" in a near-by town held "a dime social at the Union church" and debated the question, "Resolved, That the United States Should Buy and Set Aside the States of Texas and Louisiana for the Home of the Negro." Although the judges decided in favor of the negative side of this village debate, the Sioux Falls critic who attended the *Clansman* found that while it undoubtedly showed up the Negro "in his worst light with no redeeming qualities," the play should not stir up race prejudice. Why not? Because there was "nothing in the story further than is frequently found in the news of the day as printed in the daily papers."[15]

With such emotionally powerful and ultra-Southern Democratic versions of the Reconstruction myth indirectly assisting him, it is no wonder that Governor Elrod's call for repentance and repayment found many sympathizers. When some South Dakotans argued that North Carolina had gotten value received from the bonds, the *Argus-Leader* indignantly denied it and insisted that those who had heard Senator Tillman's recent lecture surely knew what the "facts" about Reconstruction were. The newspaper apologized for its 1901 endorsement of the acceptance of the bonds and now insisted that "morally the people of North Carolina do not owe this money," and "in accepting the gift, and enforcing payment in the courts the state of South Dakota did an improper and unworthy thing." When one of the more prominent Progressive Republican members of the South Dakota senate introduced a bill to restore to North Carolina the full amount received, the *Argus-Leader* backed the move as one to get rid of "tainted money" and to erase the state's venture into what the Progressive legislator called "cold-blooded commercialism," a "hold-up of North Carolina under provisions of a law passed for that purpose."[16]

[15] *Daily Argus-Leader,* Nov. 21, 1906, for Tillman; March 2, 4, 1907, for the "ladies aid" and Dixon's play.

[16] *Ibid.,* Jan. 12, 15, 1907. Former Governor Herreid explained to a

It turned out to be easier for professedly conscience-stricken South Dakotans to agitate for the return of the money to North Carolina, both in the 1907 and the 1909 legislative sessions, than actually to repay the judgment. Aside from the fact that 10 per cent of the judgment plus expenses had already been pocketed by R. W. Stewart as his fee, under the original agreement between him and Governor Herreid, there were political complications involving reputations which would be damaged and egos which would be insulted if South Dakota should go so far as to appropriate money to repay the Southern state. Finally, after semi-chronic discussion of the question which Elrod had raised in 1907, the South Dakota legislature voted in 1911 to place what was left of the "tainted money" in the general fund, where it could be easily swallowed up and disbursed without embarrassment.[17]

Different North Carolinians viewed South Dakota's agonies of "conscience" in quite different ways. Governor Glenn earnestly thanked Governor Elrod for his 1907 message. As to whether South Dakota should return the money or not, that was "a matter for your State alone in the exercise of its wisdom to decide." But Elrod's words sparkled and shone, Glenn declared, as the "chart and guide which should govern the relation of one State to another." Glenn confessed that, "Our people of course felt very much aggrieved at the

reporter that Schafer's gift through Congressman Burke had been considered "highly commendable" in 1901. The legal questions were not discussed when the state attorney-general recommended acceptance, the term " 'tainted money' had not then been invented," and Herreid still thought that Burke "was entitled to commendation, not censure, for this gift to the university." *Ibid.*, Jan. 25, 1907.

[17] *Argus-Leader*, Jan. 12, 14, 16, 18, 23, 27, Feb. 8, 12, 15, 1909, and Feb. 3, 1911. Dean Herbert S. Schell of the State University of South Dakota generously furnished copies of his notes on some of the 1909 newspaper material. By that time the Republican leader in the fight to repay North Carolina was trying to pin "near larceny" on Pettigrew and his friend Butler ("of South Carolina") while insisting that careful examination of the record showed that Burke and Herreid, both of whom were Republicans, had "absolutely clean" skirts. A great many errors of fact, such as the newspaper report that South Dakota had accepted one $10,000 bond with accrued interest amounting to $27,000, had also crept into the discussion.

action taken by South Dakota, but the sting of the judgment has been removed and forgotten in the appreciation of the splendid message that you have sent forth, refusing to accept more bonds, condemning the action then taken, and expressing your feeling of indignation that one State should lend itself to a scheme to cripple and annoy another State." The Tarheel governor only wished that he could have "the pleasure of meeting and grasping the hand of such a man" as South Dakota's retiring governor![18]

Glenn might wish to grasp Elrod's hand but Daniel Russell, despite his own increasingly poor health, would have enjoyed seizing the South Dakotan by the scruff of the neck. Russell felt quite irritated by the new agitation in Dakota. But he also intended to try his best to cut Samuel Schafer and himself in on any cash which the Western state might repay for second mortgage bonds. As soon as he learned of Elrod's proposal, Russell communicated with lawyers in Washington and in Pierre to announce that Samuel Schafer still had "good equities" in the matter; if North Carolina should get her "honest obligations back for nothing," then certainly Schafer ought to have the same amount for each of the ten bonds which North Carolina had paid for the other bonds, that is $892 per bond. "South Dakota ought not to make herself instrumental in enabling North Carolina to cheat the owners of these bonds," Russell argued. He wanted the Pierre lawyer to inform the appropriate legislative committee that "we do not object to South Dak.['s] giving back the money, but that we do insist upon decent treatment to Mr. Schafer." Privately Russell informed Schafer that, "I don't think there is much chance of my scheme amounting to anything, but if I should get something I should expect you to treat me liberally." Russell's intervention in the matter may have been

[18] Glenn to Elrod, Jan. 12, 1907, Governors' Papers. See also Busbee to Glenn, March 14, 1907, and enclosures, where Busbee describes how his acquaintance, the new governor of South Dakota, C. I. Crawford, turned down Andrews' offer to donate $1,000,000 of North Carolina bonds to South Dakota; and Glenn to Crawford, March 15, 1907, *ibid.*

one of the several complicating factors which made it more difficult for South Dakota actually to repay North Carolina than it was for certain Dakotans to propose the move.[19]

Since South Dakota never repaid the money, Russell escaped the public embarrassment which the action would have caused him and also missed the private opportunity to try to pick up additional money for himself and Schafer. The former governor and the Republican party in North Carolina came under attack from Glenn and other Democrats about the South Dakota bond suit not long before Russell died. In his public denial of Glenn's "erroneous" assertions, Russell stuck by his technically true but actually quite untrue and misleading story that he had established no connection with Schafer Brothers or second mortgage bonds while he had been the governor of North Carolina. "Governor Glenn and Governor Russell are a proud pair," Daniel Russell asserted. "Governor Glenn is proud of settling this debt by beating the creditors out of about two-thirds of their just claims by having the State to play the fraudulent debtor act in holding off its creditors. . . . Russell is proud that he was instrumental in exposing the flagrant fraud by which this [state-owned railway stock] and its incomes were kept from its owners, a fraud which shocked and disgusted the Judges of the Nation's Highest Court. He is proud of having obtained a decision which should drive robber states from the Asylum which they have sought,—immunity from suit because they are sovereigns."[20]

This was Russell's last public word about his bond suit. He died on May 14, 1908, at his plantation home in Brunswick County near Wilmington. The old kidney ailment had recurred several times since his 1904 operation, and that,

[19] Russell to R. H. McNeill, a Washington lawyer, Jan. 12, 1907; Russell to Charles E. DeLand of Pierre, Jan. 26, Feb. 10, 1907; DeLand to Russell, Feb. 1, 16, 1907; and Russell to Schafer, Feb. 10, 1907, Russell MSS.

[20] Printed handbill, "Gov. Russell Replies to Gov. Glenn. The Schafer Bonds. The Truth About Them.," an answer to Glenn published in the Greensboro *Daily Industrial News, ibid.*

probably coupled with his heart condition, killed him at age sixty-three. After funeral services at the First Presbyterian Church in Wilmington, his body was taken for burial in the family cemetery in nearby Onslow County.

The newspapers and public officials paid the proper respects to the former governor. The *Charlotte Observer* tried to keep a balance: "He was a striking personality—remarkable in appearance, an impressive individual in every way. He was not beloved of North Carolinians but he who denies to him a high order of ability discredits himself, for he was a very able man and lawyers who have practiced with him on opposing sides say that he practiced fairly. Scarcely anything operated more against him in public opinion than his infirmity of temper, for he was a violent man and was without self-control. He was vindictive, too, and unforgiving. God had been good to him in mental equipment and in other attributes, but he was possessed of unfortunate characteristics which, it is to be feared, will be remembered after his higher qualities have been forgotten."

The recently established Republican paper in Greensboro, the *Daily Industrial News,* played it safe with the controversial former governor by admitting that he was "one of the most remarkable men the state has ever produced," a "man of parts," and "steadfast in his loyalty to a friend." But the Republican daily said nothing editorially about Russell's gubernatorial administration and achievements probably because, like so many Tarheel Republicans, it was already intimidated and overwhelmed by the dominant, Democratic version of the stormy Fusion era. The veteran weekly of Russell's party, the *Union Republican,* joined the others in admitting that Russell "had his peculiarities and both his friends and enemies," but concluded almost defiantly with the declaration that Daniel Russell was "withal, an exceptional citizen, possessing many virtues and serving his day and generation to the very best of his ability—no man could do more."[21]

[21] *Charlotte Observer,* May 15, 1908; *Daily Industrial News,* May 16,

One of the most revealing insights into the complexities of Daniel Lindsay Russell is furnished by a private and personal letter which his last young law partner, Louis Goodman, wrote him about a year and a half before Russell's death. Under the partnership agreement of January 1, 1905, young Goodman was to bear all expenses of the firm and to have out of the firm's earnings whatever might be agreed on between him and Russell; "in case of disagreement, Governor Russell is to decide and his decision is to be final."

Goodman's later letter to Russell announced his desire to terminate the partnership with the thirty days' notice as provided in the agreement. Goodman's remarkable letter continued:

Never in my life have I taken a step which gave me more regret. While my association with you has not conduced to my financial benefit I shall always be grateful for the superior instruction you imparted, though like bitter physic it has always been in the most horrible form. To be entirely frank with you, my reasons for separation are not altogether confined to this— your fussiness. I want you to know all the facts.

Firstly, I borrowed $1000.00 when we entered into our agreement. Of this I loaned you $500.00 paying the interest on it myself. I furnished the office with books and furniture to the amount of $1200.00. All this I have paid for. I have helped you in every matter you had and my fees have in the division never been more than 16% and in some cases not more than 10%. I have however allowed you one-half in several small matters which I will not take time to itemize.

I have a private opinion that but for a suggestion of mine in the Bond matter you might never have gotten your money last year. You will remember that I told you that Bills for revenue could pass in five days. You and your associates in Raleigh had never thought of anything but six. You yourself had serious doubts of Glenn's ability to keep "his crowd" together over Tuesday. My suggestion was acted upon and the Bill passed on Monday.

1908; *Union Republican,* May 21, 1908. The *News and Observer,* May 15, 1908, emphasized Russell's devotion to the 14th and 15th Amendments, the "Negro Amendments," in its misleading summary of the political career of "a man who lived for the most of his life in opposition to the trend of thought of his people."

You promised me $300.00 in this matter and said you hoped to make it $500.00. You gave me $100.00. It is possible that your illness at that time warped your memory. My work for you in this case, if you will take into consideration the voluminous correspondence and the writing of interviews and the doing of typewriting and the taking of dictation, enough to keep a half dozen ordinary operators busy, was worth more than $100.00. Your last move[,] the Carlisle letter[,] was made only after a reminder from me. My delay of a day in writing the letter has again wrought you into your usual state of anger. Forgiving but not overlooking, your previous disturbances, I want to say that your telephone behavior has decided me. There was no excuse for it, though it was my fault in remaining within telephone communication when I took a day's vacation.

. . . You will from the foregoing see that you have little reason to believe that you got the worst or I the better of the bargain. I will frankly admit that my association with you so far as I am concerned was from not altogether unselfish motives, although I was working for intellectual rather than for material gain. Your lectures are worth five of the college professor's, but the method of rubbing it in is not altogether pleasant. I have always had a theory that intellectual superiority had a natural contempt for the inferior. So of course you couldn't help it.

I suppose you will be mad "clean through" at what you will consider my impudence in writing you. However, you might avoid this with the reflection that I have not the slightest ill-will towards you. You may call on me at your pleasure and I shall always be glad to help you out. . . .

The reason I write this instead of personally interviewing you is because I cannot hope to make you believe my side, or acknowledge my rights in debate. I note that you invariably become turbulent when the other side is logical and just, and then you start to bully it and generally you succeed with great applause, from the Ego. A great rule for success, I venture. . . .[22]

Young Louis Goodman may have never sent the long letter which he had typed out to his overbearing partner, or if he sent it he never acted on it. Perhaps Russell apologized for his "telephone behavior," though it seems unlikely. More

[22] Louis Goodman to Russell, July 27, 1906; partnership agreement dated Jan. 1, 1905, Russell MSS.

likely, Louis Goodman took pity and remembered, in addition to the former governor's great intellectual gifts, that Daniel Russell was a sick old man without funds and still bitterly ostracized by his Democratic neighbors. At any rate, Goodman remained Russell's partner. And when Russell died it was Goodman, assisted by Ricaud, whom financial distress had driven back to Wilmington from New York, who advised Russell's widow, the sole immediate survivor, and who undertook to settle his affairs. The last chore apparently was not an easy one, for Russell died leaving less than $1,000 in cash and debts in excess of that amount. Mrs. Russell made her living off the heavily mortgaged dairy farm which she managed. Finally, it was Louis Goodman who, through the long years until his own death in 1959, carefully guarded the old trunk full of Russell's papers about the South Dakota bond suit.[23]

Daniel Russell had finally gotten "out of it all," as he once in 1904 told Ben Duke he almost preferred to do. Marion Butler, however, still a young man, able and again politically ambitious, lived on. His long ordeal about the South Dakota bonds had barely begun when Russell died.

Butler, in the midst of Theodore Roosevelt's exhilarating presidency, had renewed his interest in politics and, contrary to what he had earlier believed about himself, he again felt eager to occupy public office and to wield political power, as he had done so dramatically in the 1890's. That fact, plus the coolness towards Russell which came with the quarrel about the division of the money from the Schafer bonds, made Butler "skittish" about having anything further to do with repudiated Southern bonds, and especially those of North Carolina. In fact, early in 1906 Butler virtually dissociated himself from the whole movement to pool the "hundred millions." He wrote to a representative of Coler and Company that he recommended against any overture or connection with

[23] Goodman to B. N. Duke, July 20, 1909; Goodman to Lindsay Russell, October 28, 1909; and Goodman to S. B. Adams, July 7, 1910, *ibid.*

the Carlisle-Andrews committee which sought so zealously a sovereign donee for its "fraudulent carpetbag bonds" from North Carolina. As for himself, Butler vowed that he would not serve as counsel or "directly or indirectly have anything to do with any effort to collect any bonds that are not honest and for which the State did not get a valuable consideration." Butler, in other words, declared that the second mortgage bonds had represented "as honest a debt as any state or individual ever owed," and he would entertain bond propositions only about bonds as honest as they had been. But he would actively oppose any effort to collect on the "fraudulent special tax bonds."[24]

Butler, in other words, quickly regretted his hastily arranged advertisement in April, 1905, for repudiated bonds. He emerged from the South Dakota affair with less profit than he had hoped for and believed he deserved. He had always been secondary to Daniel Russell in all bond matters. The Carlisle-Andrews committee, with which Butler neither had nor now wanted any connection, kept the bond question alive through its frantic activities. Yet for thirty years or so Marion Butler was to find that Tarheel Democrats, none too scrupulous about keeping such a complicated matter straight anyhow, were quick and eager to decorate his political neck, and inferentially that of the state Republican party, with a millstone hammered out of the bond affair.

By 1905 the hopes of North Carolina Republicans had begun to brighten. There were many reasons for this, but one factor clearly was the growing Southern popularity of Theodore Roosevelt. The dynamic president ostentatiously returned Confederate battle flags, prided himself publicly on his Georgia-born mother, and arduously conciliated sectional-minded and sentimental Southerners in other ways. Roosevelt received a much better Southern press during his term beginning in 1905 than had been true during his first or "ac-

[24] Butler to Judge L. H. Hole of New York City, Jan. 15, 1906; copy in the Battle Family MSS, Southern Historical Collection, University of North Carolina Library.

cidental" term, and he projected a tour through the South, including several North Carolina stops.

Southern Republicans took hope. Tarheel Republicans especially had long felt the need of a first-class daily newspaper affiliated with the minority party. By the summer of 1905 such a project had moved beyond the discussion stage, and a group of Republican leaders prepared to launch the *Daily Industrial News* in Greensboro. Marion Butler participated in this move but was not the most important leading spirit. Democratic papers, however, greatly exaggerated Butler's connection with the venture and slyly suggested that the true, albeit hidden, purpose of the paper would be to assist in the collection of the special tax bonds. The first issue of the Republican daily, edited by Robert D. Douglas, grandson of Senator Stephen A. Douglas and son of Robert M. Douglas who had sat on the North Carolina supreme court, appeared in October, 1905. It promised "our Democratic friends" to "hit hard, fighting fairly and bear no grudges" and assured the *News and Observer* concerning its bond charges that, "We could not if we would and we would not if we could." The *Industrial News* admitted that denying a charge lent it dignity, but to allay the fears of the timid the new paper avowed that its establishment had nothing whatsoever to do with state bonds of any kind. The *News and Observer* should "either go to sleep again or get up and be sensible, but not sit there like a frightened child in bed and expect the State to be shaken from center to circumference simply because you have had a nightmare."[25]

The new Republican daily quickly found, as did Butler, that denial of a wild charge did little or nothing to stop the Democratic press, and especially the *News and Observer,*

[25] For the origins of the Republican daily and Butler's connection with it, see the *Morning Post* and *News and Observer,* June-July, 1905. The first issue of the *Daily Industrial News,* which is quoted above, appeared on Oct. 8, 1905; it would later, after several changes in ownership and editorial policy, become the politically independent and widely respected Greensboro *Daily News.*

from making it. Several months after its establishment the *Daily Industrial News* was still insisting that it opposed payment of the special tax bonds, which the state constitution prohibited anyhow, and that the bond question had absolutely nothing to do with the beginning of the paper despite the *News and Observer*'s "threadbare calumny."

For his part, Marion Butler began quickly to realize that for him there might never be an end to the bond affair. Secretary of War William Howard Taft visited North Carolina in 1906 to address the Republican state convention. H. E. C. "Red Buck" Bryant, a well-known newsman of the day, reported to the *Charlotte Observer* that "the wily Butler" had come in on the same train as Taft. A man with a dark brown Van Dyke beard and ready smile, Butler was described as thinking much and laughing little, although he had lost some of the "stiffness" displayed in the Fusion era when he had "controlled" North Carolina. Bryant concluded that there was "no man in North Carolina who can spread more consternation in Democratic camps than this lean Cassius," whose "name is used more than that of any other native of the Old North State."[26]

Whether from consternation or not, Tarheel Democrats fiercely ran against Butler and bonds as the two parties campaigned in the congressional elections of 1906. The *News and Observer*'s autumnal political theme was that the Republican party's new daily paper and its "boss are tainted with the treasonable bond transaction—the worst crime committed against the State by its trustees since the days of the Littlefield regime." The attack on Butler grew so abusive that his talented wife, Florence Faison Butler, decided to act during her husband's absence on a business trip in the West. Mrs. Butler appealed to Professor Kemp P. Battle, the distinguished historian and former president of the University of North Carolina, who had been the state treasurer when the second mortgage bonds were authorized. Mrs. Butler asked for a state-

[26] *Charlotte Observer*, July 10, 11, 12, 1906.

ment from Battle about the bonds and explained: "When Mr. Butler took that case he talked it over with me as he does every big question that concerns us. I told him after I knew the facts that I approved his accepting it. He never has or never will be a party to collecting those 'carpet-bag' bonds." Mrs. Butler pled for "justice to him [Butler] as a son of the University and one that loves it, and has always come to its aid when he was needed and always will continue to do so. . . ."

Professor Battle promptly responded to the appeal with a restatement of his earlier testimony about the "high character" and completely native, pre-Carpetbag originators and sponsors of the famous bonds. "I give the 'cold facts' about the bonds," Battle declared. "I think that the public is beginning to understand the truth. You cannot go further than I do in expressing the magnitude of Senator Butler's services to the University. I have given my testimony publicly and privately." Mrs. Butler immediately sent the Battle statement to the *Charlotte Observer*, still the fairest Democratic paper in the state, and added that she "was not surprised at [Senator] Simmons and [Governor] Glenn for using a thing they knew was false to fight a political opponent," for they were "low grade men, and the State at large knows it, but I must say that Senator Overman's stooping to anything so low and underhanded was a surprise, for Mr. Butler and I have held him in high esteem as a gentleman." Mrs. Butler concluded that it went "to show how association can contaminate a man," and that "the Democratic party is very short of issues, when the whole campaign is made on abusing a man who has no political position and is not a candidate for one."[27]

Mrs. Butler shared the shrewd insight of her husband

[27] *News and Observer*, Sept. 15, 1906; see also issues of Sept. 22, 27, 1906. Mrs. Butler to Battle, Oct. 27, 1906; Battle to Mrs. Butler, Oct. 27, 1906, on a broadside which also reprints editorials from the *News and Observer* and the *Caucasian*, Battle Family MSS. Mrs. Butler to *Charlotte Observer*, Oct. 29, 1906, and the original of Battle to Mrs. Butler, Oct. 27, 1906, in the Mrs. Marion (Florence Faison) Butler MSS, Southern Historical Collection, University of North Carolina.

244 Reconstruction Bonds & Twentieth-Century Politics

into Tarheel Democratic strategy, which reached its most blatant climax during the elections of 1910. Unfortunately for himself, Butler never candidly confessed that he had once been interested in any and all Southern bonds but that he had come to think quite differently after mid-1905. He admitted and staunchly defended his connection with the South Dakota suit, about which many Democrats persistently made false or misleading statements; but Butler added to his own difficulties by trying to leave the impression that those had been the only bonds in his past.

One reason why the Democrats reserved their full-scale onslaught for 1910, rather than using it in the presidential election year of 1908, was that Tarheel Republicans were angrily divided among themselves in the year that William Howard Taft won the presidency. Butler, a stormy petrel in politics as he had always been, had fallen into an open scrap with the chairman of the state Republican party, Spencer B. Adams, and the semi-chronic outbreak of Republican factionalism helped assure the Democrats of the continuation of their ascendancy in the state. There was another and ironic reason for the Democratic, and especially the *News and Observer's*, silence about bonds in 1908. Josephus Daniels was running the national literary bureau for William Jennings Bryan's third try for the White House, and no less a personage than former Senator Richard F. Pettigrew of South Dakota figured largely as a member of the Democratic finance committee in the same re-run of the Bryan crusade. The Greensboro *Industrial News* could not resist the temptation: "Pettigrew and Daniels running the once proud Democratic party! We venture to say that when this rare spectacle first presented itself the remains of Thomas Jefferson moved uneasily in the grave." The Republican paper took it for granted, however, that Bryan's press chief would "relieve the gentleman from South Dakota of his ill-gotten gains."[28]

[28] For the Republican factionalism, *Daily Industrial News,* Aug. 23, 1908: for the national campaign, *ibid.,* Aug. 9, 11, 13, 1908.

By the time of the 1910 elections, factionalism sorely afflicted the North Carolina Democrats. They ran "scared" against a state Republican party which, despite Democratic gerrymandering, had won three congressional seats in 1908 and which gave every appearance at the outset of the 1910 campaign of having pulled itself together and found an outstanding new leader. This was John Motley Morehead, retiring Republican congressman from the fifth district and wealthy businessman, grandson of a distinguished ante bellum Whig governor of North Carolina. Morehead's becoming chairman of the state Republicans represented what a *Charlotte Observer* reporter called a political "revolution." It had happened partly as a result of something never before attempted in North Carolina—"the complete organization of the Republican party."

"For the first time in the history of the Republican party in the State," the *Charlotte Observer* reporter continued, "the rank and file has waked up and . . . has begun at the beginning—the primaries." Instead of the "back-porch conventions of postmasters" and other Federal officeholders as in the past, the outgoing Republican leader, E. C. Duncan, found himself confronted with a system of primaries where the "outs" had as much voice as the "ins." Chairman Duncan had even lost control of his own county when the Morehead City primary went against him.

What had happened to the North Carolina Republicans? Several things. But one key factor behind the "revolution" was Marion Butler. From January, 1910, on he had worked quietly but assiduously to organize every precinct in every county in North Carolina, "something new for the Republicans" whose officeholding leaders all too frequently cared little about the party's growth. Butler, then summering at the Morehead City beach where John Motley Morehead also had a residence, reportedly had "succeeded in arousing the rank and file of the party against Federal office-holder rule, and that means that the Democrats will have to face what

they never have fought before—organization." Dictating letters by the thousands and receiving Republicans from all over
the state, Butler was alleged to have two great motives—
he still loved "the game" of politics and would like to see
Morehead become governor while Butler returned to the
United States Senate. (The reporter might well have added
this point: Marion Butler had once played a large role in
thoroughly beating the Democrats at "the game." As the
twentieth century entered its second decade, and Democratic
supremacy continued unshaken, Butler not only wanted another taste of the sweet triumph, but he also loomed increasingly as the only important leader who remembered and still
believed that the Democrats could be beaten.)

Morehead, on the eve of the crucial Republican state
convention which the whole state watched with great interest,
had no statement for the press but enjoyed fishing at his "sea-
side villa." He impressed the reporter as "a plain, unassuming
business man, who was dragged into politics against his will"
and who, dreading patronage worries, "doesn't give a tinker's
dream if he don't get" [sic] the chairmanship.

Marion Butler, on the other hand, talked freely and described his arduous organizational efforts of the past months.
He predicted that Morehead's election to the party chairmanship would "thrill and arouse the Republican faithful" who
were disgusted with "ring rule" and would bring "ten thousand
recruits from the Democratic ranks." Butler insisted that, "I
have not taken charge of the campaign nor have I attempted
to do so." No Republican, except the "pie counter machine
and its henchmen who do not want a party," could resent
his efforts to advance the party and its principles. Then concluding with a proposition to which few Southern Democrats
could honestly subscribe, Butler suggested that a government like that of the United States would always be a government by parties; it seemed a "self-evident proposition that
the best government by parties can only be attained by having
two vigorous parties" of as nearly equal strength as possible.

The reporter added that Butler and his associates were "working quietly, determinedly and forcefully to evolve a respectable show out of what has long been looked upon by the Democracy as a one-ring circus."[29]

The Republican paper by 1910 had dropped *Industrial* from its name to become the Greensboro *Daily News* and, under the control of E. C. Duncan and his allies, made an especially bitter intra-party fight against the "newcomers," Morehead and Butler. It angrily charged that Butler "selected, groomed and chaperoned" Morehead and that the former Populist was "conducting, controlling and dominating [Morehead's] campaign." Morehead's election to the party chairmanship, the Republican paper prophesied, would mean that the paramount issue of the campaign would be "BUTLERISM, with all that the term expresses and implies." Who made Butler wealthy anyhow? "Are those irrepressible 'bond holders' behind him? Are they expecting legislation favorable to their contention in the event Mr. Butler's astute campaign results in a Republican legislature? Or can it be that the Whiskey Trust is backing Mr. Butler in the hope of a 'booze' plank in the platform next Wednesday?"[30]

The Democrats could and did take their cue from the embittered Republican paper which tried, as best it could after Morehead's smashing victory in the convention, to eat its words and help harmonize the party. But even without the hints and nudges from disgruntled Republicans, the Democrats were destined to be bond-minded in 1910. The Carlisle-Andrews committee still had its North Carolina bonds, had arranged for a donation to Rhode Island, and propagandized fervently against North Carolina for its refusal even to consider the matter of paying anything on the debt. Governor William W. Kitchin successfully employed Glenn's tech-

[29] Special Morehead City correspondence of R. W. Vincent to the *Charlotte Observer*, Aug. 5, 1910.

[30] Greensboro *Daily News*, Aug. 6, 1910. See also issues from Aug. 7 through 11 for other attacks and accounts of the exciting convention. E. C. Duncan resigned as president of the Daily News Company on Aug. 21, 1910.

nique to drive Rhode Island into repeal of its donation law, whereupon the bondholders turned to Nevada and ended up losing the 1901 donation legislation of that state too.[31]

Scaring off would-be South Dakotas did not, however, constitute all of Governor Kitchin's and his fellow Democrats' problems. The legislature had authorized $3,430,000 worth of new forty-year bonds at 4 per cent to be sold at par or above in order to fund the state's debt which matured in 1910. Aside from the fact that the bond market was said to be then congested, the Carlisle-Andrews committee had done its propaganda work well. When the first bids on the new North Carolina bonds were opened the total bids at par or above were only $1,768,000. The state accepted none of the bids and invited new ones. The new bids in late May, 1910, brought par-or-better bids for only $1,218,500 worth of bonds. Faced with a critical financial situation, the governor called an emergency meeting of North Carolina bankers and a special session of the state legislature. The state treasurer once more invited bids on the bonds, to be opened a few days before the special legislative session. This time strong public appeals—plus the correct rumor that James Buchanan Duke and the American Tobacco Company "had stepped into the breach, gentlemen," by a million-dollar bid—led to the oversubscription of North Carolina's new bonds.[32]

[31] The North Carolina Historical Commission arranged for Captain Samuel A. Ashe and Dr. J. G. deR. Hamilton, professor of history at the University of North Carolina, to edit and publish hastily a documentary history of North Carolina's Reconstruction bonds. R. D. W. Connor, director of the Commission, explained that the work would have not only historical but a "very present practical value for the state." He might have added that it would also help the Democratic party. Greensboro *Daily News*, June 12, 1910. A copy of the "Reply of North Carolinians to the [Carlisle-Andrews] Committee of Bondholders," Sept., 1910, may be found in the Samuel A. Ashe MSS, North Carolina Department of Archives and History.

[32] B. U. Ratchford, "The Conversion of the North Carolina Public Debt after 1879," *North Carolina Historical Review*, X (Oct. 1933), pp. 266-267. See also the New York bondholders' charge that North Carolina had used methods to obtain the subscription that were more "in keeping with the Middle Ages than the present century." *Ibid.* The "breach" quotation from Greensboro *Daily News*, June 10, 1910, as cited in *ibid.*

North Carolina had not heard much about the state's credit crisis of 1910, for the *News and Observer* announced that only Republican papers of the "baser" sort would make political capital of the matter. (It would have provided sensational headlines over a long period in the Fusion era.) But, all things considered, the state had become sensitive again about bonds. Soothing over as best they could their own deep factional divisions, the Democrats, led by the ever-faithful *News and Observer,* launched the bond campaign to end all such in September, 1910. It was true that the Democratic press accused Butler of nothing that his rivals and enemies within the Republican party had not already said; but the *News and Observer* and some of the lesser Democratic papers easily excelled in the virulence and volume of their empty, abusive campaign of 1910.

"BUTLER, BOOZE, BOODLE AND BONDS"—that was the irresistibly alliterative slogan of the Democratic campaign which moved into high gear in September, 1910. Grossly exaggerating Butler's role in the Republican party as well as distorting his relationship with John M. Morehead, the Democratic newspapers and speakers charged that Butler planned to have Morehead made governor so that the "Sampson sly fox" could then collect the special tax bonds through his "puppet." Two full pages of the *News and Observer* on September 15, 1910, gave a detailed, and highly misleading, account of Butler's role in the 1890's, with a special emphasis on how he had allegedly turned his back on "Anglo-Saxon Supremacy and good government" in order to fasten "negro rule" on North Carolina and how the bond syndicate hoped now to use Butler. "The menace of Reconstruction still threatens the State," Josephus Daniels' paper solemnly declared. "Men who really believe in White Supremacy" would have to be on guard against "Butlerism."

The type of political cartoons, crudely drawn but effective for the partisan purpose, which had been so widely used in the crucial 1898 and 1900 campaigns reappeared,

now mingling with the old "Negro-menace" threat the But-
ler-bond-Littlefield theme. One, for example, showed Butler
trying to "chloroform" the suffrage amendment while beckon-
ing hopefully to the grinning black masses behind the "White
Supremacy Bulwark." (Butler and most other Tarheel Republicans had long before abandoned all pretense of being
anything other than the staunchest "Lily-White" Republicans.) Marion Butler dominated the front page of virtually
every issue of the *News and Observer* from late August, 1910,
until the November election. Democratic candidates and leading orators repeated the themes of the party's newspapers;
even the eloquent Charles B. Aycock suggested to large gath-
erings in the eastern part of the state that a Republican victory would be a victory for the holders of the special tax
bonds.[33]

Morehead and the Republicans had written a genuinely
forward-looking state platform in 1910, something which the
Tarheel minority party had not always done. Taft had made
a significant impression by visiting the state during the climax of the 1908 presidential campaign, when he strongly appealed for an end to the self-defeating sectionalism which
had so long gripped the South. Now, in 1910, Morehead arranged for Vice President James S. Sherman to speak in
North Carolina. The *Charlotte Observer* believed that since
Tarheel whites no longer had to vote Democratic out of the
"sheer necessity of self-preservation," thanks to the Democratic policy of disfranchising the Negroes, an increasing
number of voters wished to "be an organic part of American
political life, as their fathers were, to hear national issues in
national campaigns presented by nationally representative
men." North Carolinians, according to the Charlotte newspaper, appreciated the fact that at last the state could not be

[33] *News and Observer,* Sept. 3, 4, 15, 18, 20, 22, 23; Oct. 1, 15, 1910.
An editorial in this paper on Oct. 18, 1910, dealt with an allegedly "low
down" campaign being waged against the Democratic congressional candidate in the 10th district and pointed out that "among men of character it is
never permissible to shoot from cover or hit below the belt."

taken for granted by one party while being totally ignored
by both parties.[34]

Tarheels who might have expected to hear national issues being discussed, and supposedly the nation's Progressive
era was approaching its climax, must have had a tremendous
letdown as the 1910 campaign unfolded. Democrats franti-
cally painted their dire threats about Butler, bonds, and the
time-worn but ever-useful menace to "White Supremacy."
If the Andrews bond syndicate "put up the money to elect
Morehead as chairman," the *News and Observer* slyly asked,
"has it stopped putting it up to win the election necessary for
their purposes?" To this kind of attack Butler boldly and
vigorously responded, for he had never been connected with
the Andrews-Carlisle committee. He explained and defended
his role in the South Dakota suit, insisting that he had refused to have anything to do with "carpetbag" bonds and
would at all times oppose the collection of them. Butler neg-
lected to explain, to his subsequent discomfort, that he had
not always felt that way about the repudiated Southern bonds
but had changed his mind after 1905. At the height of the
campaign in late October and only ten days or so before the
election, the *News and Observer,* with red-ink headlines
spilling over the front page, printed the advertisement for
repudiated bonds which Butler had arranged and signed,
along with his associates, in April, 1905. Senator Furnifold
Simmons, who like other prominent Democrats refused to
join in a debate with Butler, introduced the sensational advertisement in a speech at Asheville and on the following day
it was the biggest news of the state.[35]

Butler literally hired a hall in Raleigh to answer his
Democratic enemies and explain the latest charges against

[34] *Charlotte Observer,* Aug. 23, 1910. Extreme partisans in both
parties protested this paper's coverage and editorials; see *ibid.,* Aug. 27,
1910.
[35] *News and Observer,* Oct., 1910; the advertisement, which the *States-
ville Landmark* appears to have first resurrected, was reprinted on Oct. 27.
For a news account of a Butler speech, see *Charlotte Observer,* Oct. 2,
1910.

him. For five thunderous hours the veteran campaigner spoke. Aside from the attacks on Furnifold Simmons and Josephus Daniels which were said to have been "probably never equalled in a North Carolina campaign," Butler reviewed and defended the part he had played in the South Dakota suit. But as for the incriminating advertisement of April, 1905, he dodged the truth and insisted that others had signed his name to it; when he had investigated and found what kind of bonds had come in through the advertisement he had refused to have anything to do with them. He quoted his letter of January, 1906, in which he had dissociated himself from further connection with any "bonds that are not honest" and especially with the Carlisle-Andrews committee's efforts to collect the North Carolina special tax bonds.[36]

Butler's explanations doubtless convinced many who wanted their doubts settled; but his lame story about the fatal advertisement for repudiated bonds certainly won no Democrats for the Tarheel Republican cause. Even the usually restrained *Charlotte Observer* ignored Butler's Raleigh explanations in its editorials and joined in speculations about how Butler might be able to collect the fraudulent bonds through a Republican governor or legislature under his domination. Tarheel Democracy won a smashing victory in 1910, even regaining all three of the congressional seats which the Republicans had taken in 1908. The *News and Observer* on November 9 happily concluded that the Democratic triumph was more than a vote to continue "Good Government" and to make impossible "the menace of the fraudulent bonds issued by the Reconstruction Legislature of 1868-69"; it was

[36] *Charlotte Observer*, Nov. 5, 1910. Pamphlets of "Marion Butler's Raleigh Speech" were widely issued in an effort to check the Democratic onslaught. Pettigrew wired Morehead and wrote the *News and Observer* about Butler's refusal to be a party in any way to the collection of fraudulent North Carolina bonds, which attitude largely "prevented the further donation and collection of these bonds." The Raleigh paper printed Pettigrew's statement with the explanation that it was as "worthless as Butler's own denials." *News and Observer*, Nov. 3, 1910.

most of all a "rebuke of the campaign of deception waged by the Republican party this year in North Carolina."

The attack on Marion Butler had not, of course, been the sole factor in the Republicans' sharp disappointment of 1910. The elections went Democratic over most of the nation, and in North Carolina, especially, President Taft had alienated many Republicans by his clumsy patronage practices. But the largely fatuous Democratic attack on "Butler, Booze, Boodle, and Bonds," together with the even more vacuous but nonetheless fervent play to racial fears and prejudice, had undoubtedly paid off heavily in votes for Tarheel Democrats.

Butler's bond troubles were never again quite as spectacular as in 1910, but the issue dogged him with a fatal persistence. He remained an ardent Theodore Roosevelt supporter, as were the majority of Tarheel Republicans, in the 1912 campaign which split Republicans over the nation. But the old Populist apparently had had enough of third party efforts and fought for Roosevelt in 1912 and again in 1916 from within the regular Republican organization rather than throwing in his lot with the "Bull Moose" Progressive party.

As Tarheel Democrats in 1916 divided among themselves over President Woodrow Wilson's foreign policies as well as over local issues, the temptation to run against Butler and bonds seemed at first irresistible. Butler, along with other and more prominent Republicans, worked successfully in 1916 to unite the divided Republican ranks in North Carolina. "Marion Butler Controls G. O. P. Convention," the *News and Observer* headline proclaimed over a front-page cartoon with the "sly fox" motif. But the chief Democratic cheerleader in the new "Butler-bond" campaign emerged as none other than the *Charlotte Observer,* which was no longer owned or edited by the men who had earlier made the paper outstanding for its relative objectivity. Shortly after the state Democratic executive committee met and the Democratic chairman announced that Butler would "serve as a call to muster for the Democrats" and thereby "assure" their

victory, the *Charlotte Observer* published a long editorial art-
fully explaining to the "younger voters" how Butler had "betrayed" the various political parties to which he had belonged;
had betrayed "his race into negro domination"; and finally
had betrayed the whole state by concocting the "fraudulent
scheme" whereby he donated "fraudulent carpetbag bonds"
to South Dakota so that he could sue North Carolina and
win. A masterpiece in political distortion for partisan purposes, through omission as well as through sheer misstate-
ment of fact, the editorial created much discussion over the
state as the Democrats warmed to their task.[37]

"Mr. Nigger may come back good and strong and if he
does, its a cinch that the Democratic party will not profit
largely by it, for no matter how badly he has fared at the
hands of the Republican party, 'Republican' is the only word
he knows on voting days." To complement this report from
Raleigh about a call for a Negro Republican convention, the
Charlotte Observer editorialized that Butler's activity made
it "natural" that the Negroes should see their chance also;
their Raleigh meeting was "probably" called through an understanding with Butler. Naturally, too, since Republicans regarded "these carpet-bag bonds as an honest debt," it would
be safe to assume that if the Republicans controlled the state
they would advocate paying the bonds even at that late date
and despite the fact that to do so would bankrupt the state.[38]

Despite the galloping start toward the repetition of the
1910 campaign, it never quite materialized. There were several reasons why it did not, but one factor was Marion Butler's having notice served to the editors of the *Charlotte Observer* and the *News and Observer,* Wade H. Harris and E. E.
Britton respectively, as well as to both of the publishing
companies, of a suit for damages because of the allegedly

[37] *News and Observer,* March 2, 1916; *Charlotte Observer,* March 12,
1916.

[38] *Charlotte Observer,* March 18, 31, 1916. For another citizen's theory
of how Butler first concocted "his" South Dakota bond scheme, see *ibid.,*
June 1, 1916.

libelous articles which the papers had printed. In addition to the Charlotte paper's sensational bond attack of March 12, 1916, both newspapers had carried an especially vitriolic and personal diatribe against Butler which one of his fellow Republicans and an enemy of long standing, Hamilton G. Ewart, had made. Neither paper apologized for carrying Ewart's screed, but the *Charlotte Observer* hastily got its facts reasonably straight concerning the South Dakota bonds and belatedly printed the famed 1905 advertisement for repudiated bonds. Moreover, both papers became conspicuously silent, after the early spring flurry, about Butler and bonds.[39]

In addition to Butler's threatened legal action, some Democratic spokesmen quickly objected to any repetition of the noisy and empty 1910-type campaign. *Charity and Children,* an influential Baptist journal, asserted that if the approaching political campaign became one of personalities in which "mud rather than reason" was paramount not only would it be injurious to the state but the daily newspapers would be largely responsible. "Anybody can scream 'Butler and Bonds' on the one hand and 'Democratic thievery' on the other," the church paper declared, "but neither of these issues having a semblance of truth," they were not worthy of respect or tolerance by the voters of the state. Along this same line of argument, a political reporter in Raleigh learned that Senator Simmons had been told that the Democrats ought not count too heavily on Marion Butler's availability as a campaign issue and that many Democratic leaders feared the futility of a campaign with "nothing but 'Butler, Bonds and Booze.' "[40]

[39] *Charlotte Observer,* April 5, 1916; *News and Observer,* April 1, 1916. Ownership of the Charlotte paper passed just about this time from two Charlotte bankers to two out-of-state businessmen. In both composition and content the paper, at least temporarily, had come a long way downhill since Joseph Caldwell's day. When another paper asserted that the *Charlotte Observer* was no longer the fair, independent journal which it had earlier been, Editor Harris denied the charge and suggested, feebly, that the only difference was that "there is much more politics now" than earlier. *Ibid.,* April 8, 1916.

[40] *Charity and Children* quoted in *Charlotte Observer,* March 26, 1916; W. T. Bost, Raleigh political columnist, in Greensboro *Daily News,* March 1, 1916.

Butler himself also helped avoid another 1910 by limiting his personal role in the North Carolina campaign to appearances in and around his old Sampson County stomping grounds. He had fought in vain, anyhow, to have Theodore Roosevelt rather than Charles E. Hughes nominated by the reunited Republicans and felt disappointed in the outcome.[41] Do what he would, however, the bonds haunted Butler. Governor Locke Craig and other key North Carolina Democrats missed few opportunities to warn of the bond-peril and Reconstruction-Fusion horrors which would befall North Carolina if the Republicans should win. The state chairman of the Democratic party issued circulars warning that the Butler-led Republicans were making a desperate effort to regain power; if they succeeded it would mean "a restoration of Negro suffrage and as a matter of course Negro Rule" in the east. And would not the proper reward for Butler's services be payment of the "repudiated bonds held by his Collecting Syndicate against North Carolina?"[42]

On the very day of the 1916 voting, red-ink headlines in the *News and Observer,* buttressed by appropriate editorials inside the paper, blared forth a news story which must have immeasurably sickened, but possibly also grimly amused, Marion Butler: "CUBA IS TRYING TO SUE NORTH CAROLINA TO COLLECT REPUBLICAN CARPETBAG BONDS. VOTERS TAKE NOTICE." And in Charlotte,

[41] Butler seconded Roosevelt's nomination and as a member of the national convention's resolutions committee fought for planks endorsing the world court, rural credits, expansion of rural free delivery, and women's suffrage. H. E. C. "Red Buck" Bryant also reported to the *News and Observer,* June 5, 8, 9, 10, 1916, that Chicago hotel lobbies teemed with "big, husky negroes rubbing elbows with Republican leaders."

[42] *Charlotte Observer,* Oct. 22, 23, 24, 28, 30, 1916. Republican leaders took full-page advertisements to protest the Democratic chairman's Butler-bond letter as an "insult to the intelligence of our people" and a "gratuitous attack upon one individual" who was not a candidate for office, not asking or seeking anything at the hands of Tarheel voters, and who was not even taking part in the state campaign. *Ibid.,* Oct. 30, 1916. For former Lieutenant-Governor C. A. Reynolds' appeal to Professor Kemp P. Battle for a correct history of the bonds in the South Dakota case, see *Union Republican,* Aug. 3, 1916.

where the Democratic county chairman had urged the "White Voters" to cast their ballot against the party which "consistently arrayed an inferior race against the intelligence and morality of this white citizenship," Thomas Dixon's and D. W. Griffith's *Birth of a Nation* opened its "farewell engagement"—with a thirty-piece orchestra to accompany the grotesquely unfair but thrilling depiction of Reconstruction.[43]

It was enough to make a man quit in disgust. Marion Butler, however, never did. Energetic and resourceful as ever, he kept plugging away, hoping that the day would yet come when North Carolina Republicans would succeed against the Democrats just as the Fusionists had done in the 1890's. Butler took an especially keen interest in agricultural matters and still pushed modernized versions of such old-time Populist demands as storage warehouses and easier Federal credits on non-perishable crops such as cotton. He advocated a bolder program of state services in North Carolina, in such areas as road-building and education, and the old Populist insisted, "The people are not afraid of themselves—history will repeat itself if necessary."[44]

After Warren G. Harding's victory in 1920, Butler and his friends sought to get him named as secretary of agriculture. North Carolina had not ended up in the Republican presidential column but had cast more Republican votes than

[43] *News and Observer,* Nov. 7, 1916; *Charlotte Observer,* Nov. 4, 6, 1916. Cuba had come into possession of her North Carolina bonds through the Corporation of Foreign Bondholders of London and, through diplomatic pressures, was persuaded to withdraw her suit before the date set for the hearing on her petition in the Supreme Court of the United States. Not until 1934 did the Court rule that Monaco, which owned certain ante bellum Mississippi bonds, could not sue the Southern state. Chief Justice Charles E. Hughes pointed out that the Constitution was not explicit on the matter of a foreign power's right to sue a state, and since a state could not sue a foreign power without its consent it seemed only fair that the rule should work in reverse. Ratchford, *American State Debts,* pp. 240-241; 292 U.S. 313 (1934).

[44] *Charlotte Observer,* Jan. 26, 1921. For Butler's own explanation of his significant role in the establishment in the 1890's of the rural free delivery system, see *ibid.,* Dec. 23, 1920; and W. E. Fuller, "The South and the Rural Free Delivery of Mail," *Journal of Southern History,* XXV (Nov., 1959), pp. 508-509.

any other Southern state and ranked thirteenth in the nation in the Republican vote. Chief Justice Walter Clark, State Secretary J. Bryan Grimes, and other prominent North Carolina Democrats endorsed him for the post, but the state Democratic chairman, Thomas D. Warren of New Bern, Senator Furnifold Simmons' home, declared that any man who acted in the "North [sic] Dakota bond case" as Butler had to force his native state to pay "worthless bonds" deserved absolutely no support from any Tarheels.[45]

Butler did not get the cabinet post, but the Democrats continued to exaggerate his role in the opposition party and distorted his past just as they had done since 1904 and earlier. In 1928 just as the state Republican convention opened with Butler in well-noticed attendance, the newspapers carried accounts of Connecticut's proposal to sue North Carolina for almost $300,000 on special tax bonds. Although Governor Angus W. McLean and Senator Overman soon persuaded Connecticut to withdraw the suit, Democratic speakers were afforded the traditional opportunity to warn voters during the fall campaign of the dangers of Republican rule and that the "menace of the bonds still exists."[46]

Not until a few years before his death did the North Carolina press and Democratic politicians cease to use Butler and bonds as a symbol which so conveniently reached back to the Fusion and Reconstruction eras. In 1934 Butler led in harmonizing the shattered Republicans and successfully urged them, after their reorganization, to "cease fighting among themselves and concentrate upon the Democrats." Without once mentioning bonds, a reporter from the *Charlotte Ob-*

[45] *Charlotte Observer*, Nov. 19, 1920; see also the issues of Nov. 20-26, 1920.
[46] *News and Observer*, April 12, 13, 14, 1928; Greensboro *Daily News*, Oct. 20, 1928, for the Democratic warning. With Senator Furnifold Simmons constituting one of the Republicans' strongest allies in carrying the state for Hoover and against Al Smith, whom Butler reportedly admired, it is no wonder that Butler was said not only not to have campaigned but not even to have voted. Mrs. Butler worked to recruit Tarheel women's votes for Hoover. *Charlotte Observer*, Nov. 10, 1928.

server described him this way: "An old man— he will be 71 on May 20—with a huge shock of bristling white hair, an over-size white Van Dyke and stubble-covered cheeks showing pink beneath, and a portentous stomach over which his cutaway met nicely, bobbed up in the Republican state convention yesterday and in two minutes had it by the nape of the neck."[47]

The "grand old man of the 'Grand Old Party,' " as he was labeled in the 1936 state convention, had become a lonely man in the sense that he was almost the sole important survivor of the Fusionists who had ruled in a day when Democrats had not held sway over North Carolina's political destinies. Butler died at the age of seventy-five in June, 1938, thirty years after his partner in Fusion and chieftain in the bond affair, Daniel L. Russell, had escaped "out of it all." The state newspapers mostly printed kind editorials, omitting or minimizing the twentieth-century use which the Democratic party had made of Butler. The Greensboro *Daily News,* long since independent in its politics, best summarized the career of the "creature of calamity" whose national career had ended before he reached forty and whose name had been used for decades much as the " 'fear o'hell.' " Butler's real qualities and abilities, the Greensboro paper belatedly suggested, had been obscured under a legend which "personified him as a figure of malign ambitions, an abiding menace to the state." He appeared to accept his fate "philosophically" and, at the very last, "was destined to outlive" the most blatant uses of the legend.[48]

Even many of his homefolk in Clinton, Sampson County, had forgotten not only about the South Dakota bonds but also about Butler himself. As the minister of the small church

[47] LeGette Blythe in the *Charlotte Observer,* April 5, 1934. For a description of the party reorganization under younger leaders which Butler helped effect, see the *News and Observer,* April 5, 1934. For Colorado's brief flirtation with the special tax bonds, see *News and Observer,* April 19, 30, 1932.

[48] Greensboro *Daily News,* June 4, 5, 1938.

reached the especially impressive part of the Episcopal funeral service where earth is returned to earth and "dust to dust," the roar of a crowd several blocks away could be heard. While Sampson County's most famous son was being buried, a larger crowd enjoyed a "continental Sabbath" by watching a baseball game.[49]

[49] W. T. Bost in *ibid.*, June 7, 1938.

A NOTE ON SOURCES

I. *Manuscripts*

The Daniel Lindsay Russell Papers, Southern Historical Collection, University of North Carolina Library, constituted the major source for this study. The new Russell material added to the collection in 1959 deals almost exclusively with the bond affair and consists largely of Russell's correspondence, both incoming originals and outgoing copies in typed carbons or hand drafts. Some newspaper clippings and printed documents are included, and the entire collection is well arranged chronologically.

The Marion Butler Papers are also in the Southern Historical Collection. By direction of his late widow and the wishes of his heirs, the papers from the period after 1901, when his Senate career ended, are closed and are to remain so until 1975. The remarkable completeness of the record which Russell saved, as well as the comparatively small role played by Butler in the bond affair, kept the inaccessibility of the Butler papers from hindering the writing of this book.

Many other manuscript collections were examined, and some others cited, but the following were the most helpful:

1. Benjamin Newton Duke Papers, Duke University Library— Russell's letters to his powerful friend and fellow Republican, Benjamin N. Duke, afford intimate insight into the governor's political distress during and after the Democrats' 1898 white-supremacy campaign and his personal financial plight which partly motivated the launching of the bond suit.

2. Governors' Papers and Governors' Letterbooks, North Carolina Department of Archives and History—While the Letterbooks contain mostly copies of formal documents, the Governors' Papers were more valuable for this study. Governor Aycock's correspondence with Charles Price, distinguished lawyer in Salisbury, North Carolina, and the few but revealing private letters to Aycock from the North Carolina counsel in the bond suit were the outstanding items. Under Governor Glenn and his successors the bond material mostly dealt with the unsuccessful efforts of the Carlisle committee to find a state which would receive a donation of the "special tax" bonds.

3. Dean Herbert S. Schell, State University of South Dakota, generously furnished copies of his notes on the few pertinent materials in the papers of Governor Charles N. Herreid and other South Dakotans. The fact that these South Dakota items were duplicated in the Russell Papers is added evidence of the Tarheel governor's thoroughness.

The papers of Senator Richard F. Pettigrew are kept in the Pettigrew Museum, Sioux Falls, South Dakota. The curators there reported that, while there are copies of Pettigrew's letters to Butler about Mexican land and mining ventures and other business matters, none of the papers deals with the bond affair. (George and Dorothy Rogers, Curators of the Pettigrew Museum, to the author, December 7, 1959). The Russell Papers again proved invaluable by containing such gems of vituperation as Pettigrew and Russell exchanged in 1905.

II. *Newspapers*

The three most important daily newspapers in North Carolina in the early years of this century were the *Charlotte Observer,* the Raleigh *Morning Post,* and the Raleigh *News and Observer.* Other Tarheel newspapers were used, and quite a few are cited, but none to the extent of the above-named three, all of which were important sources about as well as influential factors in the story. The most useful newspaper for information about the bond affair was the Raleigh *Morning Post.* Robert M. Furman's editorials and Thomas Pence's Washington correspondence were both valuable, and the *Post* recognized the difference between a news story and an editorial. As for the editorial point of view, the *Morning Post* was staunchly conservative and Democratic in the "goldbug," Grover Cleveland style; it rather consistently took a moderate and well-informed position in the bond affair.

The Raleigh *News and Observer,* in contrast to the *Post,* was short on factual information about the bond matter but, nevertheless, a major element in the story. This was owing to the power of the editor, Josephus Daniels, in the Democratic party, and his politico-journalistic technique of mixing sensational charges, based largely on suspicion in the bond case, with selected facts.

The third important daily in North Carolina at the time, the *Charlotte Observer,* was used during important developments but less than the two Raleigh papers. Joseph Caldwell, the editor, knew less about the bond matter than did Robert Furman of the

Post and, as far as the bond affair was concerned, had no political ax to grind in his news columns and editorials in the manner of Josephus Daniels.

For South Dakota, the Sioux Falls *Daily Argus-Leader* and the Sioux Falls *Daily Press* were used. These were important mostly in a negative sense for the period from 1901 to 1905: they prove that South Dakotans simply did not read or hear much about the bond suit until after it was formally settled. The South Dakota newspapers were also examined during the 1907, 1909, and 1911 sessions of the legislatures when the "tainted money" issue was being debated.

INDEX